PERSONAL BEST

PERSONAL BEST

Denise Lewis

with

Alison Kervin

CENTURY

First published by Century in 2001

Copyright © Denise Lewis 2001

The right of Denise Lewis to be identified as the author of this work has been asserted by
her in accordance with the Copyright, Designs and Patents Act, 1988

Century
Random House, 20 Vauxhall Bridge Road, London, SW1V 2SA

Random House Australia (Pty) Limited
20 Alfred Street, Milsons Point, Sydney, New South Wales 2061, Australia

Random House New Zealand Limited
18 Poland Road, Glenfield
Auckland 10, New Zealand

Random House South Africa (Pty) Limited
Endulini, 5a Jubilee Road, Parktown 2193, South Africa

The Random House Group Limited Reg. No. 954009

www.randomhouse.co.uk

A CIP catalogue record for this book is available from the British Library

Papers used by Random House are natural, recyclable products made from wood grown
in sustainable forests. The manufacturing processes conform to the environmental
regulations of the country of origin

Typeset in Garamond by MATS, Southend-on-Sea, Essex

Printed and bound in the United Kingdom by
Mackays of Chatham PLC, Chatham, Kent

ISBN 0 7126 7737 2

This book is dedicated to my great grandmother

DUSILLA BUCHANAN

Thank you for showing me the true meaning of perseverance,

inner strength and love, and thank you for my family

CONTENTS

Acknowledgements

I'd like to say a big thank you to all at Random House for giving me the opportunity to do my first book and having the faith in me to get it finished – just! To Anna Cherrett, for long hours of editing and stressing, but we did it in the end, girl – now where's the champagne?!

To Alison Kervin, for her hard work in gathering the material together, I hope you enjoy the finished product.

To Jonathan and all at MTC, thank you for coping with all my mood swings and for all that you do behind the scenes. Your long hours of work and commitment are very much appreciated. If I've never said so before, thank you for all that you do. May our partnership and friendship last for many more years.

To my Dutch connection: Peter Vergouwen, I have never, or will ever, meet a doctor like you. When they made you, they threw away the mould! Thank you for being my ray of light in the dark moments of injury. Rick, you're the most caring person I've met, always smiling and always there to help. You deserve everything good in life. Thank you for your time and friendship. To Ineke,

Tante Lies and Fritz, thank you for making your homes my home, I would never have survived in Amsterdam without your love. I love you all dearly.

A special thank you to all the coaches I have ever worked with, no matter how small you may think your input has been, every hour and minute has been a part of this big jigsaw that has led me to where I am.

To Brian Welsby and all at Be Well, thanks for all your years of hard work and your great products. You've taught me a lot about nutrition and played a big part in getting me to where I am today.

To golden hands himself . . . Kevin Lidlow. Will there ever be a day that I don't need you? Thank you for the years of commitment, energy and care, and for always being there when I have called you, begging you to put my body back together again. I don't ever remember you failing me or turning me away for treatment even at II o'clock at night. You always seem to know what to say to keep my spirits high when facing injury after injury. Thanks for being my friend; you're one in a million.

To all my friends (I'm not listing you all, but you know who you are), thank you for making life's journey so much fun, and for never judging me. May our friendships long continue.

J.A.K., did you really think you would escape a mention? These acknowledgements would not be complete without me letting you know how much you affected my life. Throughout the last six years of my roller-coaster lifestyle you have been the one stable force guiding me behind the scenes. You're the one person, apart from my mum, who I would trust with my life. Thank you for being my friend and allowing me into your world. *Anam Cara*. I will always love you.

To Charles and Darrell, what can I say, guys, words really can't express what you've done. Both of you have sacrificed so much time and effort to bring me to this stage of my career. The hours of commitment and dedication can never be measured. We've laughed and cried and been through so many difficult times and we are still talking. But one thing is for sure, you have both inspired me to believe in myself and the power of good coaching, and have shown what having faith in someone can really achieve – thank you for never failing me. You have both been the biggest motivators in my life, but also the biggest pains in my butt! I love you.

To the little lady who made it all possible, your efforts and sacrifice have never gone unnoticed. I hope you are proud of me as I am of you. Thank you, Mum. I love you dearly. You are the centre of my world.

I would also like to thank the following for their co-operation with the book:

Jez Betts at BBC sports library, Daniel Evans, all at the *Times*, the *Wolverhampton Express* and *Star*, all at Woden Junior School and Regis School (particular thanks to Miss Leigh and Miss Dixon).

Thank you to those who supplied the images for the plate sections:

Athletics photos courtesy of Neil Loft at Allsport; Denise in 'Kiss' campaign t-shirt courtesy of Stuart Barber at Breakthrough Breast Cancer; *Parkinson* photo courtesy of the BBC, with thanks to Michael Parkinson and Sam Donnelly; Powergen modelling photo taken and supplied by Bob Carlos Clarke; *Harpers and Queen* javelin photo by Stefano Massimo courtesy of the photograher and International Photographic and Production Agency; Denise with Frank Skinner courtesy of Frank Skinner; BAFTAs photo courtesy of London Features International Ltd; Girls in Sport photo courtesy of Dave Scott at Nike.

Chapter One
My Dream Comes True

The rain had started to fall gently through the evening air as darkness descended over Sydney. Hundreds of lights illuminated Stadium Australia, and the noise was deafening. As I walked towards the track I glanced around me at the sea of faces in the stands, but my mind was focused. The Olympic gold medal was just minutes away, hanging tantalisingly in the distance.

My heart was beating loudly, my mouth was dry and the adrenaline was pumping. I was so close to the realisation of my childhood dream and the feeling was fantastic; it was completely exhilarating, but also terrifying. I knew I would have to push myself beyond my known limits to ensure that my dream came true.

I tried to keep composed, telling myself not to panic, to stick to the plan and run my own race. I knew the Russian girls would set off quickly – and I had to finish this race fewer than ten seconds behind the Russian athlete Yelena Prokhorova. If I could do that, the title would be mine.

I looked out along the first stretch of the 400m track and caught my breath. The 800m race had punished me so much over the years – in the World, Commonwealth and European Championships – and now it stood between me and the Olympic title.

The British supporters were cheering so loudly it seemed as if they were the only fans there. I could hear my name being called. I could hear the shouts of encouragement and the cries of hope. Union Jacks fluttered all around the vast, beautiful stadium. I felt unified with the crowd – we all had the same vision and the same dream.

My ankle was bandaged against an injury I had incurred in the long jump just a couple of hours earlier, but I shut out all thoughts of pain. I tried to concentrate on the crowd. They were so vocal. My spirits lifted and I felt composed.

I knew I would do my best, that I would run my heart out and finish the race. I felt the performer in me move in and take over. I had just two laps to run, that was all. Just two laps until the emotional and physical strain of the past two days and the last twenty-eight years would be eclipsed by victory or failure. This race was all about survival. It's only two minutes, I kept telling myself, anyone can run for two minutes.

The starting gun was fired, and the race began. The first lap was good, I managed to keep up with the group, but I was feeling much more tired than I usually did, and much more than I'd anticipated. Both the long, hard weeks of training that had led up to this championship, and the exhaustion from two days of gruelling competition were showing in my performance. Mental and physical fatigue were starting to crush me, and I had to fight back.

Prokhorova had set the pace from the start. It was important that I didn't let her get too far in front. I had to stay with her. At the bell I was 2.3 seconds behind her. Just one lap to go. One lap. I could do it. I had to keep going. In the final 150 metres I could hear the roar of the crowd, giving me a boost at exactly the moment I needed it the most – just when my legs were burning and I could see the gap opening between me and the Russian. Thankfully, my foot was holding out, so now it was all down to mental stamina.

Prokhorova was pulling away. I couldn't let her get too far; I had to stay with her. I began counting down the metres I had left to run: 60m, 50m, 40m, 20m. I could see the clock. I could do it, but it would be close. Then finally the line appeared. I crossed it, exhausted. I had finished.

As I crossed the line my initial thought was how much harder the race had been than expected, bearing in mind how, only eight weeks before, I had set a new personal best of 2 minutes 12.2 seconds. Then my mind turned to the result. Had I done it? I thought I had. I was aware of where the other athletes were, and was sure that I'd just made it. But, until I saw it on the scoreboard, I wouldn't let myself believe it. As I stood there, staring up and waiting for confirmation, I tried hard to keep negative thoughts from my mind – but I couldn't help thinking, what if I have just missed out? What if I've been through all this, and missed out?

In the distance I could hear the commentary team talking about two days of tough competition, then I could almost hear someone say, 'I think she's done enough.' The next thing I knew, Sabine Braun of Germany came over and told me I'd won. They had heard before me, and she asked what it felt like to be the Olympic champion. I smiled, still not sure.

Then, the moment that will stay with me for the rest of my life – my name in lights. That was when it all hit me. Relief, a moment of calm, and a thank you to my inner self for taking me through these two days. I felt a tingle through the whole of my body. This was how it is meant to be – arms aloft and fists clenched.

I looked out at the fans, who were waving flags, clapping and shouting with delight. I was the Olympic champion. *The Olympic champion.* I had to keep repeating it to make sure it was real. It was amazing – there's nothing like it. Nothing better. For me there can be no greater achievement, no greater accomplishment than winning an Olympic gold medal. The title rang in my ears and echoed in my head.

I was physically and mentally drained and I could suddenly feel the very real pain in my ankle, but I so desperately wanted to do one final lap of the track – a lap of honour – to thank the crowd for all their support, to share the moment with them. Draped in flags, beaming from ear-to-ear, still a bit dazed but thoroughly elated, I jogged around the track. And then I went around again. It was amazing to look into the faces of people and see their delight, to hear their shouts of congratulation. People were crying and smiling. That's what's so magical about sport – the unity of joy.

By the time I had finished, the crowd had started to leave, thinking the medal ceremony would be the next day. A lot of people have since asked me if I was disappointed that the ceremony didn't take place the following day when more people would have been in the stadium, but I can honestly say that I didn't mind. I had won, and I was so elated that nothing could have dulled my happiness.

It is difficult to explain how surreal it felt, standing on the podium, listening to the national anthem as I waited to receive my medal. I'd seen myself on the Olympic podium so many times in my dreams. I've heard that anthem, felt the weight of the gold around my neck and looked out into a sea of Union Jacks, but nothing, nothing prepared me for the fantastic feeling of being there for real. I didn't cry as I stood there; I couldn't bear tears clouding my vision, or for emotion to flood in and prevent me from enjoying every last second of the experience. Winning the English Schools in 1986 and 1988 was great, and I adored winning the Commonwealth Games in 1994 and 1998, but winning the Olympics was something else completely. It was, paradoxically, almost dream-like, but at the same time so utterly real.

For a moment, life stood still as I stared out from the podium into the faces of those who had stayed for two days to support me – from the moment I had walked out to find 100,000 people packed into the stadium the day before; to now. The finale. My moment of triumph.

It is hard for an athlete to convey to fans how much they mean, how much their support is cherished, and how important they are. I knew that part of this medal belonged to every one of them. But there was one person who the rest of the medal belonged to – my mum. A strong, independent, incredible woman who had given me the chance to be the very best.

I will never feel able to repay Mum for all the opportunities she has given me and the life she has allowed me to build for myself, and, as I looked around, scanning the faces, desperate to see her, I hoped to be able to tell her that this medal belonged to her.

It was Mum who devoted her life to giving me a chance. It was she who had made all the sacrifices, and she who deserved the praise. My story has hit the headlines because I've been successful, but the real story of my success is the story of a long line of strong women in my family who have nurtured and loved and allowed each other to grow. It was because of them I was standing on the podium to receive the ultimate accolade in sport. It is the motivation to succeed for them that keeps me training on cold wintry nights, it's what locks me into the gym with weights when I could be out at parties, and it's what enables me to shut out all the noise around me and focus on the task in hand – to jump higher, run faster and perform more strongly than everyone else. This book is for them, but above all, for my mum.

CHAPTER TWO
MUM'S STORY

It was early in the morning as Joan Lewis, a little girl from Hanover in Jamaica, walked slowly out of the arrivals gate at Heathrow Airport, nervously clutching a bag of her favourite toys and a few presents. She scanned the crowd of unfamiliar faces until she spotted the one she was looking for. Suddenly she was enveloped in a great hug from her mother, who had waited three years to see her precious daughter once again. That child was my mum, arriving in England for the first time on 20 July 1966.

Mum had never left Jamaica, let alone been on an aeroplane. Her journey had started badly, while at the airport. Mum and her younger brother, Jack, had been chatting as they waited for the call for the London flight. It had been subject to a number of delays, so Jack went off to the shop to get some sweets. While he was gone, Mum's flight was announced and she had to go – she wasn't able to wait for him so they could say goodbye to each other. Her sudden departure haunted her all the way to England. She kept worrying about the moment he would have returned from the shop to find her gone, and how he might have thought that she had left without waiting for him to say goodbye. She didn't know when she would see him again, and it upset her terribly for the duration of the flight. On top of this, she had been scared and lonely, worrying about what might be waiting for her when she landed. She had heard tales of a cold, dark country where all the buildings were big and grey.

Her fears about the country were realised as the plane landed and she looked out of her window at the cold, grey day. These gloomy observations of the British weather remain the strongest memories of my mum's first day in London. However, she was also struck by the white faces of the people waiting to meet friends and relatives at the airport. Of course she had seen white people before, but they had been the European tourists in Jamaica. But now, here she was in this strange country where there were hardly any black faces at all. She had not been in a minority before.

On the journey to her new home in Wolverhampton, Mum was completely amazed by everything she saw, and realised how different everything would be from now on. My grandmother had chosen to live in Wolverhampton because some family members were already living there when she came over to Britain. She had stayed with them for a while as she trained to be a nurse, then when she qualified and had saved enough money, she had bought her own house and sent for Mum.

Over the coming months Mum would learn that the voices, sounds, clothes and food were very different in England. Although, when at home, my grandmother cooked the sort of Jamaican food Mum was used to eating, outside the home the food seemed bland and uninteresting. Mum loved to come home from school or playing to the rich smells of her mother's cooking. One of her favourite meals was yellow yam and chicken, so her mother would cook that for her on a regular basis, along with another favourite, sweet potato pie.

To Mum, people never seemed to spend any time outdoors. She thought it was odd that everyone sat in their little houses instead of running around in the open air as she had done back in Jamaica. The lifestyle in England was totally at odds with the outdoor life she had been used to – a life in a tight-knit Jamaican community, a place where children played happily outside, laughing and joking in the sunshine, and getting up to all sorts of mischief. They had enjoyed nature and the wonders it had to offer; they picked fruit, played under the shade of the trees and in the water. It was a safe life and a healthy one. It was a life Mum absolutely adored.

When I go to Jamaica now to see my relatives, and I see all the places where Mum would play as a child, it's easy to picture how her life was, messing about with her brother and all the kids from the local area. I know how happy she felt there, surrounded by family and friends, and I can only begin to imagine how difficult it was for her as she left it all behind that day, to start a new life in England.

The whole experience was also very difficult for my great grandmother, Druisilla, who was left behind in Jamaica. Dusilla was a very strong and determined, but incredibly loving and unassuming woman. She was held in very high esteem within the family because she had raised her sisters, her daughters and her daughter's children, and was almost something of an Earth Mother figure, a powerful woman, always putting herself second to her family. She adored Mum and had played a huge part in bringing her up while my grandmother went out to work. As a result of all the time they spent together, Mum tended to think of Great Gran as another mum. Great Gran also adored Jack, Mum's younger brother, and there had been a lot of concern about how the departure of my grandmother, Mum and Jack would affect her. It was therefore decided that, to minimise the effect, my grandmother would leave first, and Mum and Jack would follow on, one at a time. To lose both of them together, as well as her own daughter, would have been too much for Druisilla to bear.

This meant that Mum had to travel to England alone, leaving Jack, her grandmother and all of her friends behind. It must have been so difficult – I would find it impossible to move thousands of miles away from my family but, in Jamaica in the 1960s, everyone believed that the best you could do for your children was to get them to a country where there was economic growth, where there were plenty of jobs and a 'bright future'.

Like my great gran, my grandmother, or Nanny, as I call her, was a very proud, strong and determined lady. She wanted great lives for her two children so, when she heard about the huge recruitment programme persuading the Jamaican people that their futures lay in Britain, where there were great jobs, houses and plenty of money, she, like many others, thought that this was the answer to all her prayers. She saw it as a great chance to build a fabulous new life for her and her children, to offer them the best education possible, so she applied, and her application was successful.

Nanny adjusted to life in England without too many problems. She missed home, of course, and she desperately missed her two children, but at least she felt like she was building a future for them to come into.

Unlike Nanny, Mum found the transition difficult. Once in Wolverhampton Mum joined the local school, just a short walk down the road from their home. At school she did OK. She was quite involved in sports, but says she was an average pupil, and didn't try hard enough academically. Unfortunately, she didn't have the same opportunities to develop her sporting skills as I would have years later, so she limited herself to excelling in PE lessons and on sports days.

Mum fitted in and made some new friends, but she always felt as if something was missing. She missed the friends and family she had left behind in Jamaica, and she missed Jack enormously. I suppose it's because it was where she was born, but Mum will always feel as if Jamaica is her real, spiritual home. Because the two of us are so close, I know there's no way that she would move back there now, but she still calls it home, after all these years.

But it wasn't all doom and gloom when Mum first came to England; in fact there were some new, exciting experiences, such as the first time she saw snow. Mum was fascinated as she watched it fall, her nose pressed against the window. She had never seen anything like it before, and was amazed. But this wasn't the only element of the British weather she had to get used to.

One day, Nanny found Mum waiting in the doorway for the rain to stop before she went out.

'What are you standing there for?' asked Nanny in surprise.

'I'm waiting for the rain to stop,' replied Mum.

'This is England, Joan. If you wait for the rain to stop you'll be waiting there for ever!' laughed Nanny. 'I suggest you find your umbrella and go!'

Mum had been used to Jamaica where the showers are over very quickly – once they've gone, you know that will be it, and the weather will be nice and sunny for the rest of the day.

So Mum finally started to settle into life in England, and began to accept that, while it was not Jamaica, it was certainly somewhere she could have some fun. But then, in her late teens, she discovered she was pregnant, and started planning for a new life with a baby.

CHAPTER THREE

THE EARLY YEARS

Time-keeping is not one of my specialities, but when I made my first appearance in the world it was days earlier than the midwives had predicted. It was 1972 – an Olympic year, suitably enough. However, the performances of the athletes in Munich were far from my mother's mind as she went into Hallam Hospital on the evening of Saturday 26 August 1972, complaining of pains in her stomach.

Mum explained that the pains were coming more regularly. She was certain she was going into labour. The midwife looked at her, said she was too early, and suggested she go home. The hospital had told her I was due in September, but they hadn't made the same calculations Mum had made in relation to her cycle. As a result, she knew they were four weeks out, and had to insist that I was on the way. A nurse was called and, although she agreed with the midwife, they arranged for Mum to stay in overnight and go home the next morning. But Mum was right, I *was* on my way into the world, and was born at 4.25am on the Sunday.

I was very long when I was born – nineteen inches, which is extremely long for a newborn baby, especially one weighing 7lbs 4oz. I must have been a stringy-looking thing as I lay there with my long, skinny legs! I was a great sleeper – which doesn't surprise me, as I still am. I would sleep for long periods while the other babies woke constantly, demanding their feed. Mum started worrying that because I wasn't waking up, I wasn't eating enough. She therefore took to waking me up in the night to feed me, despite the fact that the nurses told her not to, saying I would soon let everyone know if I got hungry. But Mum insisted – she thought she knew better than the nurses. I have definitely inherited her stubborn streak, and her courage to go ahead and do what she thinks is right, regardless of what other people might be thinking or saying.

When we left the hospital, we moved into the room Mum had rented in a house in West Bromwich. Mum was fiercely independent, and had decided that it would be a good idea if we moved there, rather than going back to her mother's house in Wolverhampton. She wanted the chance for us to build our own little life together.

One of the first difficulties Mum faced as a single mother was going to work when I was just six months old. This was very hard for her, and was made more difficult because she worked in a dress shop, where they had to work on Saturdays. Initially my Aunt Sonia, Mum's cousin, would look after me on a Saturday, but then Sonia got a new job, which meant that she had to work at weekends too. After that, Mum couldn't find anyone else to look after me on Saturdays – and that was when she realised that moving us both back to her mother's for a while would probably be for the best. So I went to a local nursery school during the week, and Nanny looked after me at the weekends.

But Mum never really settled back in to Nanny's house, and still wanted her independence. It worried her that Nanny was taking over too much of the responsibility of looking after me, so, when I was eight months old, we moved to a small terraced house in an area called Park Village in Wolverhampton, which was about a thirty-minute bus journey away from my grandmother's, and was a great step-up from the room we'd first moved into in West Bromwich. At last Mum had her independence, and the chance to bring me up the way she wanted to.

She got a job as a typist's clerk in Bilston, and I was enrolled at a local nursery school. It was an arrangement that worked out really well: Mum would drop me at nursery on her way to work and collect me on her way back, and the weekends were our own.

As I got older and more confident, I grew to love my nursery school. I was very happy with life there and was in my element. According to the teachers I practically ran the place, and they were convinced I was going to be the first black prime minister. The bossy streak in me – or, as I like to think of it, the helpful streak – was obviously developed at a very early age. As a toddler I was organising all the children, and would try and teach the little ones. Even those the same age as me would be dragged into my little classes. Wendy, who worked there, loved me because I made the nannies' jobs a lot easier!

Obviously, the fact that I thrived so much in the nursery school environment, coping well with being away from Mum, meant that it was much easier for her to get on and work. Had I not enjoyed it, had I cried when she left me or refused to go in, it would have been much harder for her to do every day.

But it was still difficult for her, and when she left me on the very first morning she cried on the bus all the way to work. As soon as she arrived at the office, her eyes still red from her tears, she rushed to the phone to ring the nursery to check I was coping without her. The nursery told her not to worry and explained that I was absolutely fine, not missing her at all – I don't know whether that made her feel better or worse, but she certainly didn't function very well that morning.

I even loved the bus journey to and from the nursery, and would entertain everyone by singing songs such as 'Incy Wincy Spider' and amusing them with funny tales and jokes. I would jump up and offer my seat to the people who got on, and hand around my crisps to all the other children. We would see the same people every morning, and if I wasn't there one day, they would ask my mum where I was. One of my abiding memories from around that age is of the Cadbury's Curly Wurly I was given once a week. I adored them, but was only allowed to have one on Fridays because Mum was worried about me having too many sweets. But those Curly Wurlys were well worth waiting for!

When Mum wasn't at work, we spent a lot of time with my Aunt Sonia and her daughter, Lisa. Mum and Sonia were great friends. Lisa and I were the same age and were great friends, too. We shared the same cot as babies and pretty much grew up together, spending a lot of time with each other, mainly at weekends. We would play, fight, cry and make up, then repeat the process all over again. I adored her. We often had the same shoes or a similar dress, the same dolls and toys – I suppose we were really like sisters. We were all very close, and Mum and I stayed with them in Birmingham most weekends.

Around this time, I started going to dancing classes, learning ballet, tap and modern dance. I adored it. My interest in dancing came from hearing lively music in the house – our home was always full of music. When Mum and Sonia were going out, they would get ready to the sound of reggae and Motown records. Lisa and I would dance about to the music in delight, singing along to Donna Summer and Diana Ross. My aunt was really into Diana Ross and I can remember the two of them dancing around to 'Ain't No Mountain High Enough' over and over again while getting ready to go out. I still love Diana Ross because of these good memories.

Watching Mum and Sonia get ready to go out on a Saturday evening – with their false eyelashes, big hair, skimpy outfits and awful eye-shadow – was a real treat. I used to watch carefully to see how they did their make-up, and was fascinated with the transformation.

One night, when our mums were downstairs and we were meant to be getting ready for bed, Lisa and I raided their make-up bags. Giggling and trying to keep quiet, we plastered ourselves with everything we could get our hands on. By the time we had finished we thought we looked very glamorous, our eyes caked in bright blue eye-shadow, blusher in circles on our cheeks, and lipstick smeared round our mouths like clowns. As a final touch, we grabbed a couple of wigs – mine was big and curly, Lisa's more sleek – and set off downstairs to show our mums. What a sight we must have looked. Mum and Sonia just stared at us in horror for a split second, then died with laughter!

Lisa and I used to have a great time. We did fight a lot – as children do – and would always blame the other for starting any trouble. However, according to Mum it was usually me who swung the first punch – Lisa used to boss me around a lot so I always made sure I got my own back. On one occasion, when we were around the age of three, Lisa came to stay with us and she wet my bed. I had stopped doing that a long time before and was absolutely livid. I was determined to get my revenge so, a couple of weeks later, when I was staying with Lisa, I wet her bed too. Mum knew exactly what I'd done and was furious. As she chased me round the house I was laughing about what I had done, but full of the fear of what Mum would do when she caught me!

But Lisa and I were great friends, and got up to all sorts of fun and games together. Another very vivid memory is of the time we were bouncing on the bed upstairs at Lisa's grandmother's house, seeing if we could touch the ceiling. The ceiling was covered in square tiles made from a material that looked like polystyrene. As I learned the moment I jumped high enough to touch it, it was just like poly-styrene. My finger went straight through it and left a big hole. We thought this was hilarious, so we carried on doing it for a while. By the time we had finished the ceiling was a mess. When Lisa's grand-mother realised what we had done she was furious – but luckily Mum and Sonia got more of a telling-off than Lisa and I did.

We would often dance around the bedroom, leaping on and off the bed with great energy and hilarity, singing and performing to each other for fun. Mum says that this streak – this need to perform and find an audience – is innate in me. Ever since I was standing on two feet I seem to have been ready for the limelight. There's an exhibitionist in me that's always been there, burning away, looking for the right activity.

Mum says that I was always a poser – though I find that hard to believe – and tells of how I would jump into a pose at every available opportunity, particularly if anyone took a camera out. This means that in most childhood photographs, I'm standing in some kind of modelling stance. It is in the pictures of Mum and me that you can really see the differences in our personalities; Mum is always looking very sensible, while I'm standing there with my hands on my hips, jutting one towards the camera and smiling.

I've always been more out-going and sociable than my mum. She is quite reserved and wary of people, and I think she used to wonder where on earth I got my extrovert streak. I suppose it's because I've always been more trusting than her, and find it easier to feel happy and comfortable with people.

I stayed at nursery school for five years, then went to Woden Infants' School. I thrived in the new environment and adapted to school very quickly, just as I had at nursery. I was top in most classes and still went dancing whenever I could, so all in all I think Mum was quite proud of me. We had settled into a nice lifestyle together, with just the two of us at home. Our home life was relaxed and pleasant, we lived easily in each other's company, and got along well. I adored it when Mum came home from work and we would sit in our cosy living room, have something to eat and talk about the things we had done during the day. It was a lovely time – just the two of us in our nice, safe house. I loved Mum's company and the warmth and generosity that surrounded her.

I never felt I wanted for anything, although I knew I couldn't have everything I liked. Other children would have six presents for Christmas and I'd have just a couple – but that really didn't matter to me, I knew I'd get the ones I really wanted. Mum says that as long as I had everything I needed for dance, I was happy.

Our Christmases were great fun. We would occasionally spend the day with Nanny, but more often it would be spent with Sonia and Lisa, and Sonia's mother, who I called Nanny Birmingham. Nanny Birmingham loved to cook, and her house was always filled with wonderful smells and delicious food, particularly at Christmas time. She would cook for days on end so there was always too much food, but always lots of drink to wash it down with. People would often drop round, and it was always a big, fun, happy occasion. Back at our house, preparation for Christmas always seemed to happen at the last minute because Mum was so busy, but I loved it when the two of us went shopping for presents, and I would choose her present, card and wrapping paper all by myself, and buy it with the money I had saved. Then on Christmas Eve I would decorate the tree, which stood in our front room, a light, airy space containing Mum's best chairs and our music centre. They were very happy times.

It was only at the age of six or seven, once at junior school, that the fact that I didn't have a father around even occurred to me. Sonia and Lisa, the people we spent most of our free time with, didn't have a man around either, although Lisa had met her dad, and did see him on occasion. But it is at that age when you first start questioning things, looking around you and seeing how other people's family structures differ from your own. So, for the first time, I became conscious of the fact that I had just one parent.

I never missed my father, because I never knew him. I haven't met him, or seen a photograph, and I don't even know how he and Mum came to be together. In fact, I know very little about him at all, and that's purely through my own choice. I know it might sound strange to people who come from a traditional family, or those who grew up without a father and have worked hard to find out who he was, but for me it simply wasn't important. To me, it is very simple: he wasn't there, Mum was. I had no feelings of loss, I was very happy, and everything was fine. As a child my days were always full of activity, I was always busy, always hectic. The only thing that ever bothered me was whether or not Mum was happy.

Only once did I feel the need to explain my father's absence to anyone. I don't remember why I said it, or how it came up, but I can picture the scene clearly, even now. I was in the school playground with some friends, and I made up a story that my father wasn't at home with us because he had gone off to the Far East. I don't suppose I even knew what or where the Far East was, but it sounded glamorous to me when I was young and seeking an answer to the questions I was being asked by my friends. I told them he'd been killed out there in quick sand. Quick sand? Where did that come from? I suppose I said it because it was something dramatic and final, something that wasn't within the realms of my understanding, or that of my friends, and they wouldn't be able to ask me any more about it. Although I was a creative child, and loved stories and enjoyed colourful tales, making up stories like this wasn't a consistent thing, it just seemed the right thing to say at the time and, quite frankly, I thought it was funny.

Over the years, my mother has asked me several times if I want to know anything about my father. She stayed loosely in touch with him, and could easily have asked him to see me at any stage while I was growing up, if that was what I'd wanted. Even today, I'm sure she could contact him somehow. But that's not what I want. I had the best upbringing with Mum, and there really isn't any role for him now.

I'm sure he knows who I am, and so is Mum. In some ways I think he's behaved with a lot of integrity by getting on with his own life, and not trying to enter mine now I'm in the public eye. When I hear horror stories about parents coming out of the woodwork when their children become well known, it makes me feel very uncomfortable. I respect my father for not doing that, for not trying to intervene and become part of my life just to capitalise on the success that my mother and I created for ourselves.

Occasionally, when I was younger, I did feel some anger towards my father. I suppose it was only natural that a part of me felt this way. But it wasn't because he wasn't there to look after me, more because of what Mum went through. Apparently he did take an interest in me when I was little; he was around to take me for walks with his friends, to take me out and show me off. So, one way or another, he was involved in my life until I reached the age of about six months, but when we left West Bromwich for our new home in Wolverhampton, he didn't know where we'd gone, and they lost touch. Mum has, however, bumped into him since then, but hasn't seen him recently.

What I do find strange is the fact that, because I've never known my father, and nor do I know much about him, it's almost as if he doesn't exist in my mind. I never attribute anything to him, and tend to assume that my characteristics come either from Mum or my own personal development. However, being realistic, I know I must get several of my physical characteristics from him – certainly my height. One thing I do know is that he was tall, around 6ft 2in. Mum's nearer 5ft 1in, so at 5ft 8in I must have inherited a few of his genes. But instead of thinking that I might share some physical similarity with my father, I prefer to think that I am simply my mother's alter ego coming out, that I'm some of the things she wishes she could have been, like taller and more flamboyant.

Of course Mum had other boyfriends after my father, though not many because I think she was wary of bringing a man into our relationship. I'm sure that's why she never married or developed a serious long-term relationship with anyone. Mum never got on with her own stepfather, who her mother married in Jamaica, and I think she feels her relationship with her mother was affected by this factor. So she was cautious about who she brought into our relationship; she didn't want to run the risk of me being influenced by, or not getting on with, a man she'd got to know, someone who might destroy the powerful mother-daughter relationship we had.

I suppose she felt that moving a man into a routine that was already well established wasn't the right thing to do, worrying that it would spoil the equilibrium, the balance we had. I remember a couple of boyfriends being around, and there were occasions when I felt jealous at the division of her attention. It was very important to Mum that I was happy – I was her priority and I know she sacrificed a lot of things for me. So I think it was a conscious decision for her to let her personal life take a back seat. Obviously I encourage her now, but as a child, I would worry that someone would take her away from me, and this scared me, as she was all I had.

My mum's happiness was important to me, even when I was very young. I always felt that she should be a happier person and would sometimes feel guilty, as if any unhappiness was somehow caused by me. I suppose it was because there were only two of us there. If she was upset, I felt powerless to do anything to help her. I was also very aware that she was running the family on her own and had to make all the decisions herself, without a partner to take the pressure off her and share the load.

I would often think that maybe Mum would have been happier without me. She wouldn't have had to work so much, would have had much more of a life. There were times when she seemed very preoccupied, and I knew she was worried about how she could do the best for me. But she did everything for me, gave everything of herself to me, and and I do still wonder on occasion, if things would have been better for her if I had not been born. I can see how some might find that strange, but it's true. I can't help thinking that life would have been easier, less stressful.

Mum would always be cheerful in front of me, but sometimes, later on in the evening, I would hear her crying when she thought I was asleep. I'd hear sobbing through the walls, and would wonder what had caused her tears. I would become convinced that I had let her down somehow, that I had caused her pain. I'd become so worried and distressed that I would cry too. I didn't know what else to do. I couldn't bear to hear the sobs and see the hastily wiped-away tears.

'Mum, why are you crying?' I would ask her. 'Is it me? Have I done something?'

She would say that it wasn't me, but wouldn't tell me what it was that was worrying her. As a child, seeing your parents cry is scary and upsetting. If they don't have things under control, then who does? It was at times like this that I would worry a little about our future, hoping against hope that everything would be all right.

I still worry about Mum, because she never married and doesn't have a big network of friends. She's a loner in many ways, and that's quite different from me. Sometimes I stop and think about the opportunities I have, and I wish she could have the same, or indulge more in what I have, instead of standing back from it. It's because of her that I have what I have, but she won't enjoy to the full the lifestyle she has helped me create for myself. I do think she gave up everything for me, that she channelled all her love and energy into her daughter at the expense of everything else. She sacrificed so much for me – and now, just as she feels I am still her responsibility, I also feel responsible for her.

Certainly, some of what drove me to be the best I could be, to get everything absolutely perfect, was a desire to make Mum proud, to prove to her that I was worth the sacrifices, the pain and the anguish.

By the time I went to junior school at the age of seven, I was already quite mature and responsible for my age. Because Mum wasn't back from work by the time I got home, I would let myself into the house and wait for her to come back. Some might argue that that was very young for a child to be on their own in the house, but we had spent a long time and gone to a lot of effort in trying to find a suitable babysitter to look after me for those few hours each day after school. However no one did the job adequately for both our likings. I don't think people realise the difficulties single parents face in trying to bring up their children, particularly those who go out to work full time. Good babysitters are hard to find and are expensive. It was tough back then, and I don't think things have changed much today.

I didn't particularly enjoy spending so much time alone, but didn't really mind it that much. I would have liked more of Mum's company as I was growing up, but we didn't have a choice; she simply couldn't give me any more time because she had to work. I am often grateful that I have such a creative brain, which allowed me to dream and escape from the boredom into my own thoughts and fantasies, and I do think that the time I spent alone, playing on my own, made me very independent.

Mum would get me up in the morning and I'd get ready and walk to school by myself. It wasn't far – probably between five and seven minutes away – but I had to cross a busy main road. This worried Mum a lot, and every day as I kissed her goodbye she would warn me to be careful. I never really understood what she was fussing about until a couple of children were injured. It was then that I realised why she had felt so strongly – but, as I assured her, I was always careful. My friend Karen Grant used to meet me and we'd walk to school together. We had gone to the same nursery and infant schools together, and carried on being friends through junior school.

It was at junior school that my interest in sport began to flourish. I had taken to dance naturally, and was enjoying my classes, even though it took two bus rides to get there after a day at school. But it was not only dancing I took to naturally; I soon realised it was the same with most physical activities. I was willing to have a go at everything, which is probably how I ended up getting involved in the Superstars competition at school.

When my school decided to enter into the competition, I'm sure they didn't know they were taking the first step towards producing an Olympic gold medal-winner but, looking back, that's exactly what happened. My first taste of the heptathlon, or combined events, was in this tournament. The competition involved throwing a rounders ball, sprinting, doing a standing long jump (long jump, but without having a run up), and a hurdles race over bench tops. I won the school tournament for the girls, the prize for which was a visit to Aldersley Stadium for the day.

The day I saw that stadium, my life changed for ever and I will never forget it as long as I live. I came home incredibly affected by what I'd seen, and from that moment on I was desperate to become an athlete.

When I saw Mum I ran to her in great excitement. She had never seen me this way before.

'Mum, Mum!' I cried. 'I've been to this stadium, this Aldersley Stadium. It's amazing, they've got a really big track made of tartan, and it's the real thing. It's a real surface and you have to wear special shoes on it with pointy, spiky things on the end. It's brilliant. I want to go there. They have a club. Please can I go to the club?'

We agreed that Mum would phone the stadium and get some details. It was around this time that she was thinking of moving us to Pendeford, a district of Wolverhampton not far from Aldersley Stadium. Until then I had always opposed any idea of moving because I hated the idea of being so far away from my friends. I didn't like the thought that I wouldn't be able to walk to school with Karen, and wasn't keen that my journey to school would take a lot longer, and involve catching two buses. But when I found out that Aldersley Stadium was near the house Mum was thinking of buying, the prospect of the move suddenly seemed much more acceptable.

We got a bus out to the new area, so I could see what it was like. 'Oh my God, Mum, that's it! That's it! That's the stadium,' I shouted, with my nose pressed against the bus window. 'Look, can you see it, Mum? Can you see it?'

From that moment on I was hugely preoccupied with getting myself into the athletics club based at Aldersley Stadium. I found out that the club was called Wolverhampton and Bilston, and pestered

Mum until she rang them. My fascination with athletics had developed into an obsession, and I was desperate to join.

In the end, after plenty of nagging, Mum arranged for us to go down there. They said 5pm would be a good time – which was lucky, because that was when Mum got home from work.

'OK, we'll go tonight,' said Mum. 'Make sure you're ready and waiting when I get back.'

'I'll be ready,' I promised. 'Don't worry, Mum, I'll be ready.'

Mum was convinced I wouldn't be ready, because I was hopeless at getting organised for anything. However, when she came home from work that evening she was proved wrong. I opened the door before she could get her key out of her purse, and she almost fell through it. I was standing there, dressed ready for action, head-to-toe in my sports kit. I was wearing the right socks, trainers and track-suit, my overcoat was on and done up and my bag was over my shoulder. I was poised, ready to go and grinning from ear to ear. Nothing had ever excited me more than the prospect of going to the athletics club.

When we arrived, we walked in through the doors and approached a man standing by the track. Mum introduced herself and explained what we were doing there. We were told to go to the main office, and once there, had a conversation about the club and the way it worked.

'And how old is Denise?' asked the man we had been talking to.

'She's eight,' replied Mum.

'Oh, I see,' said the man, 'then I'm afraid she's a bit too young for us. We don't take children until they're nine years old. I'm afraid she'll have to come back then.'

Mum tried to convince him that I was responsible, mature and very eager to join, but she could not change his mind. He was insistent that nine was the youngest they would take me.

As we walked away from the stadium, me dressed head-to-toe in all my best sports kit, I felt crushed.

I carried on doing athletics at school, but it was nowhere near as glamorous as Aldersley Stadium, and I couldn't wait to be nine.

CHAPTER FOUR
A NATURAL TALENT

Hundreds of children filled the stadium. As far as you could see, there were youngsters dressed in brightly coloured shorts and T-shirts, either sitting and listening closely to their coaches or running around. Some of the older athletes were stretching on their own in the corner, looking very sophisticated, self-assured and talented. The track was occupied by teenagers, running faster than anyone I had seen before, while the younger children waited patiently near the high jumps and long jumps. Adults milled around, organising, moving equipment and shouting instructions. Even behind the track, in the distance, groups of children trained on the grass. A hive of activity – little athletes and their coaches everywhere. That is my abiding memory of Aldersley Stadium on a Sunday morning. That, and the mess. Track-suits, discarded jumpers and sweatshirts lay in piles all around the edge of the track. It was such a contrast to our house, which was always so tidy. Mum had a place for everything –

if I'd have left my clothes in a big pile on the floor like these athletes, she'd have gone spare!

It was my first day at Wolverhampton and Bilston Athletics Club. I was nine years old at last, and finally eligible to join. Despite my eagerness to get involved, I was a little apprehensive that morning, because the club was so packed full of children. Wolverhampton and Bilston was one of the best clubs in the country at the time, and the success of the senior athletes had encouraged youngsters to turn up in their droves every Sunday morning and at the club nights on Tuesdays and Thursdays. When we arrived we were directed towards the far field, beyond the track. We had been told to talk to a man called Bill Hand, as it was his group I was hoping to join. As we approached the field, we saw Bill with a group of about thirty children warming up on the grass, while an assortment of parents stood by, some of them helping out, others just watching and encouraging the children to do their best. It was a nice atmosphere, relaxed and friendly.

We introduced ourselves, and Bill explained that they were doing cross-country that day – not my favourite athletic event! He said he would be delighted to have me in his group. He had a sweet face with big glasses, and was such a jolly and friendly man that any reservations disappeared immediately and I was soon totally absorbed in his class. Bill's motto was 'a lot of love, a lot of fun and a little bit of training' – isn't that great? That's exactly the right approach to take with young children, and it certainly worked with us. We all adored him. Every weekend he would have around thirty children in his group, so he had to enlist parents and other coaches to help him.

Bill was very good at making sure we warmed up and warmed down properly, and it's significant that I first met him during a warming-up session. I'm sure my ability to avoid serious injury in the early days owes much to the lessons I learned from him about stretching properly before training, and always warming down. I can remember when he took an elastic band and showed us how much it would stretch when warm, then how quickly it broke when it was cold. He explained how the ligaments in our limbs are like elastic bands, and how they need to be kept warm so they don't break. Seeing the elastic band snap in two gave us a clear idea of how much damage we would do to ourselves if we did not warm up enough, or do it in the right way.

Bill says he saw very early on that I had a natural talent and an innate aptitude for athletics. After just one session I was put in the top group for all the events I did. I certainly wasn't the best in them all, but I was up there with the top ones. In fact, the only criticism he has of me from those days is that I wouldn't join in all the cross-country or long-distance runs. He believes that if I'd made more of an effort with them then, I'd be better at the 800m today!

After the first session, Bill told me about the training nights during the week, and said I was welcome to come along on Tuesdays, and Thursdays if I wanted to. He finished by adding, 'Why don't you ask your sister if she wants to join in next time?'

'That's my mum,' I replied. A lot of people made the same mistake when I was younger, and I was really proud of that. I thought it was great the way Mum looked so young.

Bill coached the youngest girls the club would take, who stayed with him between the ages of nine and thirteen. He later told me I had been turned away from the club when I was eight years old because he was determined not to run some sort of baby-sitting service where busy mums could dump their kids on Sunday mornings. He wanted to provide a sensible, safe and loving environment in which young aspiring athletes would thrive.

I thoroughly enjoyed myself for those four years. I went down to the club on Sunday mornings, from 6.30 until 8pm every Thursday evening and every other Tuesday evening. I was still dancing at the time, and did that every Saturday and the Tuesdays I wasn't training with Bill. Once at senior school, I also joined the netball team, so most of my evenings were filled with sport. It was a lovely time.

I can only remember one thing that spoiled the great fun I had during this period at the club. It came in the form of some comments from two sisters who were in my group. I can't even remember their names now, and maybe neither of them meant any harm. They started excluding me, I think, because I was good. They had been at the top of the group until I came along, and they didn't like the fact that I knocked them off their self-constructed perches a little. Their parents came down to help out on Sunday mornings, so I suppose they felt a little bit protected and thought they could say whatever they liked. The younger of the two girls made a silly remark of a racist nature. I can't even remember what she said, which is odd; maybe they didn't mean any real harm, but I was quite hurt by it at the time. This was one of the few times I had ever come across racism. I told Mum about it, who told me to ignore the girl, saying that she was just jealous because I was better than her. This made me feel much better, and Mum suggested I just get on and enjoy the classes regardless of the girl. Thankfully her behaviour didn't make me want to leave, or stop athletics; on the contrary, it made me more determined to kick her ass. And I did: by the end of my first year at the club I was voted the Outstanding Athlete of The Year. I was given a special certificate and Bill told me how proud and pleased he was. He told me that, with a little application, I could make it right to the top.

As time went on I became very friendly with one of the girls in my group. She was called Joanne Taylor, and she was the group's star, very talented, small and athletic. I really admired her and was in total awe of her – it seemed as if she won everything in which she took part. We got on extremely well, and were very good for one another, both competing in the triangular tournaments against two other clubs in the area: Bromsgrove and Redditch, and Worcester. We had a tartan track at Wolverhampton, there was a cinder track at Bromsgrove and Redditch and a home-made shale track at Worcester, so it meant the athletes from across the three local clubs got to compete on different surfaces. My first entry into this competition took place in my first year at the club, and although I didn't win, I finished in the top three in everything, which got our club points.

It was in one of these competitions that I first encountered Joanne

Wise, the long jumper and current Commonwealth champion. She was a year older than me and was the golden girl, always better than everyone else in the field. I took part in the long jump and hurdles at the time, and Joanne was always jumping about a metre ahead of me. It was incredibly frustrating – I was always second, and couldn't quite get near enough to her to compete for her crown. Joanne just seemed to ooze raw talent. She was only small, but it was as if she had springs in her heels. It was always my goal to get closer to her because she had so much ability. I was really quite in awe of her because she was so talented. By 1997 I had managed to close the gap from metres to centimetres, but still had a lot of work to do!

While I was in Bill's group, one of the biggest competitions I competed in was the All England Indoor Club Championships final in Nottingham. I was around eleven years old and our team comprised athletes from all over the West Midlands area. My events were the standing long jump and the standing high jump. The standing high jump involved standing next to a wall, where a mark is made by the tips of your fingers when you're stretching upright. You then bend your legs and jump as high as you can, and another mark is made at the highest point your fingers reach. I won and broke the record. I was so proud – it was a huge success for the club, and for me as an individual. Our team even went on to win the competition. Sadly, Bill wasn't able to go to the competition because he had to work, but the first thing he said to me when he saw me later on was, 'You look after yourself, Denise, keep yourself fit and healthy and away from boys, then one day, when you're on the television receiving your Olympic gold medal, you can wave to me.' In fact, the first thing he said when he saw me after Sydney was, 'Denise, why didn't you wave?'

It was around this time that a television crew from Central TV, the ITV company from the Midlands, came to the club. They were doing a series of half-hour programmes featuring six 'stars of the future' from the West Midlands in different sports, and Wolverhampton and Bilston chose me as the little girl with the most potential in athletics. Unfortunately I was so shy and said so little that the programme's editors were unsure whether or not they would be able to use any footage of me! But Bill was quite insistent that I should be the one featured in their programme so they persisted, and even came to my house one day to see if I was any more chatty in familiar surroundings. I wasn't, and left them with practically no footage at all after two attempts. In the end, Bill gave them another girl who was more confident than me, and she was the one who starred in the programme. I wonder what she's doing now?

This was around the time that my cousin Lisa moved away to Switzerland. Aunt Sonia was a nurse, and a couple of years earlier she had moved to Germany. Lisa had been looked after by her grandmother while Sonia worked and got together enough money to give the two of them a new start – in much the same way as my grandmother had done when she left Jamaica for Britain in the 1960s. Sonia was now settled in Switzerland, and the time had come for Lisa to join her. Lisa's departure left a big void in my life, things just weren't the same, and I reacted to the situation by becoming quite introverted. Some nights, when I was feeling particularly lonely, I would go into Mum's room to sleep. She would tease me about it, saying things like, 'Denise, you're too old to sleep with your mummy, what would your friends say?' But I didn't care, I felt I needed the comfort and security.

Luckily, my athletics was more vibrant than my personality at the time, and I started to really develop my long jump skills. On one occasion we started practising in the car park because another group were already using the long jump pit, so we did long jumps between the white parking lines. A senior male athlete came along and showed us how he could jump from line to line, and challenged us to do the same. I crouched down and in one quick bound covered exactly the same distance that he had. Apparently, it was a key moment for Bill, because it was then that he realised just how determined and competitive I was, and what reserves I had – how I could pull out a big performance when I wanted to.

At the age of twelve, it was decided I should move on from Bill's group of fun and games and join a more serious group at the club. My friend Joanne had moved on by this stage, and so had some of the other girls. It was therefore my turn, and I really felt as if I was losing the cosiness that had existed in our close little group. Bill had been so nice to me; he was kind, patient and thoughtful and used to drop me back after training because he passed my house on his way home. It was therefore always going to be difficult to move out of his group.

Unfortunately, I had particular problems with the next group I moved in to. It was run by a man called Bob King and I didn't find it quite as much fun as Bill's group had been. Because I hadn't wanted to leave Bill's group in the first place, I found it difficult to adjust to Bob's coaching style. As a result, athletics stopped being fun and started to feel like a chore. In the end, I told Mum that things weren't working out with my new coach, and she came down to the club to try and calm the situation down. We agreed that it would be best if I moved into another group, but Bob wasn't happy about my decision. I think he thought I was being ungrateful for the time he dedicated to the track and to coaching me. However, he did prove to be quite a saviour of mine a few years later, stepping in to help out when Mum threatened to pull me out of the club.

I was about fourteen and had lost my track-suit – again. Every time I came back from the stadium I had forgotten something. I was always losing things – even my bus passes. One month Mum said she would make me walk if I lost my pass again. Unfortunately I did and, true to her word, she made me walk to school the next day – a journey that took me just under an hour. Thankfully Mum took pity on me the following day and replaced it, but it certainly taught me to be more careful – until the next time! But the main problem at Aldersley Stadium was that all the track-suits would get put down after training and we would forget to pick them up again afterwards.

Because we didn't have a great deal of money, Mum, understandably, would get furious with me for losing the things she had worked so hard to pay for. On this particular occasion she completely lost her temper and told me that that was it – I had to leave the club because she couldn't afford to keep replacing the kit that I lost. When I told the coaches some of them rushed round to persuade Mum to let me stay, and one of the men who convinced her the most was Bob King.

So after just a couple of months in Bob's group, I was put into Richard Whitter's group. Most of the girls in this group were about three years older than me and they tended to be sprint specialists because that was Richard's favourite discipline. It was therefore quite daunting being with Richard – but he was a very nice, hard-working man, who was eager for all his athletes to do well. I stayed with him for the rest of my time at Wolverhampton and Bilston, and it was with him that I started to develop the wide-ranging skills across the disciplines that would prove so invaluable in later life. Because Richard was the sprint group specialist, I worked with him on my 100m and 200m, but when I wanted long-jump input I would turn to Alan Jones, who specialised in the event. Alan often took me to Telford where we would make use of an indoor area to practise long jump take-offs and jumps. With Alan's specialist jump knowledge and the sprinting I was doing with Richard, I started to become very good at the 200m, hurdles and the long jump. I went to the hurdles and long jump trials for the English Schools Athletics Championships and, to my delight, I was selected to represent the West Midlands. Unfortunately, you were only allowed to enter one event, so I chose the long jump. It was every aspiring athlete's dream to get to these championships because it was the stage where you would get noticed by coaches and selectors who would turn up to assess the new talent. By working my way through the system while at senior school, I learned a lot about athletics that would prove crucial later on.

Chapter Five

A Winner on the Sports Field

When I was ten years old and in my third year at Woden Junior School, we moved across Wolverhampton to our new home in Pendeford, a nicer, quieter area. The house was within walking distance of Aldersley Stadium and was more spacious than the one we'd come from. It had a long front room, a large kitchen and front and rear gardens. It was on a friendly street in a tight-knit local community with lots of shops nearby. It was the house Mum had set her heart on, and she'd worked hard to get enough money to buy it. But for me, it was a mixed blessing.

As soon as we arrived I ran into the house, claimed my bedroom and started organising all my things. I certainly loved the new place, but I desperately missed being close to all my friends, having them scattered along the neighbouring streets where I could call them up and visit at a moment's notice. I didn't want to be on the other side of Wolverhampton, where everything was new and unfamiliar, miles from anyone.

Getting to school was also a problem. Instead of being able to walk with Karen every morning, I now had to travel on two buses. This meant that getting together with friends after school became difficult because I had to contend with the big journey back. Moving so far from the catchment area around Woden School also meant that, when it came to choosing my senior school, I couldn't go to the same one as my friends. As a result I found the concept of leaving junior for senior school very difficult, and wondered how I would ever make any new friends in a different part of the town. I worried that I would have to spend all my time alone, and that the friends from my old school would all find new ones. It's odd that I should have felt that way, as I was a sociable little girl with lots of interests and lots of mates outside school. I didn't really have a good reason why I should have worried so much about making new friends.

It was finally agreed that I would attend Regis School, a popular mixed comprehensive in the leafy suburb of Tetenhall in Wolverhampton, not far from Pendeford. It sits on a tree-lined street, tucked away from the hustle and bustle of the main roads. Regis had a good reputation, which appealed to Mum, while I was attracted by the status it had in the area for turning out winners on the sports field.

My nerves at starting at a school where I didn't know anyone weren't calmed by what I had to wear. As a rule I hated wearing skirts because I was so skinny, and this became a particular problem when Mum and I went shopping for my new uniform. Because I was in a single-parent family we were on a tight budget, which meant we could only go to one particular shop. I remember walking up to the main shop window and thinking, 'Oh God, do I have to go in there?' I had seen some of the Regis girls wearing lovely skirts that were neat, short and pleated, and I wanted one like that. However, Mum wasn't a fan of short skirts and anyway, you couldn't buy the ones I liked in the shop we had to go in. I ended up with a dowdy A-line skirt that hung down past my knees. I would roll the skirt up at the waistband, but it didn't make it look much better and I'd have to make sure it was back down again by the time I got home. Although in the first couple of years of secondary school I hated wearing that boring uniform, I'm a huge fan of the concept now. I now know how hard it can be when there's any element of finance controlling the choice of clothes you wear, and I think uniforms provide a level playing field which is of great comfort when your choice is influenced by your parents' income.

So, in September 1983, I arrived for my first day at senior school. I was just a little first year wearing an unfamiliar and slightly oversized school uniform, mildly overwhelmed and surrounded by strange people, strange sights and strange smells.

That first Monday morning we were met by Miss Dixon, who looked after the first years. Miss Dixon was also the head of the PE department, and would become very important in my school athletics career. She was extremely popular, but was not the sort of person you messed with. I would later learn that she was a lot of fun and easy to get along with, but you had to know where to draw the line, to respect the distinction between teacher and pupil. But I knew none of this on my first day, nor did I know how much fun I would have at Regis School, and how much the teachers would help me in achieving my sporting goals. After Miss Dixon's welcome, we were taken through to our classrooms and spent time getting to know our new form teachers and the other pupils with whom we would be spending the next five or so years.

After that first day, I quickly established myself as a rising sports star. The sports scene at Regis was incredibly vibrant. There were 900 children in the school, and I think around half of them must have thrown themselves into sport on a regular basis, making use of the school's excellent facilities.

The first time Miss Leigh remembers spotting me was during a netball lesson, when she saw me 'glide' across the court. But Regis was full of girls who were good at netball, so she didn't really give me a second thought. Then, during one PE lesson, we were given a rounders ball – we were going to learn how to throw. According to

Miss Leigh, that was when she realised they had something special in me. I threw that ball further than she had ever seen a girl throw a ball before. She believed I had a real talent, that I was a great natural thrower – which very, very few girls are. She talked to me afterwards and made sure I knew about the school's athletics club.

I certainly did! I also knew about the rounders club, the netball club, the tennis club and the hockey club, and was involved in all of them by the end of my first year. In fact, swimming was the only sport I didn't get involved in; although the school had a pool, I didn't enjoy swimming at all. I hated getting my hair wet and just paddling from one end to the other.

One of my favourite days of the year was sports day, when we would all troop round the field behind our house flags. The school would try and get a celebrity to come and open the day, and I can remember the year Tessa Sanderson turned up and threw her javelin across the rounders field. We were all completely entranced. The sports events would take place during the afternoon, and the certificates were awarded on a three-tier pedestal before home time. It was a lovely idea, and a day we really looked forward to every year.

I made lots of friends at Regis, girls with whom I am still in touch today. Denise Nelson was one of my best friends. We met when we were thirteen, and she soon became my comrade-in-arms. We spent most of our time with each other, playing in every sports team and hanging out together. I've always had girlfriends around me. I had some male friends, but they were never as important to me as my female friends. People have asked me if I think this is because I came from such a female-dominated family. It's an interesting question, and one I don't really know the answer to, but I certainly tended to form closer, longer-lasting bonds with women than I did with men. I suspect a lot of women are the same – your best female friends are such an important part of your life. Denise was certainly important to me when I was growing up. We hit it off straight away. We had similar interests, and for a couple of years she came down to

Wolverhampton and Bilston and got involved a bit, but it was mainly just for fun.

Jayne Finch was another very close friend of mine. She lived a couple of miles away from me and our friendship got closer in our second year of school when we would travel to and from school together on the bus. She played hockey and netball and did a bit of athletics. At school we were seen as the 'sports girls', and were at the centre of a group that dominated the teams. We loved our sport and ruled the roost. There were seven of us: me, Denise and Jayne, Tonia Wilbrey, a talented athlete who unfortunately lost interest in sport when she found boys, Maree Hendricks, a great netballer who was also good at javelin and shot, Sharon Hughes who did netball, athletics and tennis, and little Lizzie Holland who played netball, hockey and tennis. Lizzie was the delicate one, and she was hopelessly in love with Bruce Springsteen, or 'The Bruce' as he was lovingly called.

We really were *the girls,* all seven of us. We were very competitive. Being in a school that encouraged sport, and having a group of friends like that, I never felt as if it was at all odd for girls to be interested in sport. We loved it and we were good at it – why should that have been so strange? But I know I was lucky. I had PE teachers like Miss Dixon, Miss Leigh and Miss Tranter. They put a lot of effort into encouraging girls to get involved, and created a system in which girls could succeed and an atmosphere in which they could thrive.

I am amazed that so many girls see sport as a male preserve. People say I'm a role model for women in sport – and that's great, because I know how beneficial sport can be for girls. And although it is flattering to be asked to model, go on television and attend award ceremonies, it's more important to me if one girl takes up sport, or one school considers sport for girls more seriously because of what I have achieved.

But it wasn't just the girls who excelled in sports at our school – the guys were sporty too. Those who did well and liked to get involved were definitely seen as the cool ones, the sporty scene was where it was at. Some of the boys were good at football and cricket, and we'd go along at break time and join in with them, kicking the ball around on the grass.

It seems there is a preconception in schools that, for games such as football, the boys are good and the girls are bad. It was never that way with us – the boys had more experience, but we were all quite fit, so we girls picked it up and did well. The boys didn't seem to have any problem at all with us playing football; they saw us as good athletes and knew we were capable of running rings round them on the track, so they had a certain respect for us. Again, much of this was down to the way the school dealt with us, we were publicly rewarded for everything we did; we were handed our trophies in assembly and the whole school would applaud us. Because our sporting achievements were highly recognised, we were motivated to do the best we could, and were respected by our peers for having done so. I think the boys were proud of us. Isn't that refreshing?

I competed for the school in athletics every year. In the first year, I represented the school in the town championships, competing in the hurdles and long jump, which Regis won for the sixth consecutive year. I then went on to win the county championships, and therefore qualified for the English Schools Athletics Championships, where I would represent my county.

In June 1985, in my second year at school, I qualified for the West Midlands team again. That was when I came across a coach called Darrell Bunn. Darrell was a selector for the West Midlands squad and I remember meeting him after I competed for the town in the county championships. He must have been watching me because at the end of the competition, as I ran across the grass on my way to pack up and say goodbye to a few people, he called me over to where he was standing. He said he'd seen me in the long jump, thought I was very good and asked me who my coach was. Because he was one of the West Midlands selection team, I was extremely flattered. When I said I was working with a group at Wolverhampton and Bilston, coached by Richard Whitter and Alan Jones, he said he knew them well.

The West Midlands squad meetings took place at Birchfield Harriers Athletics Club, and were run by Darrell. He said he would see me there, and added, 'When you come down for squad meetings, why don't you come and do some long jump practices with me? I'll have a look at your run-up if you want – it's a little bit inconsistent, and I'm sure we could do something with it.'

'Yes please,' I replied delightedly. 'That would be great.' And I ran off to tell Mum I'd been talent-spotted!

While I was at the sessions at Birchfield, Darrell would help me with my long jump, pointing out the simple mistakes I was making, and allowing my jump to flow much better. After working with him I could not believe how much I improved. He took the jump apart and looked at every component of it; no one before had analysed so closely what I was doing. I was only thirteen at the time and quite a bit younger than everyone else, but I managed to come third in the long jump, after reaching 5.35m, and took part in the relay, in which we came second. Performing in the English Schools competition was a fantastic experience, and it taught me a great deal about competing at the highest level. The competition was structured like the Olympic Games, with a parade of the teams, team meetings, a call room where you had to go before competing, dress fittings, rules of conduct, overnight stays away from your family and the nomination of a team captain. There was a real emphasis on team effort and bonding, and I thought it was wonderful.

The following year, in my third year at school, the English Schools finals were held in Portsmouth, which was miles away from the Midlands. We went down the day before and stayed there overnight, which was great fun. The next day I won the under-14 long jump competition with a leap of 5.45m. Winning the competition brought me to the attention of all sorts of people, and suddenly everyone was starting to pay an interest. I was awarded a National Dairy Council Scholarship which helped me pay for clothing and training fees, such as my club membership and entry to the track.

I was really starting to feel like a somebody. I felt as if I was excelling – an athlete who was special and starting to shine, not just taking part. I was having lots of fun too, but I really was beginning to see the improvements and feeling the competitiveness. On top of all that, I was starting to forge new friendships across the country.

Athletics was really starting to take over my life at this time, but that was fine by me. I still went out with friends and did 'normal' teenage things, but my athletics was most important to me. There were no boyfriends in my life; I simply didn't have the time for them. In addition, Mum was very strict, and I wasn't allowed to go out very much.

Through the first two years of senior school, I was still dancing as well as going down to Wolverhampton and Bilston athletics club. All my spare time was full of activity, and Mum was starting to worry that I would wear myself out and lose my concentration at school. The final straw came when I was fourteen. Richard, my coach from Wolverhampton and Bilston, was driving us back from an English Schools competition in the evening when the car suffered a blow out on the motorway. We'd been in an enormous rush to get back so I could get to the rehearsal for our annual dance show.

Mum offered me an ultimatum. 'Right,' she said. 'That's it. Something's got to go. You have to give one of these up – dancing or athletics. Which one is it to be?'

'I can't do that,' I cried. 'I love them both!'

But Mum was adamant. 'We're racing from one side of the country to the next all the time, Denise. This can't carry on.'

I eventually agreed, with great reluctance, to give one up – but told Mum that she would have to choose which one as I couldn't bear to do it myself. Mum refused to choose, and said I was old enough to make the decision on my own. In the end I decided to give up dancing, but we compromised by agreeing that Mum would explain the problems to Shirley, the lady who ran the dance school. I was so close to her, I couldn't face telling her I was giving it all up after ten years.

So, athletics became my major preoccupation, and I threw myself into it wholeheartedly. I did, however, have lots of fun off the athletics track, and recall lots of house parties and get-togethers with friends from both my school and the other local schools. But there was never any question of me favouring socialising over my athletics.

Other girls at that age were into boys, but they were never a big deal for me. I was so caught up in the world of athletics that any other interests were secondary. I was lucky I was involved in such a good club at the time, a club that seemed to be so vibrant and optimistic. I saw it as the place of champions. I can remember Kathy Cook, the highly acclaimed 200m and 400m specialist, turning up at the track with her husband, Gary Cook, a successful British International 400m runner; Sonia Lanaman would come as well, and I would watch in awe from the sidelines as this super sprinter trained on the same track as me. Then there was Tessa Sanderson, and Joan Baptiste. All the names and faces I had seen on TV were there, at the stadium, and I'd see them training and think, 'Wow, they're all real!' I wouldn't say that being famous was a motivation for me, I was just interested in being good. I wanted to be a great athlete. I wanted to see if I was as good as I thought I was, and as good as everyone else had started to say that I was. When you're told you're good at the age of thirteen you obviously want to know *how* good. You need a measuring device. Athletics is perfect for that, because you can compare exactly how good you are, you can measure improvements and you can see, at any stage, how far off the best you are.

With the long jump, I found the challenge of having to jump further and jump your best intoxicating. I felt as if someone got up and drew a line in the sand after every jump I did and said, 'Now run down and jump past that.' I was always challenging myself, always pushing myself further. I'd be determined to do it, and once I did, of course I'd want to draw another line in the sand and jump past that. I always wanted to be the best, and to answer questions such as, What is my maximum? How far can I stretch myself? How good can I be? I still do.

It takes a lot to keep driving yourself, especially as you get older and you find other things you want to do and new pressures upon you. In some ways you have to ignore those other pressures if you really want to excel. I'm afraid I ignored the demands of school work. I know I could have performed better in the classroom, and I'm disappointed that I left with worse grades than I was capable of. I should have had the same ambitions for my school work as I did for my sport, but somehow it didn't happen. Academically I was a failure, and I hate that. But something prevented me from having the discipline or the real desire to push myself further in something other than athletics. Although I knew how important the study was, my passion was for sport – and I suppose that it is passion, ultimately, that drives you to challenge yourself.

The fact that I didn't do as well as I should have still plays a lot on my mind, and sometimes I think that maybe I would have been respected more if I'd gone on to be a teacher, as I had planned to do originally. In my more reflective moments I wonder if Mum would have been more proud of me then. She took my education extremely seriously; she was eager for me to do well because she hadn't finished her education because she became pregnant with me.

If I had gone on to be a teacher I would have taught PE, but would also have taught English, as it was always my favourite subject. I used to be good at maths, too, when I was younger, but then I let it slip. I should have done better, and could have done so with a bit more dedication. I know how frustrated my teachers were, they knew I could achieve so much if I just put in the time. But once I'd started seriously training for athletics, time was something I didn't have very much of – I hardly had the time to do my homework.

The GCSE results came through, and I had passed just three: English Literature, English Language and PE. Although I was devoting a lot of my time to athletics, I still didn't think it would be possible for me to pursue it as a career, so I toyed with the idea of re-sitting my exams. But then I decided against it. Instead, I stayed on in the lower sixth, and did a B-Tech in Technology. During the course I won the Women in Technology competition, which was sponsored by Digital. The brief was to make a video talking about the problems companies face in encouraging women into careers in technology. The prize was a visit to their parent company in Boston, to look around and see what they were doing to tackle the issue. Winning the competition really lifted my spirits and I started to believe that it was my application that was letting me down – I just needed to spend extra time studying, and if I did, I would see the results.

When I finished at school, I went on to Wulfrun College where I studied A level English and PE.

There was definitely something of the rebel about me when I was a teenager. I wasn't unpleasant, it was more that I didn't always conform and do as I was told. My friends and I just liked to have fun. I remember once we decided to play blackjack in the middle of a French lesson. We had a great time, but unsurprisingly it really upset the teacher and we had to stand up and apologise to her. Then we were sent to see the head of languages and explain our behaviour to him. I was terrified of the consequences and what Mum's reaction would be, but luckily it wasn't taken any further. We could be dreadful at times, and I know the teachers would call Denise Nelson and me the 'terrible twosome'. The interesting thing was that they were never sure just who was the leader and who was the follower – although she would deny it, I think it was definitely Denise who led. Although we weren't model pupils, we weren't unpleasant, we would never have bullied any of our fellow pupils or caused any real trouble.

I did have a tendency to be a bit stubborn – I still do. Both Miss Dixon and Miss Leigh found me incredibly frustrating when there was something I really didn't want to do. I think they found me particularly exasperating wherever long-distance running was concerned. When it came to running the 800m, I'd think of a million reasons why I didn't want to take part. I would say I had a big competition coming up and had to rest my sore knee or ankle, or hamstring, or whatever injury I was pretending to suffer. I would then walk around with a big grin on my face, knowing there was nothing they could do to make me. I must have been so annoying! Luckily they also recognised the positive side of this stubborn streak, the side that would have me practising and practising each lunchtime, as I tried to improve my long jump.

On these occasions, I wouldn't give up and wouldn't stop training until I had my technique exactly as I wanted it, my run-up spot on. I would – and still do – use my innate ability to pull on my inner reserves. It would show in competitions when I was at school – I might have two no-jumps, and when most people would feel really low and want to pull out, I would draw on something inside, on my determination, and would often manage to do a great jump on the last attempt.

I don't know what it is that's inside me that makes me so resilient, but it is an ability I have had to draw on time and time again in major championships, and it has allowed me to turn the most bleak and desperate situations into a success.

Chapter Six
Birchfield Beckons

The three things Bill Hand feared most in life were 'boobs, boys and Birchfield'. He would tell us how he'd nurture his young female athletes for years, then suddenly one day they'd arrive at the club as fully grown women, and find that running the 800m wasn't quite so comfortable in their 36Bs. And for those of us who weren't over-developed in the bust department, and still quite comfortable running that 800m, he'd worry that boys would come along and distract us. But neither of those happened to me, and athletics continued to play a major role in my life. However, eventually I did fall prey to the bright lights of Birchfield, which I suppose was only natural.

Birchfield Harriers was a big, reputable club based at the Alexander Stadium in Birmingham, one of the country's leading athletics venues. The first time I went there to meet Darrell Bunn for extra long jump practices before the English Schools competition in 1985, I was impressed with its bigger stadium, nicer long jump pits and better hurdles. It appealed to me immediately.

I went to Darrell four or five times for extra coaching before the competition. I loved working with him because he had a different style of teaching – it was more detailed, and at a higher level. Generally I was good at following instructions and was a quick learner, but Darrell seemed to have a knack of explaining things so that I understood immediately what he was expecting. It was a good relationship, and was very comfortable and effective from the start. We did the sort of work on my jumping that had never been done before, examining it in detail and working out exactly where I was going wrong. My confidence levels rose, and I knew I was jumping better than I ever had before.

The day of the competition dawned. That morning I was too nervous to eat a proper breakfast and couldn't do much more than pick at my toast and cereal. When I arrived we had a big team meeting. These sessions were great – excellent pep talks for us all that really boosted our confidence levels. We were told how the West Midlands team was a force to be reckoned with, that we were superior regardless of our performance. We were made to feel that we were at an advantage just by wearing our kit, and were given fluorescent stickers to plaster everywhere saying 'West Mids, Best Kids'. It created such a fantastic atmosphere and a sense of belonging.

We were organised into event groups, and walked on to the field in single file. At the pit I put on the special long jump shoes I had borrowed from a triple jumper. It was great to wear these specialist shoes, which were more supportive than regular sprint spikes. Darrell was in charge of our group, and I was very appreciative of the words of guidance and encouragement he offered me right up to the moment when it was my turn to jump. I had already marked out my run-up, so I stood at the end of it, took a deep breath, and started running. I accelerated as I approached the board and took off. I knew my take-off was good, I felt as if I would be airborne for ever, and as I landed the crowd clapped enthusiastically.

That day I jumped a personal best of 5.35m. I had no doubt that Darrell's contribution had made all the difference, giving me the extra edge to jump my best ever and win a medal. Afterwards I introduced Mum to him, and as we went home that evening I talked of nothing but what a great coach Darrell was, and how much I enjoyed working with him. I was only twelve years old, but I knew how much he would be able to help me. I kept asking Mum whether we could get Darrell to coach me every week at Birchfield, but she explained that he was based in Birmingham, which was too far away. I insisted that it didn't matter, that I'd catch the train to Birmingham, but she was adamant that it was too far. In the end, as much to placate me as anything else, she said that if I was still interested at the end of the season, she would call him. I suppose she expected me to forget all about it. She must have thought it was an absurd idea, to move from the club based down the road to one miles away. But as far as I was concerned, being part of such a big set-up could only enhance my progression further. To me, it was a small sacrifice if it meant I would improve.

I continued to come across Darrell at other competitions and he would always pay an interest in me, ask how I was doing and speak to Mum. All this time I never stopped wanting him to coach me, so in September 1985, just after my thirteenth birthday, I persuaded Mum to ring him to see if he would. Darrell was quite surprised by the request, and worried about the logistics of me travelling from Wolverhampton to Birmingham. I admit it was a long way. At best, the journey would involve a fifteen-minute bus ride from school to the station, a twenty-five-minute train journey to Birmingham, then another bus ride of at least twenty minutes from Birmingham to Birchfield. And of course the whole journey back again – at about nine o'clock at night.

None the less, Mum explained my enthusiasm and commitment: 'She's willing to do it, and she's quite insistent, so I'm happy to give it a try if you are,' she said, and in the end Darrell agreed.

'Tell her to come down on Wednesday,' he said.

And that was that – I had the coach of my dreams! I started going to Birchfield for long jump practices twice a week on Wednesdays and Sundays, but stayed as a member of Wolverhampton and Bilston where I continued to go for running sessions on Tuesdays and Thursdays.

I quickly realised how monotonous my jumping had become at Wolverhampton. Although I'd done a lot of work on it, never had I been able to break the event down into easily manageable chunks. Darrell analysed a long jump differently, making me understand the link between the run-up, take-off, flight and landing, not treating them as separate sections. But he didn't change too much of my style, too soon, because he liked what he saw and thought the way I was jumping was effective. He could see I was athletic and commented on my good 'jump-ability' and speed on the runway. It was the consistency he thought needed work. Still he recognised a talent in me – but also something more, something special.

There were two jump groups running simultaneously when I arrived, one headed by Darrell, the other by his friend Kevin Reeve. It was a bit of a free-for-all in many ways, with us all mucking in and warming up together on the track. I remember lots of people from that time: Steve Phillips, a long jumper; David Emanuel, the triple jumper; Kevin Liddington and Paul Hibbert; but it was Sharon Bowie to whom I took an instant shine – she was the star of my age group, and became almost like a sister to me.

Sharon was a long jumper and had competed for England in senior internationals; I desperately wanted to be like her. She was *the* girl of the moment, about eight years older then me, and I idolised her. She had a slim build and was taller than me, but very leggy, with long arms and long fingers. She had an infectious laugh and was very friendly. Much to my delight, she took a shine to me, and treated me like a little sister. In a way, I always felt that Sharon, Darrell and I were like a special party, a mini team within the group: I was the little protégée, Sharon was the senior sportswoman and Darrell was the boss. We worked together in this way for three years.

It was during those years that things started to happen for me.

After coming third in the English Schools in 1985, I won it in 1986. And, although I dropped to third place in 1987 because I had moved from the under-14 to the under-16 group, I won again in 1988.

Joining Birchfield Harriers for my training – and mixing with athletes like Sharon Bowie – was very good for me. I was surrounded by people I wanted to emulate, and felt that these people had a chance of making it to the top. The national triple jump and long-jump squads were there, training had become exciting, and I felt as though I was getting real benefits and making real improvements.

Darrell was an inspirational coach, encouraging, thoughtful and knowledgeable. He introduced discipline on the runway and made sure I didn't foul. He introduced check marks, so I knew exactly where I was at any point in my run-up – when I had to accelerate and at which point I should hit the board. My run-up became more structured and reliable, I knew that if I followed the check points I would always hit the board at the right point, at the right time, and always at optimum speed. Darrell used 'trigger words' which got through to me. He was an excellent motivator and managed to convince me that one day I would be the best.

While training at Birchfield I had stayed at Wolverhampton and Bilston but I was at the club in name only. So, at the age of fifteen, after two years of working with Darrell, I signed to the Birmingham club exclusively. Once I started training at Birchfield I spent almost every night there – Tuesdays, Wednesdays, Thursdays and Sundays – and Darrell, Sharon and I grew closer and closer, socialising together after training, talking to one another, sharing all our hopes with one another. After training on Sunday mornings, the two of them would often come back to my house for lunch, then we'd all settle down in front of the TV.

I was learning new things every day, and having some successes. Unfortunately for Sharon, things weren't going as well as she'd hoped, as she was having to contend with some recurring injuries. It seemed to me, rightly or wrongly, that Darrell was channelling most of his energies into me and my progression, and not paying Sharon as much attention as he had done in the past – and I noticed some tension creeping in between the two of them. Sadly, our once-happy threesome now seemed to be in jeopardy, and I don't think training was as much fun for Sharon as it had been previously. Slowly, she stopped coming round for lunch, stopped socialising with us, and became less involved with the group. It finally came to a point at which she stopped coming to training altogether, and focused more on her career as a teacher. Darrell and I became a twosome instead – and our relationship really started to blossom.

Darrell astutely limited the amount of work he allowed me to put in. He was incredibly cautious, refusing to let me train too much or too hard, wanting me to peak at the right time, rather than be a child star who blew out, or got injured before I was out of my teens. I'm really grateful to him for that. He knew when to wind me up and when to calm me down.

There is always a close bond between athlete and coach, and I think the relationship Darrell and I had was closer than most tend to be. Because Darrell coached me throughout my teens, he saw me develop into an adult, and really got to know me and understand me.

I think with a male coach and a young female athlete the bond can be particularly strong because the coach can feel almost paternal. Darrell and I had that sort of relationship, and people often ask me whether that was because I didn't know my own father. Was I looking for a father figure in Darrell? That's hard to answer, but I don't think so. He was someone I could really talk to; he didn't judge me, and more importantly, I really believed that he was the person who would guide me to my maximum potential. I certainly looked to Darrell for guidance. He was fun to be around and there was a good atmosphere between the two of us in training. I saw him as my mentor, and I trusted him completely.

He certainly showed me extraordinary commitment. To save me from having to get the bus, whenever he could he would meet me from the five o'clock train in Birmingham and take me to Birchfield.

He also ended up driving me home after most sessions, so I didn't have to get the train. It meant he had an incredibly long journey, from Birchfield to Pendeford, then back to his home in Birmingham again, and I was very grateful to him.

Another question that people have asked me is what Darrell's motivation was during these early years. What was he getting back from it? I think his motivation was a huge passion for the sport, and the ambition to take someone to the highest level possible. What he got back was the sheer pleasure of seeing someone succeed, and knowing that he had been a part of it.

To an athlete, the value of a good coach is immeasurable. It is what makes the difference between an average performer and a champion. For years the role of athletics coaches in Britain has been under-valued, especially at club level. These people give up their time freely to mentor or inspire and motivate young athletes, week in, week out, fifty-two weeks a year, with little in return apart from the hope that one day that athlete may go on to become something great. I think most coaches see their role as being in some way akin to that of a sculptor. A good coach sees a talented athlete as a piece of stone, recognises its potential to be a fabulous creation. A great sculptor knows that he has the ability to make it extraordinary, to carve it so that it can stand alone and be great. We are lucky that for most of them, the motivation isn't financial reward.

Most coaches in Britain don't get enough respect for what they do, which is a terrible indictment on our sports system. Without coaches and helpers, sport stops. We rely on them to keep sport functioning, yet they are offered little support and practically no money. The question really is how many more years these volunteers can keep doing what they are doing with such a lack of recognition. We're lucky that so many of them keep going when they must feel inclined to give up. It is crazy that there is no senior pay structure to encourage coaches into the sport, and that so many of them have to carry on voluntarily to a very senior level. Athletics is worse than most sports because it doesn't have a tradition of paying – and I know of just a handful of coaches throughout athletics who receive proper financial support. If we lose these vital pillars, the future of our sports will be jeopardised.

If things weren't going well at school or at home, I'd talk to Darrell. He was a PE teacher at a school in Birmingham, so he understood when I complained about school and my teachers. There were never any big problems, and I was never in any serious trouble, but when you're a teenager you often feel the need to moan about things, and when it was just Mum and me in the house, and she was always working really hard, I suppose I felt the need to confide in someone else about my problems.

Throughout my teenage years my mother and I did occcasionally suffer from turbulence in our relationship, as teenagers do, but for me it felt particularly bad because there wasn't anyone else, no intermediary to turn to and let off steam, so the tension between us would sit in the house like a dark cloud. I'm sure at times it was difficult for Mum too – she only wanted the best for me, but of course I couldn't see that at the time. Mum didn't have anyone else to talk to and discuss problems with, no one else she could bounce ideas off. And on top of all that, she had to go out and work to support us both. My rows with Mum were about the usual teenage things – whether my room was tidy, whether I wore appropriate clothes, whether I was working properly at school and what time I got in – and a lot of our problems were caused by a lack of communication. Unlike my relationship with Darrell, Mum and I never talked very much, and as a result I felt she didn't understand me. Darrell would often step between Mum and me when our lack of communication was making life harder and harder for both of us. Just by telling my Mum how upset I was, by urging me to see things from her point of view, or simply by saying, 'come on you two – sort it out,' he was able to dissipate the tension a little and help us to work together. We'd all end up going out and having some dinner and everything would be OK afterwards.

As I got older, moving from my early to mid-teens, I became much stronger as an athlete and a person, able to say what I wanted and what I thought. Darrell reacted brilliantly; he could see that my needs as an athlete were shifting, and he changed his approach. He adopted a less prescriptive way of coaching, and started to incorporate my views and opinions. Slowly, Darrell and I moved away from child and teacher to become two adults working together. Darrell handled the changes in me incredibly well; he allowed me to take more responsibility for my actions, and allowed me slightly more independence – which kept me interested in the sport, preventing me from feeling like a schoolgirl at the track.

The English Schools competitions were the biggest events of my early years, particularly in 1988 when I won, at the age of fifteen, and was invited to partake in a British Schools International, in which I would be competing for England against Ireland, Scotland and Wales. It was still a schools competition but now I was representing England, something which seemed terribly exciting. I can remember being handed my red and white England kit for the first time, fingering the material and examining every inch of it.

We benefited from a strong team spirit at the competition and it was fabulous to be part of something so big. There was a great atmosphere as we travelled down on the train together. I was slightly nervous, but I did well, and came second in the long jump with a distance of 6.02m, helping the England team to victory. But it is the socialising I remember most clearly from this event, particularly staying overnight in Wiltshire and having a great pool party. I hadn't been to a pool party before and had a fantastic time. I partied the night away with Donna Fraser, and we hit the dance floor in our swimming costumes and bikinis, dancing around to Wham's greatest hits and Salt 'n' Pepa's 'Push It'. Donna and I had rehearsed the dance routine to the song from the video, and executed it perfectly to the music.

Later that year I competed in my first 'proper' international. I was selected for the Great Britain juniors team for long jump. The Great Britain team travelled all over the world, particularly round Europe, but where was my first international? Cwmbran, Wales. I didn't even get to go on a plane!

I remember the letter coming through to tell me I had been selected. The envelope was stuffed full of forms I had to fill in. I was thrilled.

The letter read, 'Dear Denise, We are pleased to inform you that you have been selected for the Great Britain junior squad to compete next weekend in Cwmbran. Please return the acceptance form below.' I used to keep all the selection letters in a scrap book when I first started, it was so exciting to get them.

The envelope contained forms about competitors' sizes, so they could organise kit for you, the flight details, an expenses form, and a medical form so you could notify them of any injuries you had, so the team doctors were fully up-to-date on everyone's level of fitness. The kit was sent out as soon as they received the completed forms.

I was extremely excited about going to Cwmbran. But it didn't work out how I had hoped it would. I didn't compete very well, and it was nothing like the exciting international debut I'd dreamed of. Darrell assured me there would be bigger and better competitions, and that this was just a small junior tournament, but I was starting to get restless. I'd received a big shock at the competition, realising just how much more I had to do to succeed at the next level. It was clear that there were a lot of talented youngsters across the world – there's nothing like an international to show you that, and Cwmbran was mine.

Still, I knew I had talent, and felt that one day I might make it. But when?

CHAPTER SEVEN
THE TEENAGE YEARS

When I was a teenager I wanted to be Whitney Houston and marry Clint Eastwood's character, the Man With No Name in *A Fistful of Dollars*, with all his icy ruggedness. I thought he was the greatest, and every time I saw him on screen or in a magazine, I dreamed of the day I would walk down the aisle towards him. One of my favourite British athletes was Steve Cram. I was a huge fan of Steve's, and loved his blond hair, sweet face and long legs! He seemed such a nice guy, and I would sit glued to the television every time he ran against Sebastian Coe and Steve Ovett, desperately hoping he would win. I would cut out every picture I could find of him in the newspapers and magazines, and stick them into my favourite athletes' scrapbook, along with the likes of Heike Dreschler, Evelyn Ashford and Daley Thompson.

I was also incredibly taken with Morten Harket from A-Ha, something which will, no doubt, do great damage to my reputation! That had started with the 'Take On Me' video, which I loved. A-Ha were the first group I went to see in concert. It was at the NEC in Birmingham, and was going to involve me travelling on my own – as A-Ha were far too uncool for my friends. Mum said there was no way I could go, but after lots of begging she relented – and it was worth it!

I had a great time in my teens. People think that if you're an athlete there are no opportunities for socialising or having fun – but that was far from true in my case. Most of your time is taken up with events at the track, but there is certainly the chance to go out and enjoy yourself. Athletics was always the number-one priority during my teens, but I still managed to do all the things that other girls my age did, like partying, drinking and dressing up.

When I went out for the evening, I would say goodbye to Mum wearing simple clothes that looked decent and respectable. However, my party outfit and make-up were always stuffed into my pockets, so I could make myself beautiful either in the ladies' loos or at a friend's house. Occasionally, if I thought I could get away with it, I would wear my party clothes out, covering them with the biggest coat I could find so Mum couldn't see them. That meant all I had to do was nip into the ladies', apply lashings of lipstick, and I was ready to go.

Sometimes I would shout goodbye to Mum and run off down the street before she had a chance to check what I was wearing. By the time she made it to the front door I had usually sprinted to the end of the road (being an athlete had its uses!) and was re-applying my lipstick just around the corner. My coat would come off the minute I was out of view, revealing the full splendour of my chosen outfit – sometimes a mini skirt, sometimes a pair of tight trousers, or even my favourite black lycra mini-dress. If I couldn't manage to get out wearing my latest trendy outfit, or smuggle it out in my pockets, I would borrow clothes and make-up from Denise when I got to her house. Denise had a very liberal mum who didn't mind us getting ready there, and would tolerate us on the occasions we came back having had quite a lot to drink.

I had so much fun as a teenager because I had such great girl-friends. We'd go everywhere together and always had an excellent time, whether we were just sitting in each other's kitchens, chatting and eating, or out on the town. On nights out, I had to rush back from training in Birmingham having laid out all my gear that morning. The girls would go out at 8.30pm, and I needed to be home, showered and dressed before joining them. I'd race back, belt through the door with my sports bag, throw it into a corner, wash and change and fly back out through the door before Mum even knew I was home. On many occasions she was still at work, so I could get away with dumping my stuff and jumping into my mini skirt, just leaving a note on the table to say I would be back late.

We all loved to dance, so that was the number-one night-time activity – particularly at Picasso's or the Mermaid pub in Wolver-hampton. We would also gossip madly about everyone and every-thing. We used to drink as well, and we went through the usual stages of experimenting with, and getting drunk on, horrible concoctions such as sweet wines, before progressing on to Diamond White and Black.

I remember one particular afternoon drinking session when I was sixteen. We were all having a great time when we should have been sitting in lessons. I was happily laughing and joking with the others when I suddenly remembered I had training that evening, and realised that if I didn't leave soon I would be late. So I said goodbye to the girls and staggered out of the pub towards the bus stop.

I have no idea how I made it on to the bus or even the train, but I do remember that the bus to the track was packed, and every time it moved I would fall into people. They all stared at me, and even started tutting. I just gazed back at them through glazed eyes, smiling stupidly. I finally managed to get myself, and my giant kit bag, upstairs. (That kit bag was enormous. Whenever I think of myself in my younger days going to training on buses and trains, I remember the bag really annoyed people because the damn thing took up half the floor, and everyone had to stand around it.) Having staggered up the stairs to the top deck I eventually found myself a seat and plonked myself down. The combination of the alcohol and the movement of the bus meant that, as soon as I was sitting still, I fell fast asleep. Somehow I managed to wake up just before my stop but, to my horror, I had my head on the shoulder of the guy next to me. Luckily, there wasn't enough time to be embarrassed and I grabbed my huge bag and headed off down the stairs as carefully as possible. Walking back into the fresh air made me feel horribly drunk all over again, and by the time I got to the track I knew there was no way I could pretend to be sober. I had to confess to Darrell that I had been drinking, and apologise for my behaviour. He told me I was impossible, put me in his car and left me there for a couple of hours to sober up while he worked with the rest of the athletes. But he made me train afterwards. I felt dreadful by then, and it was certainly the last time I drank before training!

When I was eighteen, I had my first serious relationship with a boyfriend, Tim, whom I'd met at the track in Birmingham. He was nineteen and worked shifts as a computer operator. We would go out and have a great time drinking and partying at clubs all over the Midlands. 1990 and 1991 were certainly two of the best summers I've ever had, full of fun, great music and a brilliant atmosphere. I'd stay out late, then go back to Tim's house when I could – even though Mum didn't like that very much, as she believed that if you went out, you came back to your own home. Sometimes I'd defy her and stay at Tim's anyway, but most of the time I knew it was far easier to get myself home at the end of the evening.

As our relationship grew, I did spend a lot of time at Tim's. He lived with his parents and his sister in Birmingham, and I enjoyed the family atmosphere of his home. His dad was really funny and I got on really well with all of them. Mum began to worry, feeling that all the time I was spending with him would have been better spent on schoolwork. She probably had a point, but at the time I felt she was being too strict with me, that she didn't understand. I was training hard in athletics, and I needed to have some fun. I still feel strongly that you have to have a release from hard work. I am a disciplined athlete and I lead a disciplined lifestyle, but every so often I have to let it go – I go out, have a few drinks, relax, then get back to the training the next day. It's just a case of knowing when to stop and where to draw the line.

My friends got away with so much more than me; even when I was sixteen I was under an 11.30pm curfew. This meant I had to be on the last bus which left Wolverhampton town centre at about 11.03pm, getting me to the end of our road by quarter past. I missed it once, and had to take a bus that didn't go past my road. I had to jump off two miles away and run home through dark streets that I wouldn't even go down on my own at night now. My heart was pounding hard in my chest, and I knew that I'd be in all sorts of trouble with Mum, and that would be it – I wouldn't be allowed out again for weeks. Luckily, I arrived in only a few minutes late. But after that I certainly made sure I caught the 11.03.

I don't really know how I kept everything together during those years; I would get up, go to school, come back, get changed, leave for the club, catch four buses and two trains getting there and back – and after all that I'd want to go out partying. On a few occasions I would promise Mum that Darrell would bring me home after training, knowing full well that I had already made arrangements to go out that night.

It meant that homework was being done late at night when I got back, and was hardly ever handed in on time. Mum used to get so annoyed when she found me downstairs late at night trying to get my work finished, after I had assured her that I'd be home earlier. A couple of times she had to go up to Regis to see my form tutor because of missed essay deadlines, constant lateness, that sort of thing. It was a trying time for Mum, and she knew it was because I was trying to fit too much in.

But she didn't want me to mess up my schooling, and we'd have terrible rows about it. She would rein me in, the curfews got tighter, and I'd work a bit harder – for a while. I would also play Mum and

Darrell off against each other. I'd tell Mum that Darrell was giving me a lift home so she shouldn't worry, then I would disappear off with my friends having told Darrell I was going straight home. On one occasion, when Denise and I were stuck in Birmingham unable to get home, I called Darrell at 3am to ask him to pick us up. He was not impressed, but he came to get us. Darrell would always try and help me out because he would worry about what might happen to me if he didn't. I hope he realises how grateful I am for all his support and how much I appreciated the way he put himself out for me, as I may not have said it at the time.

Both Darrell and Mum found this a difficult time. Sometimes, I would worry Mum by not phoning to explain where I was. I would simply crawl in late at night, saying someone had invited me somewhere and I'd had to go. When she would ask me why I hadn't called, I'd shrug. I don't really know why I didn't phone, maybe it was because I knew I'd get told off!

I must have been incredibly irritating and difficult, but I suppose it was my way of testing everyone, seeing how far I could push the boundaries. I resented being treated like a child. In my eyes, Mum had trusted me to take care of myself and be responsible ever since I was a child, so I couldn't understand her over-protectiveness in my teens. I just wanted to dictate my own time – where I went, and who I went with – have a certain amount of freedom and be left to get on with things myself.

I didn't just argue with Mum; Darrell and I had our fights, too. They were mainly about the amount of time I was spending going out, and I would give him a hard time for siding with my mum against me. When I stop and think about it, poor Darrell was often the piggy in the middle between Mum and me. When he sided with my Mum and I got angry with him, he would calmly explain her side of the story, telling me how hard it was to be a parent – and a single parent at that. Equally, on the occasions when he tried to justify my behaviour to my mother, she would give him a hard time and tell him not to interfere in the way she brought me up.

I know there were times when Mum resented Darrell's presence and his constant involvement in our life. After all, she *was* my mum, and wanted to retain a certain amount of control and discipline on her own terms. But having said all that, when we weren't having our disagreements, the three of us did spend some really good times together. I remember Darrell spent most of one summer helping us to decorate our lounge. The two of us would train at the track in the morning, and we'd paint in the afternoon. Darrell was decorator, taxi driver, coach and confidant. I don't know how we would have survived without him.

CHAPTER EIGHT
THE FIRST RUNG OF THE LADDER

I always believed that my future, and any chance of international sporting success, lay in the long jump. It was the event I had always excelled in, and the one that I thought I could crack one day. But the people around me saw things differently.

Darrell had spent time thinking about how good I was at picking up new skills, and how challenged I was by learning them. So, in 1988, when I was sixteen, he began incorporating other tasks into our regular training programme. His initial motivation was just to get me working on new motor skills, challenging myself physically and mentally to keep me alert and thinking. But what he had effectively started was the journey to an Olympic gold medal.

I already had some experiences as a hurdler, sprinter and long jumper, but I only had limited experience of the throwing events or high jump, and was certainly not skilled at the 800m – I loathed running anything further than 200m; even today I dread that race. Some heptathletes feel the same, as we tend to come from dynamic and ballistic events such as sprinting or jumping. The 800m is the only race in the heptathlon that demands endurance. It's the solitary stamina event, and needs aerobic fitness, so we all find it incredibly tough.

Darrell and I started by introducing a small amount of throwing into our practices, and we started with the rounders ball. Just as Miss Leigh had noticed in my first year at school, Darrell spotted straight away that I had a natural throwing arm.

We moved on to the proper equipment soon afterwards, starting with the javelin. I was no Tessa Sanderson, but the javelin certainly went further than you would imagine for a first-time throw. Darrell was amazed. He claims he stood there in awe, watching the javelin sail through the air. It went further than he'd ever seen a novice throw. I had this fantastically elastic arm that was both supple and strong, which lent itself perfectly to the task. I just found it all felt very, very natural, and with a little practice I was soon throwing it a reasonable distance.

Not long after starting, Darrell and I realised that, far from these extra sessions simply being fun, keeping me motivated and alert, they might well be the start of something big. I enjoyed learning new skills, and up until that time had always hoped I could continue to compete in the hurdles as well as the long jump. But now I thought trying the heptathlon was a good idea – I had watched Judy Simpson compete in the 1986 Commonwealth Games, and had also seen a local heptathlete, Joanne Mulliner, competing on the TV. But up until then it had not crossed my mind that this might be something I could do. It was my success with the javelin that truly made up Darrell's mind.

I was also quite quick at picking up the basic skills of the high jump. I already understood the importance of the run-up and the phases of jumping, but I now had to learn a different take-off technique for jumping up rather than along. I also had to learn the Fosbury flop, which was unlike anything I had done before. My first couple of attempts were not great, as I flopped in an undignified heap on to the high-jump bed with the bar clattering around my ankles. However, once I worked out what needed to be done I was able to make the changes quickly, and soon found I was jumping to around 1.5m, which was quite a reasonable standard. Technically, I wasn't the best high jumper in the world, but I managed to clear the bar through sheer strength and determination.

The shot was more difficult to pick up. I was very aware that I would have to keep working away at this, because I found it heavy and the throwing did not come to me as easily as it had for the javelin.

While I was working on these new events, I was still perfecting my long jump, and continuing to hurdle. The only event of the heptathlon that I hadn't looked at was the 800m. The 200m was not a problem because I had been sprinting as part of my long jump practices, and running flat races in preparation for the hurdles and relay. I was, however, aware that I would now be requiring a different training programme to tackle the speed-endurance element of the event. The 800m was more of a problem, and it took a long time before I was able to achieve a respectable time and speed in that.

But, after nine months spent working on my new skills, and with six good events – the long jump, high jump, shot, javelin, hurdles and 200m – Darrell suggested I enter a heptathlon competition, just to see how I was doing, and compare myself to the opposition. So, in September 1988 I entered my first ever heptathlon competition – the Midlands Championships in Birmingham.

I didn't know what to expect but, perhaps because there weren't any expectations, I don't remember being nervous at all. My abiding memory of the event is a feeling of total exhaustion half-way through day one. My other memory is how well all the athletes got on with one another. There was a great atmosphere. Obviously everyone was tense before the first event, but once that had passed, people opened up a little and started chatting. I soon realised that heptathlon is as much about overcoming and surviving the events as it is about beating your opponents. Don't get me wrong, the girls are competitive, but unlike the regular, single-event competitions where you spend maybe thirty minutes together, heptathletes spend two days in each other's company, sometimes even sharing the same recovery room or the same physiotherapy rooms. I don't know whether this attitude is shared by all heptathletes, but I have always felt a sense of belonging, understanding and respect for my fellow competitors while still allowing myself to be aggressive for competition.

I spent a lot of time watching the more experienced heptathletes, learning from them. I noticed how the other athletes were counting up the points and working out what they had to achieve in every event. By contrast, I didn't have a clue about points, and was simply giving it my best in everything, relying on Darrell to let me know how well I was doing, and hoping it would all sort itself out in the end.

Just before the 800m, Darrell came over and told me that everything was going really well, and that I was in the lead with one event to go. If I could do well in the 800m, I was in with a good chance of winning the whole competition. But that was a big 'if', as the 800m was my worst event.

The pain I felt during that race almost put me off heptathlon for life. I was sick beforehand with the sheer fear of what I would have to go through, and the race itself was awful. I finished somewhere near the back, and thought every bone in my body was about to crumble. I felt weak from the neck down and had a raging headache.

But, despite all that, I did enough to win the competition, and became the Midlands champion in my first heptathlon. I was thrilled. From that moment, Darrell and I knew that heptathlon would be my number-one event, and any hurdles and long-jump competitions would be to supplement my main goal – to become the best heptathlete I could.

The next stage was the National Championships, to which I was automatically invited in my capacity as Midlands champion. There, I would have to put my skills against the best in the country, a slightly unnerving prospect for a novice. It was here I met Yinka Idowu, a supremely talented athlete and a tough competitor in my early days. I used Yinka as a marker to judge how well I was doing during that period, because my hurdles, long jump and javelin were on a par with hers, while her high jump really surpassed mine, as did her shot. However, at one competition, Yinka's long jump had improved dramatically, so she had a noticeable edge over me there too. We would battle like crazy in those early years, and I would usually lose out to her at the end of the competition – but you learn as much, if not more, from losing, and I was certainly not downcast by the result, I just needed to work harder. If you win everything easily, you don't experience the thrill of competition, which is such an important component of sport.

I got selected and represented the Great Britain juniors team for a few competitions, but my main focus was the European Junior Championships in Varasdin in July 1989. That would be my chance to show Europe what I could do. The day I found out I had qualified was the highlight of my career so far. Here was an opportunity to really make my mark. I knew that I would come to the attention of the hierarchy in athletics if I could perform well, and it would probably be a good opportunity to attract some sponsors. It was the event that had sat tantalisingly in the distance while I trained every evening in an effort to perfect my new skills.

A few weeks before the European Juniors, I was selected to compete for Great Britain in the long jump in a small international juniors competition in Italy. This was very much a warm-up for the main event in Varasdin three weeks later. I flew to Italy with the rest of the team, and settled myself into my room, which I was sharing with Donna Fraser and Geraldine McLeod. I was thrilled to be there, and was looking forward to competing and having some fun. I was not nervous about the competition, just hugely excited at the prospect of competing in the forthcoming European Juniors.

I have always loved being away at athletics events. For someone who hadn't travelled much, those early years were fantastic. I was getting to see lots of Europe – places I had seen only on maps and on the TV – while doing something I really enjoyed. I liked the camaraderie, the excitement and, above all, the challenge of testing myself.

The competition began with the men's long jump, which took place the day before the women's. I went to watch them competing, and heard the competitors complaining about the board being slippery. Some of the athletes had sustained injuries, but at the time it didn't worry me unduly.

The next morning saw the start of the women's competition. I was determined to do well and get enough points to help the team and do myself justice for all the preparation and practice I had put in. On my turn, I stood at the end of the run-up and focused. I took a deep breath and started my run, but at the board I slipped, forcing me to run on through the sand pit. I wasn't injured, but I was concerned about the board for my next jump. Unfortunately Darrell wasn't with me, so I was unable to discuss the situation with him. I knew I would have to be careful not to foul again as I had to get a valid jump in the first three attempts.

For my second jump, I ran towards the sand pit at full speed. At take-off my foot slipped right across the board and I went flying into the air, landing in a heap in the sand, screaming and rolling around in pain. I had never felt anything like it, and it seemed to take for ever before someone came to my aid. My whole leg had gone numb, and I couldn't feel anything except a searing pain shooting through my knee.

The physios put an ice pack on it, and as they laid it on the injury it was as if a knife had been stuck into me. The pain was unbelievable, and I lay there, devastated and crying my eyes out.

I was taken off to hospital, where the doctors took X-rays and scans of my knee, all the time trying to calm me down. I felt very scared because everyone seemed to be talking Italian around me and

I didn't understand what was going on. Finally I was asked if I would give my consent for surgery. However, the British team doctor advised me to wait until we returned to the UK – despite the fact that the Italian doctors were keen to operate on me there and then. I couldn't bear the thought of having surgery so far from home, and was desperate not to have any work done unless it was really necessary, as I knew it would rule me out of the European Juniors.

Everything had happened so quickly, and all I could think about was competing in the forthcoming competition. I hadn't had a serious injury before, so I couldn't judge the severity of the situation. I was on a lot of painkillers for the journey back to England, but was clinging to the one bit of good news – the cruciate ligaments were intact. It was the tracking of my kneecap that was out, exacerbated by trauma in the knee joint itself. Even today, I find myself holding my knee when I talk about it or think about it. I was numb from the whole experience, and didn't really want to think in detail about what was happening inside my leg – thank goodness I had Geraldine there to look after me throughout the flight and keep my spirits up.

Arriving back in England at Birmingham International Airport, I was put into a wheelchair. Darrell was there to meet me. He had heard from one of the team managers that I was injured, but I don't think he was really prepared for what he saw. He took one look at me sitting in the wheelchair, with all the protection, strapping and padding around my leg from my foot to my knee, and asked me what I had done to myself. At that point, it all became too much for me again, and I burst into tears.

That night I stayed at Darrell's in Birmingham, and the first thing next morning he took me to the hospital where I had an appointment with my physio at the time, Mike Garmston, and a doctor that he knew well. When we arrived, they looked at my injury straight away. I had to explain in great detail what had happened, and I told them how the doctors in Italy had wanted to operate immediately. By now my knee was huge, and rock hard because the joint had filled with blood. Mike and the doctor took scans and told me that the knee looked far worse than it actually was. They explained how I had an infusion of the knee joint, which means that blood and fluid gather in the joint, causing it to swell. This is the body's way of protecting the injury from further damage. However, they agreed with their Italian counterparts, and told me I would need an operation.

My heart sank. I desperately tried to explain how eager I was to compete in the European Juniors, and begged them to reconsider. I asked if intensive physiotherapy would be enough to get the inflammation out of the knee joint and avoid surgery.

Mike looked at the knee and conceded. It was agreed that we would give it four weeks. I was so relieved.

In order to have regular physiotherapy I had to visit the hospital every day, which involved taking lots of time off college. The journey was horrendous – I had to travel from Wolverhampton to Birmingham on the bus and the train, then hobble all the way up Corporation Street to get to Birmingham's General Hospital. That walk must be a good twenty minutes if you've got two legs, but I had to do it on crutches. Hobble, hobble, stop, hobble, hobble, stop, all the way up the road. My hands were eventually blistered and sore, but I had to do it because I needed my treatment.

Rehabilitation was incredibly painful. The first thing I had to do when I was recovering from my knee trauma was start to regain extension and flexion – but I couldn't move my leg beyond ten degrees either way. Every day the physio would look to see if I had gained any more movement, and the pain this caused was excruciating. In the end, the physiotherapy did not work well enough for me to enter the European Juniors, or avoid surgery. The injury put me out of action in June 1989, and finally, in February 1990, I had the operation.

Surgery was a more terrifying time for Mum than it was for me. She was very nervous and concerned, but I remained as calm as I could be, stressing to her that it was now the only solution to my problem. The operation involved having my lateral ligament released in order to realign my patella. They also did a lot of scraping underneath the kneecap because there was a lot of debris under the surface. Although I trusted the doctors completely, you never really know how your body will recover. It could quite easily have meant the end of my athletics career, and if the injury taught me anything, it was how much my sport meant to me, and how much I had missed it while injured.

After the operation I had to learn how to walk again. Even before the swelling had gone down I was trying to walk around as much as I could. Once I was able to jog I had to wear a thick, ugly knee brace for lateral support. It was a bleak time for me; I had to take time off college and travel to and from Birmingham in the mornings to have rehab for a good couple of hours. The focus of my existence had been taken away, and everything else seemed to pale into insignificance. I had certainly had better times.

Rehabilitation was a slow process, but I had been warned that if I tried to move too quickly, I would do myself more damage. It was also incredibly painful, as I was almost having to force the knee to do things it didn't want to do, and the last couple of degrees in the 'good range' of movement were always the hardest part.

The injury was to my right leg, the take-off leg for my jumping, so it was crucial that I got back my confidence to jump again if I was to have any chance of getting back into heptathlon, or indeed athletics.

One day, when I was gently jogging round the track, testing my knee, Darrell called me over. 'How about trying to jump off the other leg?' he said simply, as if it were the most natural suggestion in the world.

'I can't,' I responded, horrified. 'I can't possibly.'

But Darrell was very persuasive. He'd given it a lot of thought, and had decided it would take me too long to regain the strength in my right leg. If I put too much pressure on it, too soon, I would be vulnerable to further injury – so in his opinion it made perfect sense to get me jumping off the left leg instead. He was sure I could re-learn all my techniques because I was so quick at picking up physical skills.

He also believed my dancing background would help, because dancing uses both sides of the body. I just had to give it a go.

Initially I thought Darrell was just trying to keep me entertained, that he was setting me a new challenge because he knew I was a determined character. I think he always thought in the back of his mind that I might move back to my right leg once my confidence returned. In the meantime he reassured me that it wasn't an impossible task, that I could do it – so I believed him.

We worked at the change-over throughout the summer months. It was a fun but tiresome process, but we began to see results. At first it felt peculiar. I had jumped off the 'wrong' leg before, but that was just messing around, seeing if I could jump further than the youngsters when using my left leg. But actually relearning skills and competing on my left leg was an entirely different matter.

We started gently, which was Darrell's way. Eventually I developed the confidence to extend my running on the runway, and I slowly committed more speed on take-off, until the jumping was going well. When you're jumping you have a real sense of where your body is in the air and what it's doing, so the most difficult thing for me was having everything reversed; sometimes I would find that my arms were doing their own thing, while my legs were doing something else.

In the summer of 1991, at the age of nineteen, I was selected to represent Great Britain in the European Junior Championships in Thessalonica, Greece, two years after the one I had missed. I was delighted to have made the team having struggled through the previous eighteenth months.

We would be away for just over a week, and the atmosphere was bright and cheerful. We were a good team of junior athletes and were optimistic that we would bring back some good medals. Donna and Marcia were there too, so I knew we were going to have some fun. They were both favourites for medals, while I was going there in the hope of finishing in the top five.

The heptathlon began well for me, as I ran a good hurdles race. However, I had a disaster in the high jump. I just couldn't get my run-up right. I was shaking like a leaf as I prepared for my third and final attempt to jump 1.66m. I failed it, and as I walked back to my kit I could feel the tears stinging in my eyes. I had messed up, and it seemed as if that was all I was capable of doing. However, I pulled through in the rest of the events to finish in fifth place with a score of 5484 points. The recovery was officially over, and I was back.

1991 to 1994 was a strange time for me. My training was improving and I was competing whenever I could, but my results were in no way reflecting the amount of effort I was putting in. It was almost as if I had reached a plateau. Darrell and I both knew I should be scoring more points in competitions but even my best scores did not reflect the progress I was making.

I knew I was injured and had to build myself back up again, and I knew it wasn't going to happen overnight. Being selected for the European Juniors in 1991 certainly gave me a boost, but I knew I really made some mistakes out there in the high jump.

I refused to let it eat away at me even though I was quite frustrated and disappointed. I knew one day it would all come together. I really believed that in my heart. However, I continued to make mistakes during competitions and I wasn't showing much consistency. I suppose I was still learning.

In the 1991 European Juniors I had scored 5484 points. My personal best was 5758, but to qualify for the 1992 Olympic Games in Barcelona I needed 5950 points. In July that year I took part in the National Combined Events Championships in Sheffield. Although I finished in second place, I couldn't quite make the necessary points to get my place in the Olympic team. It meant I missed out on the chance to compete, and it was Clova Court, my club mate and Britain's number-one heptathlete who flew the flag for Great Britain in this event, while I stayed at home.

It was not a nice feeling to watch the Olympic Games on television and not be there. Every time I heard the Olympic theme tune,

'Barcelona' by Freddie Mercury and Montserrat Caballe, a tingle went through me and my hairs stood on end. It was so close to home, and I really felt I could have been there, been a part of the games and competing in that electric atmosphere. I felt tantalisingly close to being at a major championship. I had such a great belief in my ability, yet I just couldn't get it together. I watched every event Clova was competing in, and was convinced that I could have done at least as well – but when was I going to get the chance to prove that?

By 1993 I was desperate for a break. It was the year of the European Championships in Stuttgart and, once again, I entered the National Championships with a view to making the qualification mark. But I didn't manage it. I just couldn't pull together all seven events in the same competition. I'd do well in one, then completely mess up in another, missing the qualification by the smallest margin. It was incredibly frustrating.

While the team from Great Britain were competing in the European Championships I went to Stuttgart anyway, to compete in long jump for the Midlands team in a totally different competition. On one of the days we went along to watch the championships and I was overwhelmed by it all. It was amazing – an enormous stadium, filled with atmosphere and more people than I had ever seen at a competition in my life. This was how it looked from the inside; this was what I wanted. I wanted to be a part of all the excitement. Some of my friends had competed in Stuttgart and they came back with lots of funny stories and fascinating tales. I felt joy and jealousy at the same time, hoping that I would be able to recall tales of my own one day soon.

The big events of 1994 were the Commonwealth Games in Victoria, Canada, and the European Championships in Helsinki, just four weeks before. I was selected for the hurdles and long jump at the

Europeans and for the heptathlon in the Commonwealth Games. It was an amazing feeling. The European competition did not go well, but I had a good time. I relaxed and enjoyed myself, and watched the stars up close. It was fantastic, and I felt part of the sport at the highest level. I was really just there to make up the numbers, finishing in nineteenth place, but I loved being a part of my first major competition. The number of people and the phenomenal noise were astounding. I remember standing at the beginning of the long jump in Helsinki in the freezing cold, unable to believe how anyone could focus properly in the noise. But it was an amazing experience, and made me all the more eager to get out to the Commonwealth Games and compete in my number-one event – the heptathlon.

CHAPTER NINE
GOLD: THE
COMMONWEALTH GAMES, 1994

The 1994 Commonwealth Games were held in Victoria, Canada, in August, a couple of days before my twenty-second birthday. This was my big chance, the opportunity to show the world I was a talent to be reckoned with and to prove to myself that I could compete on the big stage. Having missed out on the Olympics in 1992 and the World Championships in 1993, I felt ready for these Commonwealth Games – in fact I felt more than ready, I was keen to get involved. I was burning with ambition, and yearned to go to a big competition and perform at my best. For a British athlete, the Commonwealth Games is the event at which you want to 'launch yourself' into the world of senior athletics, your first opportunity to make a name for yourself.

As the games approached I was training hard – at least five days a week. I had started asking myself the questions that constantly spin through a determined athlete's mind. Am I going to make it? Am I going to move myself out of being one of the best in Britain to being one of the best in the world? Do I have what it takes to make that extra step, that giant leap into the highest echelons of the sport?

The first step is the one that takes you out of the category of 'prospect for the future' and up to the level of world-class performer. It is the biggest step to take, and one that necessitates you pulling together all the disciplines and focus you may have learned thus far. It is one that demands that you are mentally and physically prepared to grasp the opportunity and go for it.

Jane Flemming, the Commonwealth record holder and Australian golden girl, was the favourite for the heptathlon gold in Canada. It seemed unlikely she would be beaten. England's hopes for a gold medal lay in the hands of Clova Court, Britain's number-one heptathlete at the time. I was not considered a likely medal winner, in fact most people believed that a top-six finish would be a major achievement for me. But my personal goal was much higher than that – I desperately wanted to become Britain's number-one female multi-event athlete, and therefore had to beat Clova.

I was both nervous and excited when the time came to pack everything up and head for Victoria. I laid the team kit proudly on my bed and looked at it – the red and white England track-suit, my red competition gear, a few socks, my trainers and all my spikes. I also had lots of freebies from the sponsors of the England team such as baseball caps, shower gel, sun block and sunglasses. I neatly folded it all into my suitcase and hoped that when I next wore my kit, I'd be excelling myself in North America.

The flight to Victoria took eleven hours, the longest I had ever been on. It was an odd trip in many ways because, while it was like every other team journey I'd made, it was also unique. The team had completely taken over the aeroplane, and I was surrounded by my friends, laughing, joking and giggling non-stop. From the moment we left British soil I had a good feeling about this trip. I was incredibly excited to be going on my first big international trip and was hoping to do well.

When we arrived in Canada I experienced every traveller's nightmare – you arrive, but your bags don't. It was not a good start, particularly for me as I tend to have more spikes than everyone else and replacing them is not always straightforward. After the long flight, and with the prospect of such an important competition ahead, it was the last thing I needed. But I wasn't the only one – one of my close friends, Jacqui Agyepong, couldn't see her bags either.

We reported the situation to the airport staff and team management. A couple of days later, when I was just about to get the money to go out and replace everything, my bags finally turned up. I was lucky, but Jacqui wasn't – she never saw hers again.

As with most trips, I hardly saw anything of the beautiful country, but did see a lot of the athletes' village with all its amenities – a hairdresser, games room, shops and the communication centre where you could phone and send faxes home. I shared a room with Geraldine McLeod, the sprinter from the Midlands and a good friend. The weather was glorious, and a special reception had been put on for us when we arrived, which was marred only by the fact that I was quietly panicking about having to replace my shoes.

Day one of the heptathlon competition was dull and windy, despite the fact that we had been assured good weather. I had to get up around five in the morning to make the short walk to the warm-up track and begin preparations to compete. At 8.15am we all filed into the call room where they checked our spikes, numbers and bags. Then, forty-five minutes later, we walked out on to the track for the 100m hurdles, to the sound of rapturous applause. I couldn't believe it, I was really here at the Commonwealth Games for all eyes to see. It was such a fantastic feeling.

We pulled the blocks down, ready for the start of the race. As I took my place in lane six I was full of apprehension. I knew that Clova Court was on exceptionally good form, as she had run a personal best in the hurdles in the European Championships just a month before, but I tried to put this to the back of my mind. At the gun, Clova got off to a great start, and won the race in 13.07 seconds. Jane Flemming came second with a time of 13.32 seconds and I was third in 13.66 seconds. It was a good omen for me.

The high jump was next, an event I knew I needed to keep my focus on. Not one of my strongest events, it is a place where you can start to fall in the rankings quite considerably if you're not careful. I made a good start, jumping 1.74m, but when I moved up to 1.77m I ran into problems – missing two of my three jumps. I had to make the third one count.

I ran, too fired up and eager to jump, and, once again I took off too close to the bar, tipping it off on my way up.

I felt a little dismayed, but Jane Flemming had jumped only 1.77m, which was a long way below par for her. In the end, Cathy Bond-Mills won with 1.86m – Clova had a bad time, only jumping 1.53m.

Clova had a long history of back problems, which made high jumping quite difficult for her. Part of me felt so sorry for her, she was older than me and desperate to win, or at least come away with a silver medal. She was devastated at setting herself so far back.

Next up was the shot put, an event I had difficulty with, but had done a lot of work on before the games. I hoped I would at least be able to improve on my personal best. I always found it hard to score good points in this event because I didn't have a very good technique. But now I had to do my best and pull myself back into the frame before the 200m, the final event of day one. To be in with any real chance of a medal I had to get into the top four.

I picked up the shot, cupping the heavy weight in my right hand, willing it to go a long way. I knew I had worked hard, and knew that if I focused, I could do a good throw. I walked inside the circle, took a deep breath, then went for it. The shot flew out of my hands; it was almost effortless, and I knew straight away, as you often do, that it was good. Sometimes you can 'brute it out' and get a fairly decent distance, but not as efficiently as if you add some good technique to it. This throw went 13.22m, a personal best. Things were looking good.

I went into the 200m race lying in third place, behind Jane Flemming and Cathy Bond-Mills, and eager to keep hold of that position going into day two. At this stage I was still measuring myself against Clova, and I knew she was fast in the 200m. If I could hang on in, stay close to her in this race, I was sure I could get the better of her in day two, which is always a better day for me.

The 200m was a straight fight for the line between Clova and Jane Flemming. For the entire race the two women were neck and neck ahead of the field, with Flemming eventually nudging ahead to finish in 24.06 seconds, and Clova a tenth of a second behind her. I came in at around fifth place, with a finishing time of 25.11 seconds. It wasn't a very good time, but I was still in third place overall. I felt quietly confident.

Considering it had been such a dreadful, miserable day, I was pleased; my high jump had let me down, but I'd pulled back some ground in the shot. Physically, I was feeling OK. As predicted, Jane Flemming was in first place, closely followed by the Canadian, Cathy Bond-Mills.

Unfortunately Clova was not doing quite so well and later that day she announced she was pulling out of the competition because of a niggling injury that had got the better of her. She was so devastated that she even talked of retirement. The news upset me greatly, and I felt desperately sorry for her. Even though we were keen competitors she was my club mate and a senior person to me. I also considered us to be friends.

So, after the first day I was in third position, knowing I had my best day ahead of me. I just had to try and consolidate now, not make any mistakes, and stay in touch with the leaders. I went back and had a massage and treatment from my physiotherapist, Kevin Lidlow. Kevin was my knight in shining armour. It was the first time I'd had a physio working on me solidly for two days, someone who 'belonged' to me, and he really made a difference. Then I had dinner and went to bed, knowing I had to get as much sleep as possible. As I lay there I wondered how tomorrow would go, and willed myself to achieve the good long jump result I knew I needed.

Day two was beautifully sunny, a welcome contrast to the rain and wind of day one. I woke up feeling a bit stiff, but after I had warmed up, I started to feel good. The track-suits came off and the sunglasses went on. I was having some problems with my left ankle that morning, but still I managed 6.44m in the long jump, out-jumping the leaders, Jane Flemming and Cathy Bond-Mills, who finished with 6.29m and 6.22m respectively. Because the final event – the 800m – was my weakest, I knew that to make sure of the bronze I had to throw the javelin like I'd never thrown it before.

After the long jump Kevin strapped my left leg up to my shin as my ankle was still slightly tender and he wanted me to have the extra support.

As I walked over to the javelin area, I bumped into Mick Hill and Steve Backley. They wished me good luck and I asked them for some last-minute advice: 'Come on then, Steve, give me some tips, give me some tips. I need to really throw this javelin.'

And Steve simply replied, 'Just chuck the thing as far as you can. Give it some welly, mate. That's all you've got to do, Denise. That's all.'

That didn't sound like very technical advice to me! That's all? Just a 'chuck' of the javelin between me and a very real chance of a medal at the Commonwealth Games? But I knew I was capable of a big throw – prior to the tournament I had been doing some extra work with John Trower, a javelin specialist and Steve Backley's coach, and I was ready to put all his advice into practice.

I was the first to throw, which is always a nerve-wracking experience because everyone is watching you as you go out there to set the standard. The stadium was full, but quite quiet. I picked out a red and white Apollo javelin – my favourite. Stay with the point, stay with the point, I kept thinking to myself. That's the way we describe the alignment needed between the javelin, the body and the direction in which you need to throw. As I prepared myself, I felt the warmth of the sun on my face, and felt composed.

I launched it. The throw felt effortless, everything was channelled into that moment when I let go of the javelin and it flew out of my hands. At one point, when it seemed to be coming down, it suddenly appeared to take off again and continued to sail through the air for another three metres before coming down. The whole stadium erupted, and I couldn't control myself. The javelin had travelled 53.68m, smashing my personal best by 6m. I think it is the only time that I have completely lost my composure. I was running around, excited, dancing and smiling, jumping up and down, unable to fully digest what I had just done.

Suddenly I was the talk of the stadium and I became the focus of everyone's attention. I wanted to stop myself from grinning, but I just couldn't. I was completely beside myself. My throw had catapulted me into first place, over Jane Flemming, who threw just 39.76m – nearly 14m less than me. With just one event to go, suddenly the eyes of the world were on me.

We usually have two or so hours before the 800m race, but on this occasion we had less than one and a half hours. I think that this was a blessing. Any longer than that and I would have been in more of a state than I was already. Suddenly I was trying to hang on to gold – one false move and I would lose it. I felt dizzy, sick, and had diarrhoea. Kevin made me a temporary bed by the toilets so I could lie down and try to compose myself between dashes to the toilet. It was almost as if I didn't want to go out there because the enormity of the opportunity ahead was so terrifying. I couldn't bear the thought of messing up this great chance. I felt a massive weight of responsibility on my shoulders. I was so scared, and all I could think was, I'm too young, I can't cope with this kind of pressure. How am I going to get through this? No one told me it would be like this. I just didn't think it would be this hard.

Finally, it was time to head out to the track, and Darrell gave me a little talk before I went. 'Denny, you've done your best to get to this position, now you've got to run your heart out. You can't let this moment slip – you might regret it for ever.'

I walked out on to the track for the start of the race, staring at the floor in front of me, trying to cut out all the people in the stadium and the athletes standing alongside me. I could feel tears stinging at the backs of my eyes. I was petrified. Completely petrified. I had no idea whether or not this was going to be my one and only chance. Darrell was right: if I messed up the 800m I might regret it for the rest of time. I might spend the rest of my life talking about the time I almost won the Commonwealth Games. I couldn't blow it, I had to succeed. The pressure was almost too great to bear.

The sun that had been so warming earlier started to feel too intense, reflecting the situation I was now in. I forced myself to focus on the race ahead, and the prize that lay at the end of it. I was in lane five, with Jane Flemming inside me. I knew she had to beat me by five and a half seconds to win gold. I kept staring down, breathing deeply, waiting for the instruction to move towards the line and prepare for the start. The points difference between Jane and me equated to the difference between our personal bests in the race – so, the person who ran the best race of their life would win the medal. Simple. Except this was my least-favourite event, the one I always dreaded so much.

They kept us on the track much longer than usual, and I began to wonder if there was some plot against me. I was really feeling sick by now, and just wanted it to be over. Then, after what seemed like an eternity, we went towards the line, and we were off. I had to stay with Flemming, I couldn't let her get away.

For a lap we were next to each other, then at 500m she started to pull away. I knew I had to stay with her but she was really turning on the speed as she headed down the back straight. I was some 40m behind her and began to wonder whether or not I had lost the medal. The gap seemed to be getting wider and wider and my legs were heavy and tired. When Jane crossed the line I was still struggling down the home straight, but I knew I had to stay on my feet and drive myself on. As I fell over the line I was suffering from serious oxygen deficit. I collapsed on the grass, staring straight up, trying to breathe deeply. I felt pain everywhere: I had a splitting headache, my lungs were on fire, my arms and legs were in agony, and I thought I was going to cough up blood.

Kevin was there – before the race I had begged him to be at the finish to help me, as I knew I would be completely exhausted. He took my trainers off, checked my ankles and started massaging my legs. Slowly I felt life returning to them. I had forgotten about the medal at this moment and was more worried about whether or not I would ever be able to stand again. All around me I could hear cheers and shouts, but I had no idea whether I'd done it.

Then I heard Darrell's distinctive voice shouting, 'Yes, yes! She's done it!'

Then, more cheers.

It was official. I had run a time of 2 minutes 17.6 seconds – a personal best – to finish with a points score of 6325. I stood up slowly and smiled from ear to ear, waved tentatively to the crowd and tried to register my initial feelings. I desperately wanted to see Mum and Darrell.

This victory was a huge mark of approval for Darrell as well as for me. All the work he'd put in, for no reward, for all those years, had finally paid off. Together we'd produced the performance that had won a gold medal in the Commonwealth Games. But as I began to walk towards the crowds, looking for him and Mum, I suddenly found I couldn't move anywhere – every journalist in the world seemed to want to talk to me.

This was my first experience of dealing with the media, and it was some introduction; everyone was talking at once, all wanting to get a few words with me. I could hardly hear the questions because they were all talking over one another, all shouting louder and louder to make themselves heard. I was pulled in many different directions: a lady had to take me to doping, another person was insisting I did a live broadcast for the BBC immediately, and journalists were stopping me at every opportunity. This was all so new to me. I wasn't drugs tested there and then, but I had to sign a form to say that they had notified me, which meant that I had to return as soon as I could. I was then marched off to do my live BBC broadcast with Paul Dickenson, whose voice I had heard on the TV for years. Suddenly we were face to face underneath a dazzling white light. I was exhausted, and panicked that I was going to be incoherent. But I pulled it together, still breathing heavily from the race and conscious that my lips were sticking together because my mouth was so dry!

From there I was ushered into the press conference where the British media were waiting for me. They fired questions at me, which I did my best to answer. Was I surprised? How did I feel? No one prepares you for this. How was I supposed to answer? When you're completely overawed with emotion things can sometimes not come out the way you intend them to, and seeing your words in print can sometimes give you a big surprise, but I think I handled things well.

No sooner had I said my last words than someone was whispering to me that the medal ceremony was about to take place and that the other girls were waiting for me. As I walked out I saw Mum and Darrell for the first time since I had won the race, just under an hour ago. Mum was in tears – she had worried that something serious had happened to me after I had been lying on the grass for so long, attended by Kevin. Her fears were added to by the fact that I had been out of the stadium for so long afterwards. But after a long embrace she could see and feel that I was fine. Darrell's face was red with happiness, and I could see that he had shed a few tears of his own.

I was just so happy. Delighted and thrilled. However, Jane Flemming wasn't delighted. In fact, it would be fair to say she was devastated. You could see that she had been crying and was still very emotional by the time the medals ceremony took place. She had wanted the gold so much, and had to wear dark glasses to cover her eyes. The Australian papers said things like 'Australia's golden girl gets beaten by freak javelin throw'. Charming – but that's sport.

Great Gran with Mum, my Uncle Jack and Rosebud the doll in Jamaica, shortly before Mum came to England, 1966.

My christening, November 1972. My gran is holding me, Mum is standing behind us.

Me, aged seven months, March 1973.

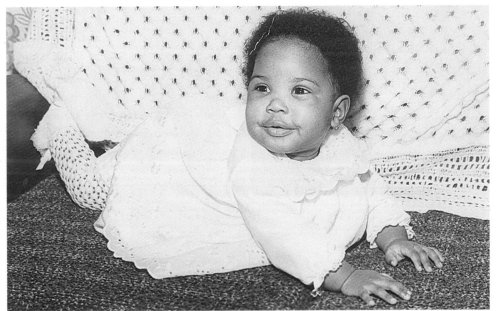

Don't laugh! Me, aged two, trying my hand at shot put!

Me and Mum, Christmas 1979.

First day of junior school, September 1979.

The New Supremes! Me and my cousin, Lisa, in our wigs, 1978.

Me, Mum, my
Aunt Sonia and
cousin Lisa,
Christmas 1982.

Turning Mum's
lounge into a dance
studio! Me, aged
eleven.

First day at secondary
school, September 1983.

A star is born! Me with my champion's rosette after the Superstars competition, 1981.

The wonderful Bill Hand, my first coach.

Me with my trophy collection, 1984.

The four generations: me, Mum, Nanny and Great Gran (and Richard, a cousin!), Jamaica, 1991.

One of my last pictures with Great Gran, Jamaica, 1995.

Clockwise, from left: me, Sonia, Jack, Mum and Lisa, Dunn's River Fall, Jamaica, 1980.

The long jump,
Commonwealth
Games, Victoria,
1994.

Me with my gold
medal at the
Commonwealth
Games in
Victoria, 1994.

Me and Darrell, my first time at Gotzis in
1995, where I was delighted to finish sixth.

The shot put, Olympic Games,
Atlanta, 1996.

The long jump, Olympic
Games, Atlanta, 1996.

Standing proud in bronze position after a difficult two days of competition, Atlanta Olympics, 1996.

My name in lights on the scoreboard.

Me and Mum, just after the medal ceremony.

The closing ceremony for the Atlanta Olympics, 1996. From left to right: Donna Fraser, Geraldine McCleod, Stephanie Douglas, me, Marcia Richardson, Jacqui Agyepong.

Fifty per cent of 'the girls' on our way home from Atlanta – from left to right: Geraldine McCleod, Marcia Richardson, Michelle Griffith and me.

Me and Michelle doing our warm up at the warm-weather camp in Lanzarote, January 1997.

Me and Michelle, Lanzarote, 1997.

Me and my long-time buddy, Donna Fraser, at the Europa Cup, 1997.

Preparing to long jump, Gotzis, 1997, where I broke my own British record for the second time.

Long jumping 6.77m to win the competition.

After the 800m!

Awaiting the start of the 800m at the World Championships in Athens, 1997.

Darrell, Mum and me with my silver medal at the World Championships, Athens, 1997.

Welcome home. Friends and neighbours decorated Mum's house after the Olympic Games in Atlanta in 1996 and the World Championships in Athens in 1997.

The hurdles, European
Championships, Budapest, 1998.

The 800m, the Commonwealth
Games, Kuala Lumpur, 1998.

What a big year – completing double victories in the European Championships
and the Commonwealth Games, 1998.

Loyal British supporters
at the European
Championships, 1998.

Kevin Lidlow, my fantastic
physiotherapist.

The high jump, the
World Championships,
Seville, 1999.

I found the press attention very intense. First of all there were a lot of one-to-one interviews, then the requests for me to speak to more journalists, basically answering the same questions over and over again. The articles then began to appear, and the process of looking through to see what had been written about me was funny and very interesting. Never had I received such media attention. Most of the articles were extremely positive about my performance and the Commonwealth Games, but there was one piece I remember to this day, the only negative piece, an article which said how very lucky I was to have won. It implied that I was a one-hit wonder whose result was nothing to do with the hard work that had been put in.

By contrast, one of the best moments in all the coverage I received took place at the end of *Grandstand,* that someone recorded for us while we were away. Des Lynam said, 'and the surprise of the day was a young heptathlete called Denise Lewis,' and when the credits rolled they showed Linford Christie and Colin Jackson, who had both won medals that day, and then me, looking back and smiling at the crowd. It was amazing, and really captured just how special that day of the championships was.

Straight after the ceremony I had to do my first drugs test at a major championship. It was all completely new and quite daunting. You know that you are clear, but you still worry that they might make a mistake, and you desperately rack your brains for any medication you might have taken recently. It is an incredibly serious moment.

The athletics world is very eager to stamp out drugs in athletics, and heavily punishes anyone who is caught. This is a stance I endorse wholeheartedly. All national athletics federations are required to adhere to rigorous testing programmes, therefore accusations of cheating whenever an athlete pulls off a good performance are sometimes a little unjust. But drugs have no place in sport. I would like to believe that none of my contemporaries in the heptathlon have ever considered the option. Naturally you hear rumours about some athletes, but I have never heard anything about any of my current competitors in the event. It would turn the occasion sour for me to discover that any of my competitors had taken anything.

The only time I even remotely came into contact with the drug issue at the Commonwealth Games was a couple of nights after the heptathlon. I was lying in my bed when I suddenly heard screams coming from down the corridor. They were deafening and gut wrenching, as if someone had just received some awful news. I heard raised voices, then talking, and more screams, then it went quiet. The next morning I heard that one of the female athletes had been told that her drug test was positive and she was being thrown out of the competition. By the time I went down to breakfast she'd been flown out of the village and it was a major talking point among the other athletes. Thankfully though, she was subsequently cleared of any suspicion of taking drugs. Generally drug abuse, although an issue in athletics, is not as widespread as imagined.

After my victory I had a fabulous time. I received faxes, telegrams, cards and flowers from all my friends back home. When we got back to Wolverhampton my mum's house had been decorated with banners, balloons and cards. Lots of people, many of them kids, were out in the streets wanting to see me, staring at me and probably wondering if I was the same woman they had seen madly dancing around after throwing the javelin, and winning the gold medal.

There was a huge reception at Birchfield Harriers – we all had a great time, and I really seemed to be the heptathlete of the moment. However, I did feel slightly embarrassed at my success because Clova and her husband and coach Howard were also members of the club – and there seemed to be little recognition of her and the devastating problems she had experienced out in Victoria.

So 1994 was a great year for me, and it taught me a great deal – first, how people can be incredibly kind and supportive and that self-belief can really work if you believe it can. I also learned about the demands that are put on you after such a win. Winning the gold medal in the Commonwealth Games was a wonderful experience, but I would sometimes dream of that 800m race and everything it stood for, and have nightmares about just missing out. The pressure associated with that competition had been immense – with Flemming having to beat me by five seconds in order to take gold away from me, and then the media attention and the reaction of people back home.

I knew I had set a new level for myself, and that I would have to prove I was at that level in every subsequent competition I entered. And I was ready to rise to that challenge.

CHAPTER TEN
TRACK SIDE

After the Commonwealth Games I went back to the part-time job
I had at Birmingham City Council, as a secretary and helper in the
Community Development Office, visiting schools and helping
them teach games. I had been working there since the summer of
1992, and it worked brilliantly for me – I had regular working
hours, plus the freedom to get out of the office, doing something I
really enjoyed. I was allocated a few schools in the south
Birmingham area, where my role was to encourage the children to
get involved in physical activity. I would teach netball and athletics
during school time, and help run courses after school and in the
holidays. I produced posters on my computer advertising events
and schemes and undertook the general clerical and administration
work associated with the job. It was great to be able to get out there
with the kids and show them how much fun sport can be. I got a
lot back from it, and I loved it from the moment I started.

I joined the council when I finished my A levels at Wulfrun

College. I'd studied English and PE, and had enjoyed them both. However, my results were not as good as they should have been. I thought I wanted to become a PE teacher but unfortunately my results meant the job was closed to me unless I re-sat my exams. In the end I chose not to do that because I wanted to focus on my athletics, at least in the short term. The job with Birmingham Council was therefore a great way for me to work with children and in sport, without needing the exam results. It was perfect.

The only part of the job that I didn't enjoy was the journey to work every morning. I had to get a bus to Wolverhampton town centre, a train to Birmingham, then a bus to the south of Birmingham. On average it took just under two hours, the same amount of travelling as to Alexander Stadium, and the final stage of the journey was much slower because the bus stopped everywhere. Sometimes I'd try to have a little sleep so I felt refreshed when I got there, but most of the time I just looked out of the window at the familiar landscape drifting past, and wished that I was driving through it instead of sitting there at the mercy of a bus driver.

I longed for the day I would be able to drive myself around. I knew that getting to the track, getting back afterwards, and getting myself to the various tournaments would be so much easier. So, at the end of 1992, I decided to learn to drive. I had ten lessons in quick succession, because I believed that ten lessons would be enough for me – I wanted to drive, and I wanted to drive now.

Fortunately I took to driving very easily, as Darrell had predicted I would. He always said that my ability to pick up physical skills was very finely tuned, and that I would find driving a breeze. There was an exception, though – parallel parking and reverse parking – they didn't come to me quite as easily, and I had to do a lot more work until I perfected the technique.

I passed my test the first time, and by 2pm the same day I was driving around in my boyfriend Tim's car, enjoying life to the full with the stereo on and the windows open. I bought my first car a couple of months later, a white E-reg VW Polo Coupe S, and was no longer dependent on Darrell driving me to training, collecting me, and dropping me home again. I had freedom for the first time and it was wonderful. It was great for me, and it must have been a huge relief for Darrell, too.

Suddenly life was much less complicated. My days slipped into a comfortable, quiet routine, driving myself to work, to the track and then back again, and working hard on my athletics. And it continued in this way until a few months after my return from the Commonwealth Games. Then everything started to change.

The first change was in my job. The council moved me across from community education to sports development. My role on the sports development team seemed to be purely administrative, which wasn't really what I wanted. Although the people were really nice and supportive, it didn't work for me because I didn't get the same enjoyment out of it as I had with my community work. It was a bigger team and the hands-on work in schools disappeared. So, after a year of returning from the games, having given it some thought I resigned and became a full-time athlete. It was a daunting decision, leaving myself at the mercy of the sport, but I had reached the stage where trying to fit training into a work schedule was no longer adequate. I needed to push myself further.

It was around this time that I started to think very seriously about my athletics, and what I could do to improve. Winning gold in the Commonwealth Games showed me I had the ability to be the best, but I knew that to really capitalise on the win I would have to focus on every part of my training.

Diet was another area I knew I needed to work on. I had an understanding of nutrition, and I knew which food groups I should and shouldn't be eating, but I didn't take it seriously enough. Sally Gunnell had demonstrated how much an athlete can change shape when she turned from being quite bulky into a leaner, more toned figure towards the end of her athletics career. I decided that I wanted to have the advantage of that lean, muscular figure – which meant that some changes needed to be made.

Darrell and I had discussed my food and nutritional requirements before the Commonwealth Games, and he had introduced me to a stamina drink called PROBUZ, an effective protein drink I had started taking. It was incredibly expensive because I needed to take so much of it, so regularly, but it did make a real difference. I was also aware that there were many other nutrients and supplements I should be taking. This put us in a dilemma, because I could not afford to buy them all on my income.

Darrell suggested we contact Brian Welsby, the owner of Be Well, the manufacturers of the drink, and ask him if he would sponsor me, providing me with the drink in return for my endorsement of it. Brian agreed, and we met at Alexander Stadium to discuss how the arrangement would work.

Brian arrived with piles of paper, information leaflets and scribbled notes. He took my approach seriously, and outlined the various things he could do to help to improve my training and recovery from one session to another. Much of it was mind-boggling, but basically he was trying to get me to understand that you are what you eat; the more efficient your diet, the higher your energy levels and the more you can get out of your workout. I liked him and trusted him from the beginning. He asked me whether I was prepared to tackle my nutrition properly, and he asked me what I really wanted to achieve. Without stopping for a moment's thought, I told him I wanted him to be my nutritionist and I wanted a gold medal in Sydney. Brian laughed and said that he could do the first thing, and that he was confident that the help he'd give me would set me on my way to the second – but he couldn't make any guarantees. I left him that day armed with leaflets to read and bottles of drink to take.

After the meeting he sent me lots of information on the body, covering such subjects as how it digests and converts food into energy, and giving me a greater understanding of what happens to athletes' bodies during and after training.

As soon as Brian and I began working together I became aware of everything I was eating – the type of food, the quantity and the times that I ate. I had to write down everything that passed my lips, and Brian would analyse it in detail. I was sometimes horrified when I re-read my lists. I soon found the type of food that I had been eating was invariably of the 'quick fix' variety such as KFC and sandwiches full of mayonnaise, which I loved. I'd buy food that was easy to get hold of and tasted nice. I realised very soon that it all had to stop. Bye bye pizza, bye bye kebab and chips! Brian gave me a list of foods to avoid such as red meat and dairy products. My mum was a bit alarmed when I showed her the list and sent her out shopping, as everything had to be reduced fat or zero fat from now on, and sugar had to be avoided completely.

So I had to wean myself off excessive eating of cheese, my milk had to go from semi-skimmed to skimmed, and I had to make my portions smaller. I had to increase my intake of fish, as well as vitamins. I am not a good tablet taker, so getting used to that was hard. Junk food also had to go – no more hot chocolates, apple pies and McChicken sandwiches. Alcohol intake also had to be reduced. It seemed as if everything had to go. But I knew that if I wanted to continue to be a champion I had to start eating like a champion, giving my body the fuel it needed to be the best.

One of the first things Brian wanted me to change was the pattern of my eating. Instead of eating three large meals a day he wanted me to become a 'grazer' – eating much smaller meals at regular intervals of four hours or so throughout the day. The small meals were sometimes just pieces of fruit, other times just drinks he designed specifically for me, containing exactly the right nutrients. These drinks had to be taken at specific times of the day, one in the morning, one during exercise, one after exercise, and one last thing at night. Some of them tasted unpleasant, but I did get used to them – after a while, drinking them became second nature. But one of the hardest things initially was getting used to taking in so much liquid during the day. There was a different schedule for training days and competition days, with the overall focus to get my body functioning at its optimum level, at which my metabolism would be able to convert the food into energy for training with more ease, repair itself while I was resting, and keep all my internal organs ship-shape.

Breakfast was very different. Before my new diet I would eat cereals sweetened with sugar, so it was a big change to move on to boiled eggs with the yolk removed, to ensure I got more protein. I also had to get used to drinking the juice of a lemon first thing every morning, which makes my stomach less acidic and more alkaline.

Brian suggested I have an afternoon sleep, 'a power nap'. He said that chemicals released by the brain after sleeping help recharge the body and would therefore give me an extra natural boost for when I had a second training session in the afternoon. It seemed logical to me, and as I sat there listening I was more and more convinced that training full time (which would mean training twice a day for two and a half to three hours per session), together with the introduction of my new eating regime was the way forward. I felt quite proud of myself for taking the first steps towards being a more responsible and possibly a 'professional' athlete, but I could see it wasn't going to be easy.

The power naps were quite difficult to master at first because I had to relax my mind and body totally to induce sleep, rather than thinking about all the things I should have been doing. But Brian told me that it would be beneficial so I had to learn how to do it. Sometimes I would picture a black box and put all my thoughts in it, other times I would focus on the sound of my own breathing. Eventually it became instinctive, and now I don't even have to think about it. I am now able to sleep anywhere, just for a few minutes, to revive myself. If I drive to training and arrive early, I can put the seat back, doze for twenty minutes, and feel refreshed when I train.

Soon after I first learned this skill, I would tell Mum I was going upstairs for a nap. When I'd come down fifteen minutes later she would say, 'I thought you were going to sleep,' and I would tell her I had slept. But she simply didn't believe me.

There is no doubt that the changes to my nutrition and sleeping habits gave me more energy. I was more alert and refreshed and could get more out of my training sessions because I wasn't as tired.

Athletics was now a big part of my life. I trained full time, ate sensibly, slept well and didn't go out late at night. I was more determined than ever to improve myself. I spent more and more time focusing on athletics – and less and less on my relationship with Tim, which had deteriorated. I suppose Tim was the archetypal 'first love'. We'd spent some really happy times together, having great fun, but I could now feel us slipping apart. We seemed to have less in common, something I had felt for a while, and I felt that he wasn't taking life seriously enough. We had started arguing a lot and I could see that we were going in different directions.

The grand finale came when I found out that he had been sleeping with one of my fellow athletes. She lived in London, and the two of them had met at a competition abroad. I had had my suspicions a year earlier in 1993, when I found a postcard she had sent him at his house, and heard from a friend that she had been flirting with him. Tim denied it at that stage, but it became more and more obvious when she called the house a few times. I remember one particular occasion when she rang. Tim pretended it was one of his male work colleagues, but I knew he wasn't telling me the truth because I had heard her voice. Finally, a few weeks before I left for the Commonwealth Games, he admitted it. I was furious and felt totally betrayed – naturally with him, but also with her, as she was a member of the Great Britain team too – it wasn't the sort of thing you would expect from your teammate. But, looking back, I reckon she did me a favour. I closed the chapter of my life that concerned Tim, and from that moment on, my training went from strength to strength and my life really took off.

Chapter Eleven
Taking On the Main Players

Life after the Commonwealth Games was fantastic, and I could have drifted around, enjoying the after-effects of victory for months, wining and dining to my heart's content at awards lunches and evenings. But I knew that this victory had to be the start of something big, not the highlight of my career; the gold medal had to act as a platform from which to launch myself on to greater things. It was important that I got another big competition under my belt, to show the world that my win was not just a one-off, that it had not been a 'freak javelin throw'. I was a talented all-round athlete, and I needed to show everyone just how good I could be.

I knew the Commonwealth victory would make life on the track harder for me, because now I had an air of expectation following me around. The public who lived locally to me were aware of who I was, and I knew that there would be a certain amount of pressure on me to succeed, pressure I had never experienced before. I wasn't frightened by this and I never felt worried about not meeting people's expectations, but it was something I was definitely aware of – and I hoped that I would be given enough time to prove myself, because the step up from the Commonwealth Games was huge.

The next big competition on which I set my sights was the World Championships in Gothenburg in August 1995, a big competition featuring the best heptathletes in the world. Even though I had won gold in Victoria, my score of 6325 points had only put me in tenth place in the world rankings, behind such heptathletes as Shouaa and Braun, so I knew I was a long way from the best. I decided that my aim was to secure a top-ten finish and cement my position as Britain's number one, in time for the Olympic Games in Atlanta in 1996.

But before that, I was due to compete at Gotzis in Austria. I was thrilled when I received notification that I had been invited by the organisers to compete in their annual heptathlon and decathlon competition. The competition had been running for about 25 years and throughout this period it had seen all the great legends from the two disciplines compete there. Numerous world records have been set in Gotzis, and the standard of competition is as high as you would expect it to be in any of the major championships. It is a great privilege to be invited, and if you are, you know you have arrived!

Darrell and I flew from Birmingham to Zurich, then took an hour-long bus journey over the border into Austria. It was a beautiful day, and the scenery was spectacular. As we drove through the mountains I was struck by how clean and perfect everything looked. Upon our arrival at the hotel I was greeted by the meet organiser. Once I had put my bags in my room, my first task was to write down my personal bests in all seven events, which helps with each athlete's seeding for the competition. Before lunch I was shown around the small and compact complex, and afterwards I went to my room for a sleep. That afternoon I spent most of my time sizing up my opponents.

I felt like the new kid on the block. Charles van Commenee was there with his athlete, Sharon Jaklovsky, but apart from that I didn't know anyone. Charles and I had met a year before at a competition in Spain and had got on well. He had been there coaching some Dutch athletes and had watched me compete. Sharon was a Dutch heptathlete who would become my training partner a couple of years later.

I went to bed that evening thinking about the events of the next day and feeling quite nervous. I knew the girls I would be competing against were some of the best in the world and I just hoped I could be up to the task.

Somehow I managed to fall asleep, and the next morning I woke bright and early. I got ready, prepared my spikes and met Darrell downstairs for some breakfast. I could only just eat because I had butterflies in my stomach. As I looked around the room at some of the other athletes, they all seemed to be so much more in control.

We got to the stadium at 8.45am so I could start my warm-up at nine o'clock. The first heptathlon event, the 100m hurdles, was due to start at ten. As I walked into the stadium I was struck with how amazingly beautiful the setting was. There was a small stand along the home straight of the track, and for the other 300m there was an open grass area with the most beautiful backdrop of mountains, and a steam train in the distance. The air was fresh, and it was incredibly peaceful and calm. As the start of the competition got closer and closer this peaceful setting was transformed into an amazingly lively sporting venue.

I tried to take every event as it came, eager to show that I deserved to be there, doing my best – but at times I found myself just watching some of the fine athletes there. The whole competition seemed to be so well organised. There was always something happening – first the girls were competing, then the guys were competing, and the crowd was able to move around the stadium accordingly. Presentations were made for the best performances in each event, and it was traditional to award those winners with a gold coin – which I thought was a nice touch.

By the close of the competition I had thoroughly enjoyed myself.

Charles had predicted I would finish sixth and I did. I felt very satisfied with myself.

Perhaps it was because I was so happy with my performance at Gotzis – my success in securing a top-ten finish and confirming my position as Britain's number-one heptathlete – that I was able to go into the World Championships hopeful and determined.

I had learned a lot from my sessions with sports psychologist Alma Thomas – particularly how important it is to set realistic targets for yourself. I had first met Alma in 1993 on a pilot course being run for women on the British athletics team. Its aim was to try to address the problem of why British female athletes were underachieving in relation to the men. I thought it was a good idea, so I went along, and it was here that I began to understand the role of psychology in sport, and the power of the mind.

It became clear that each individual has their own coping strategy for success and failure, and we identified our 'triggers', such as words and colours, that can pick us up. It was fascinating to realise how failure can take place before it actually happens, and that your mindset plays an incredibly important part in how you deal with events and situations.

It is important that you have realistic expectations, which is where sensible goal-setting comes into play. You have to be honest with yourself and set an overall goal for the year, but also set daily or weekly short-term goals you can use as a measuring device.

But sports psychology is also about identifying where your mental blocks or problems lie. For athletes they can be about injury, your perception of yourself as an athlete, or your basic ability. Sometimes, though, your problems can be to do with you, what's happening in your life.

Identifying your problem areas doesn't mean you'll never fail, but it does go a long way to enabling you to understanding yourself and what drives you, and maybe if you can get a good grasp of that, you will be able to ensure that you don't make the same mistakes.

The goal I had set myself for the World Championships in Gothenburg – the top-ten finish – filled me with confidence and resolve. In the first race, the 100m hurdles, there were no signs of me being slowed down by any nervousness; I began with such a blast away from the blocks that I was given my first false start in a major competition – certainly not the sort of 'first' I was after. But, still full of confidence and determined not to let that setback affect me in the re-start, I made an excellent start out of the blocks to win it in 13.53 seconds, just six-hundredths of a second outside my personal best. It was a fantastic start to the competition, and one that really gave me confidence.

The hurdles are a particularly difficult way to start the heptathlon – a tough speed event in the morning, over hurdles that can easily be knocked over and end your heptathlon before it's really begun. It is difficult to make up for huge errors at this level. The key to being a good heptathlete is not to have any particularly weak events, but to strive for a good consistent standard in all seven events – consistency is everything.

However, the high jump had been difficult for me for a couple of years. I think I had built up mental barriers with this event because of failures in the past. 1.8m is a benchmark for good high jumping in heptathlon, and high jump is also a good points scorer. Any mistakes in this event can prove to be quite costly and you can be put at a real disadvantage. So, when I jumped 1.74m, which I only just cleared on the second attempt, I knew I was in trouble. I didn't manage the next height of 1.77m although I did attempt it. It was very disappointing for me, and it meant that I was in tenth place as I went into the shot, another of my weak events. Suddenly the confidence with which I began the day seemed to vanish. The pressure was piling on.

My final result in the shot was just 13.24m. The competition was not going as well as I had anticipated. I had one final race before the end of day one in which to pull myself up the table: the 200m. As I stood at the starting line, poised and ready to go, I tried to shut out the noise of the crowd and focus on the finishing line, only 200 metres away. The gun went off and I ran like my life depended upon it, finishing about fifth, with a time of 24.88 seconds, a personal best.

At the end of day one I was lying in seventh position and my disappointment was huge. While I accepted that the World Championships involved competing at a level that was much more intense, I simply wasn't competing to the best of my ability.

But the American heptathlete Jackie Joyner-Kersee, the reigning world record-holder, had pulled out before the championship started, and Sabine Braun had had to retire after the high jump with a wrist injury. I then found out that Heike Drechsler had also withdrawn because of an injury. So, if ever there was a chance for me to make an impact upon a big competition, it was now.

I went back to the apartment I was sharing with triple-jumper Michelle Griffiths, Jacqui Agyepong (100m hurdler), Simone Jacobs (100m/200m), Stephanie Douglas (100m), Donna Fraser (400m) and Marcia Richardson (100m). The girls were changed, waiting for me to get back, and we walked the ten minutes to the restaurant together. It was great to have their support, and to know that no matter what was going on, or how the competition was faring, once you got back to the apartment at the end of the day there would be six people telling you what you had done wrong, encouraging you, telling you you had done a good job, and giving you their opinions – whether you asked for them or not!

The girls were always sensitive and you knew that if things had gone badly someone would be there to crack a joke to pick you up and make you smile. In that way, we were all reliant on each other. That has been consistent feature throughout the years we have competed together: my 'girls' are almost like sisters to me and have made all my trips entertaining in some way, shape or form. Having such good friends is very important. We have a great time, we respect one another and we pep each other up. We are there to watch each other as much as we can in the competitions, even though we all compete at different times. I believe we'll all be friends well after the athletics is over as we have shared some very special times and memories. I love them all dearly.

That night as I lay in bed I thought about the next day and hoped it would be a successful one. My long jump had been going well, so I was optimistic about my result in that. I knew I needed a good throw in the javelin, and after that I would know exactly what I needed to do for the 800m. Although I felt relaxed, I was unable to get to sleep because of the noise of the disco on site. It finished at 2am and I eventually dropped off.

Day two began with the long jump and with a first-round foul. But eventually I jumped 6.57m, which pulled me up into sixth place as we went into the second event of the day, the javelin. After my astonishing Commonwealth Games throw I think most people at the competition were expecting me to pull back a lot of points, and it certainly would have been a thrill to have done that. However I managed just 49.70m, and retained sixth position going into the 800m.

There was no real prospect of a medal, so I was running for the highest position I could achieve. After the 800m my overall position was seventh, which was hugely disappointing because the gap between seventh and fourth places was only a matter of a few points. A young Eunice Barber had been the one to finish in fourth place, and Ghada Shouaa of Syria won.

On the whole, Darrell and I were pleased that I finished in the top ten in my first World Championships, because that was the target I had originally set myself. Although I did feel initial disappointment, by the time I got home and had thought about it properly, I could see exactly where I had gone wrong, and realised that seventh place wasn't so bad after all.

It was in 1995 that I had my first proper go at modelling, when I was featured in the *Britain's Girls of Sport* calendar for 1996. However, Mum claims that my interest in clothes and posing goes back to many years earlier. When I was around five years old there was a children's modelling competition in the paper, so we decided to send in my photograph. The organisers of the competition rang Mum to say that I'd got through to the next round. I therefore had to go to a hotel in the centre of Wolverhampton to have some photos taken. Mum and I trooped in to town, and waited ages with lots of other girls until we were called into a room where my picture was taken. I thought it had all gone very well, but apparently the organisers didn't, because I never heard from them again!

Luckily things were a bit different in 1995. The calendar was the idea of Sharron Davies, and it was she who called me and asked if I wanted to be involved. The calendar aimed to do two things: first, show that sportswomen could be sexy, and second, raise money for women in sport. I agreed to do it because a few of my friends were involved – Michelle Griffiths, Geraldine McLeod and Jacqui Agyepong – and I didn't want to let the team down by not joining in. Besides, I quite fancied the idea and we all thought it would be fun.

Before the shoot I was quite nervous, so I decided to go out and buy something I knew I would be happy wearing. We had been told to bring something flattering and sexy with us, so I went into town and bought myself a lovely peppermint-green balconette Wonderbra because I loved the colour, and thought that a bit of help in the bust department might be helpful before venturing on to a glamour calendar! I then went to the hairdressers and had my hair done up.

The next day, I turned up at the photographer's studio wearing my new purchase. I expected something a bit more glamorous than the studio I found myself in, but the photographer was excellent at getting me to relax and do all sorts of different poses while he clicked away. I had expected the shoot to be over fairly quickly, but I ended up staying there for hours while he took the photos. By the time we had finished I was absolutely exhausted, and frustrated that I was going to have to wait for months before I could see the finished product.

When the calendar came out I was quite pleased with the results. They had decided not to use any of the more seductive pictures of me in my green outfit, opting instead for one in which I was wearing a wig I had also bought for the occasion that made me look very young and cheeky! I thought the photo looked nice – it was a bit raunchy, but not offensive or crude. I thought the calendar did us all justice and never thought any more about it.

Unfortunately, though, a while later the photos of me in my green underwear were picked up by the *Mirror* and were run in the style of page three pictures. I heard that they would be appearing in the paper three days before they went in, so the first thing I did was talk to Mum, and explain to her that the pictures were about to appear, and that she might not like them very much.

She raised one eyebrow when she saw them, and wasn't very impressed. 'Look at your chest,' she said. 'Did you have to stick your chest out?'

I told her the pictures were supposed to be for a calendar, that that was the point of it, but she wasn't very happy with the whole thing. Her look said it all!

1996 was Olympic year. Every athlete's dream. I had always maintained that Sydney was going to be *my* Olympic Games, but that Atlanta would be a significant dress rehearsal. How prophetic of me! I suppose it was wishful thinking at the time, because all athletes would love to look back on their careers and measure their progress by Olympic performances.

Popular belief was that Atlanta was going to be the greatest Olympic Games ever. I was sure that the Americans, who like to think they are the best at sport, would pull out all the stops to host a games to beat all others. It would be a good one to star in, and everyone involved in sport was determined to be on top form for it.

The Olympic year began well for me. The lifestyle changes I had made after the Commonwealth Games were definitely having an effect: my diet was now as good as it could be, my fitness was better than ever, and I was training full time. I also had some major competitions under my belt, and was starting to understand myself and the nature of the heptathlon much better. In April I went to Tallahassee in Florida to do some warm-weather training before the annual heptathlon-decathlon competition in Gotzis at the end of May.

Training went well in Tallahassee and gave me the opportunity to spend some quality time with my boyfriend, Jonathan, who was a keen long jumper for the Irish national team. I had met him the year before in Tallahassee on the same training camp. Unfortunately, since then we hadn't been able to spend very much time together due to personal commitments, and the distance between Wolverhampton and London, where he lived.

The first time I met Jonathan I felt that there was something special about him – it was his manner, his movement, and the things that he said. Initially he had been aloof, but he seemed so self-controlled and thoughtful. He was dark and I was particularly struck by his soft eyes. His accent was incredibly mysterious; he was Irish, but had acquired a slight American twang from his days of study at Princeton University. None the less he had very much retained what I would refer to as his Irish 'isms'. He wasn't my usual type, but he had a strength, an almost mystical power. He was different, and I had never met anyone like him before – nor have I met anyone like him since. I put him on a pedestal and adored him.

We managed to spend a lot of time together during the camp, and talked about a lot of things. We were both hoping to qualify for the Olympic team and had a lot of shared hopes and dreams for the future. We could see our careers and lives merging and both realised that we wanted to make more of a commitment to each other. He enriched my life immensely, and when we were together we had a wonderful time.

A month later we were in Gotzis for the 1996 competition. It was here that I broke the British record, achieving a points score of 6645 to beat Judy Simpson's record of 6625 that had stood for ten years. It was a phenomenal achievement and meant that I soared up the world rankings from just inside the top ten to second place. The best thing for me was that the improvements came in the events I was not traditionally good at. In the 100m hurdles I ran 13.18 seconds, and made 14.36m in the shot against a previous best of 13.58m. For me this was one of the best results of the competition because I had worked quite hard at developing my technique and had really started to feel the event. I had placed a lot of emphasis on trying to develop my strength and build up the amount of weight training I was doing, and it was fantastic to see such a direct result of my efforts. It made me realise that if I trained hard I really would see the improvement in my scores. I ran the 200m in 24.06 seconds, and equalled my personal best in the high jump. And most surprisingly of all, I ran the 800m in 2 minutes 16.84 seconds.

In the long jump I reached 6.60m. This was only 7cm short of my best of 6.67m, and we had been competing in rain and into a head wind, so I knew there was much more to come when I could get the conditions and my form to collide. Supporting my own beliefs, Darrell was convinced I would have jumped 6.80m if conditions had been right. My javelin throw was 47.86m, which wasn't that good considering that my throw at the Commonwealth Games in 1994 was 53.68m. If I had thrown 55m, which I knew I could have done, that would have given me another 130 points.

Still I was ecstatic. All the promise and self-belief had at last started to show. Sometimes, when you set a good score as I had done at the Commonwealth Games, you wonder when you will show such good form again, or if it was only a one-off. I had been quietly working behind the scenes, and at last I had put together what for me seemed like a dream performance. I had set five personal bests in one competition.

At the end of the tournament, Darrell was thrilled. I had broken the British record when I was not at my best and he was convinced there was much more still to come. We both hoped I would be able to pull it all together in Atlanta.

Before heading for the three-week British Olympic training camp back in Tallahassee, I wanted one final chance to compete. I was very optimistic about my chances in the Olympics, but needed to affirm my good form by entering another competition. So when the opportunity arose to compete in a domestic meet in Gateshead, I was pleased. I wanted to practise my hurdles and, as I had one of the fastest times in the country, I felt that on merit I deserved a lane at the meet.

Unfortunately, Malcolm Arnold, Britain's chief coach, did not see things the same way. He told me I couldn't run because he wanted to leave a lane open for any of the hurdles specialists who might be after one last chance to get the Olympic qualifying time. I totally understood his point of view, and would never have wished to get in the way of anyone else's preparation, but I also had to think of my own. What I didn't understand was why they could not find a place for me as well. My blood boiled as we exchanged words, but he wouldn't change his mind and I couldn't alter the situation.

I think it is much harder for a multi-eventer to get the same recognition as a single eventer. There seems to be a perception that, just because we are not the best in a single event, we are somehow less valid. We have been described as 'Jacks of all trades, masters of none' but in fact it takes a very high level of fitness, co-ordination and mental toughness to do seven events. It can take years to perfect all the skills and training is much more intense than for other events because you frequently have to combine your sessions, maybe tackling three disciplines in one day.

Many people don't understand how an athlete who wins only one event out of seven but keeps a reasonable standard in the other six can still become the champion overall. They make comparisons with running events in which the person who comes first is the victor, or the high jump where the person who jumps the highest is on top. But the heptathlon is an event that requires a range of skills and disciplines, and this can really thrill and excite spectators. Following the up and downs of the events, calculating the points and working out how many points a competitor is above or below their best, can be more exciting than watching a race that lasts for a matter of minutes or seconds.

For a long time, the media has paid little attention to multi events. For example, for two consecutive years, in 1996 and 1997, I travelled to Gotzis as Britain's number-one heptathlete, but there was no media awareness of what I was doing, what was happening, or when I was competing. On both occasions I broke the British record, elevating me to the level of the leading heptathletes, but there were no media there to cover the event, thus missing the great atmosphere and excitement of the two days of competition. Instead there was a frenzy of journalists calling me up after the event trying to get information about the two days and trying to get me to convey my feelings retrospectively. I felt disappointed, almost like a second-rank athlete, and wished that, like any other leading performer, I had got the coverage I deserved.

The Europa Cup for combined events – the heptathlon and decathlon – is another competition that I feel should get more media attention. It takes place every year and the top six to eight countries compete against each other for the cup. Exactly the same competition is held for single events – a competition of which most people are aware because it is publicised in the media and televised. They share the name but their status is very different.

Since the likes of Daley Thompson there has been very little emphasis on combined events and few efforts have been made to develop the standard of coaching or to maintain the profile of the events. I do hope, though, that I have gone some way to raise the profile of combined events over the past six years – through my newspaper articles, and particularly through my successes in the sport. I hope I have showed the public the character-building qualities that are needed, qualities that can also be applied to real-life situations. One event in the heptathlon can go badly but, like everything in life, you have to pick yourself up and rise above the disappointment in order to get the best out of yourself for the next one. Sometimes you have to dig deep down into your reserves in order to get a personal best and personal satisfaction, and giving up should never be a realistic option, as tomorrow may be your greatest day.

In the end, I flew to Tallahassee without competing at Gateshead. I gave myself a two-week period in which to refine all my events before heading on to Atlanta. It was a good opportunity to focus hard on the championship ahead, to think clearly about my aims and goals. I felt good on the camp, the only nagging doubt being a shoulder injury which just wouldn't go away. I could feel it when I threw javelin and did certain upper-body exercises, so I was being careful not to over-train and aggravate it further. Kevin Lidlow, the physiotherapist I had met in Victoria for the first time, was in the States with us as he had come to be my personal physio for the games, and he spent time working on my shoulder, trying to ease the tension and keep the pain at bay.

From landing at Atlanta airport to arriving at the athletes' village, everything was very organised and went very smoothly. Each team had its own delegation to look after them and see them on to the next stage of the journey. As we entered the village I was aware of how big everything seemed, and wondered how long it would be before I got lost. The teams were housed in blocks on this incredibly large university-style campus.

We were a large British team, and we seemed to share the euphoric feeling that we were a part of something big, something united. I was staying in a four-bedroomed apartment with the girls – Michelle, Marcia, Donna, Jacqui, Simone, Geraldine and Stephanie. When we walked into our apartment's lounge we were struck by its spaciousness; but in contrast the bedrooms were tiny. However it was great fun to have us all together in one place. For most of us it was our first

Olympics, and I intended to absorb and enjoy the atmosphere to the maximum.

The first day of the heptathlon dawned. The temperature was around 80 degrees and the first heat of the hurdles took place in glorious sunshine. I was in the second heat, the same as the world record-holder and two-time Olympic champion Jackie Joyner-Kersee. This was the first time I was to compete against her, and that thought alone had me spellbound. Then the lane draw was issued and I realised I had been drawn in lane seven, next to her.

As we waited to be taken into the stadium, everyone tense and ready for action, Jackie turned to me and smiled. I was so surprised – this legend had actually acknowledged me! This gave me enough courage to speak to her and wish her well for the competition.

Finally it was time for our heat to be led out into the arena. I felt my adrenaline pumping as I stepped on to the track and looked at the Olympic flame burning high above us. Although it was just half past eight in the morning I felt ready and focused. We stripped off and took our places on the starting line.

Not long before we had entered the stadium, the glorious sunshine had been eclipsed by a sky full of dark and threatening clouds, and suddenly, as we waited for the start commands in our blocks, the heavens opened and the pouring rain drenched everything in sight.

The race went ahead regardless, but we began with a false start. As we walked back to our blocks for a second time, a very loud American male voice started shouting, rooting for Jackie: 'Come on, Jackie, show 'em who's boss! You're the greatest, show 'em you're twenty-one again! Let's go, Jackie . . . come on!' He just wouldn't stop. And this – combined with the rain and my own idolising of Jackie – was more than enough to distract me; my focus was not as sharp as it should have been.

The gun went, and my start was lousy. I hit most of the hurdles on the way down, but Jackie was in the lead, and I was trying to catch her instead of running my own race. I crossed the line in second place with a time of 13.45 seconds. The time wasn't too bad under the circumstances, but the race itself was awful. Jackie had won but she seemed to be in distress: she had been heavily strapped around her hamstring for the race, and had obviously aggravated it further.

From the hurdles we went straight into the high jump, and heard the news that Joyner-Kersee had pulled out of the competition with a hamstring injury. Despite what people might think, this was no real consolation to me. All athletes want to beat the best at their best, and a great champion pulling out through injury was bad news as far as I was concerned.

This was probably her last big competition, which was a real shame. She had been such an excellent ambassador for the sport that it would have been good if she could have at least finished the competition on home soil. But at least I can say that I raced with the great Jackie Joyner-Kersee.

Although the rain had now stopped, the whole of the high jump area was soaking wet. There were huge puddles everywhere, and officials were running around with big sponges, soaking up the excess water and squeezing them out. High jumping is always a little tricky when the area around the bed is so wet, as it makes me concerned about planting my foot aggressively for take-off. According to Darrell, this was clear as he watched my warm-up jumps. I wasn't too bad at the lower heights, but as the bar went up and I needed to commit myself more, my uncertainty was evident. I finished on 1.77m.

After two events, I had dropped back into tenth place overall. Again I was bitterly disappointed – my high jump had really let me down.

Shot put was next. I threw 13.92m and was starting to lose confidence. But I managed to edge myself up into seventh place.

Going into the final event of the day, the 200m, Ghada Shouaa was in the lead. As I stood in lane three, waiting for the gun, I felt I at least wanted to finish the day off better than I had started it. I ran a good race – not a world record-breaking performance, but I came in second place with a time of 24.44 seconds. Natalya Sazanovich from Belarus was in first place with 23.72 seconds. I would be going into day two in sixth place.

It was a late finish that night, and when I finally got back to the village I went to the restaurant for some food but couldn't find anything. The Atlanta Olympics clearly hadn't been organised with the comfort of the athletes in mind. It had been set up to make as much money as possible, and while the corporate sponsors were no doubt loving the show, for athletes like me the reality was that at one o'clock in the morning, having travelled back to the tiny little apartments late at night, all you could eat was McDonald's. I got into bed that night feeling quite low and hungry. I kept telling myself that tomorrow would be much better for me, had a quick chat with Jackie, my room mate, then fell asleep, exhausted.

On the morning of day two I woke feeling positive, knowing I was starting with the long jump, the event in which I have most experience and a good degree of confidence. But this time I suffered a disaster. No one in the competition jumped particularly well, but I doubt anyone was relying upon the event quite as much as I was. It felt like the end of my world. I fouled the first jump, and made a distance of 6.32m for my second – well below par. My third and final attempt was another foul. I could not believe it, and was in a real state of shock as I dusted off the sand and put my Olympic kit back on. I couldn't make eye contact with anyone; I felt embarrassed and a failure. So much support and encouragement from my friends and family and now my chances of a medal had surely evaporated.

I went to meet Mum and Darrell behind the stands after the competition. Also standing there, waiting to greet me was my great friend Denise Nelson and her fiancé Glen. Denise had been living in New York for the past five years, and she and Glen had made a special trip to Atlanta to come and watch me compete. I took one look at the people I cared so much about, and promptly burst into tears. I can only recall one other occasion when I felt so much disappointment that I was reduced to tears, and that was in Thessalonica as a junior, when I did badly in my high jump. But now I was beyond that, this was an Olympic disaster! I told everyone I was going home. Mum, Darrell and Denise had tears in their eyes as I spoke, but told me not to be silly. Darrell walked me to the bus back to the athletes' village and suggested I calm down and wait and see what the afternoon session had in store.

I didn't have much time before the javelin, so back in my room I took a quick shower, changed my clothes and repacked my kit bag. I gazed at all my cards from my friends, fans and well-wishers, and began to feel sorry for myself again. I told myself I would do one more event, and if that didn't go well I would pull out. I met up with Kevin on the warm-up track so he could take a look at my shoulder. He tried desperately to cheer me up, in the end promising to strip naked and run around the stadium if I managed a throw close to 60m. This made me laugh – but you would have to know Kevin to understand!

The time for javelin approached and Darrell and I sat down and talked everything through. He assured me that it wasn't all over – there were two events left – but reminded me that I did need a big throw. The pressure was on. But I'd done it before, and I could do it again.

I went to the javelin still feeling that if things didn't go well I would pull out before the 800m, with the amusing thought in the back of my head of Kevin running around the stadium naked. I sat there feeling non-committal. Shouaa had thrown already and looked as if she was going to win the competition. I stepped up on to the runway for my first throw. It landed just over 46m – the confirmation I was looking for, my excuse not to run the 800m.

On my second attempt, the crowd was so much behind me that I felt I owed it to them at least to focus on trying to throw well. On release, the throw felt better technically than the first one, and this was confirmed by the distance of just over 50m. I got a rapturous applause from the crowd, but I still wasn't that pleased. I was caught between two worlds: one saying don't run, don't finish, go home, the other, the competitor in me, saying come on, throw it, give it some welly and go for it. If I was going to go on, I wanted to minimise the pain of the 800m, because I knew I would have to run more quickly than I had ever done before.

So many thoughts were running through my mind as I went to take my final throw. I felt as if everyone had created a star that had not yet been born. I felt I was mentally unprepared for all the pressures and expectations that were upon me. Winning Gotzis did not, in my opinion, make me number two in the world. The pressure was simply overwhelming.

I took a deep breath, took my run-up and launched the javelin. When my score came up on the board I shook my head in disbelief. I had thown a personal best of 54.82m. How had I managed that? At that point I still didn't realise the implications of my throw, although I could see Darrell jumping up and down and clapping. It was then announced that I had moved into third place. Sabine Braun came over to me and asked me where the hell I had pulled such a throw from! I couldn't answer her, but looking back, I think that maybe my pride was bigger than my will to be defeated.

So, once again, all the pressure was on the 800m. Once again I was in a major competition and I had everything to lose by not pulling an astonishing win out of the bag. I knew that if I didn't run well, the Polish athlete Urszula Wlodarczyk would beat me and I'd lose the medal. I couldn't win silver because the gap was too big. It was bronze or nothing.

It was raining gently and I felt quite tired. It had been a long day – we'd had an early start with the long jump, and it was now approaching 10pm. My race plan was not to go out too hard, to run my own race and not to commit myself before the back straight of the final lap.

At the gun I started off well, keeping myself in touch with the rest of the pack. Then, with 250m left, Wlodarczyk pulled away. I could see the gap opening up and, tired as I was, I knew I couldn't let it get any bigger. I had just seconds to play with. So I rallied. 60 metres, 30 metres, 20 metres to go. I threw myself at the line and made up around half a second. It made all the difference. I finished in 2 minutes 17.41 seconds and Wlodarczyk came in at 2 minutes 12.35 seconds.

The statisticians got to work, and after what felt like an agonisingly long wait, I discovered that I had beaten Wlodarczyk by five points to take bronze. Shouaa took the gold and Sazanovich the silver. I don't think I have ever felt such relief. I had made so many mistakes, yet it had all come together in the end and, aged 23, I had won Britain's only Olympic medal for a female participant.

After the 800m I struggled to recover. I felt exhausted, light headed and sick. I went to the medical room with Kevin, who kept asking me if I felt OK. I told him I felt terrible and very strange, and at that moment he handed me his mobile, telling me someone special was waiting to talk to me. It was Jonathan, a very croaky and emotional Jonathan. I couldn't speak, but he told me he was proud of me and that he loved me. It was wonderful to hear his voice, and I just managed to tell him that I would call him later.

I felt dreadful. One of the doctors came over and looked at me. I was incoherent, and before I knew what was happening I was lying on the bed. It all happened so fast; it was like a scene from *ER*. I had a team of doctors around me and they put a clip on my finger and pads on my chest to monitor my heartbeat. I couldn't open my eyes and was burning up, but I felt freezing. Kevin had gone to find the British team doctors, so there was no one there I knew.

But my heart was fine, and slowly everything returned to normal. They said it might have been heat exhaustion, but they weren't sure. When I was strong enough to walk I went off to do my drugs test and press conference.

It was well after 1am as I travelled back to the apartment, with just the bus driver on an empty bus to keep me company. I was hit by a real loneliness. I was looking at the moon, thinking, 'Gosh, girl, look what you've done, you've won a medal at the Olympics.' I wasn't presented with the medal until the following day, because we finished so late, so

I couldn't even hug that for company. It was an odd time, just me, an anonymous bus driver and the full moon, but all the pride in the world.

Although the two days of the heptathlon were not much fun and full of anxiety, there was a lot of fun to be had during the rest of my stay in Atlanta. From the day we arrived and saw the little transport carts, like golf buggies, that were used to get the athletes and bags to the apartments, Marcia and I were determined to hijack one. So on our penultimate night in Atlanta, with the rest of the girls in tow, we sneaked out after dinner and found one with the key still in the ignition. It was excellent – we went racing off through the night, screaming with laughter. We kept going round and round the campus. Every time we went forward too quickly, the girls would fall off the back. If whoever was driving went too slowly, the others would cry, 'Faster, faster!' Later on that night we found an excellent club on the other side of town. We danced the night away to some great R&B and hip-hop tunes and had a fantastic time. Guys tried to hit on us throughout the night but we weren't interested, we were too busy enjoying each other's company and entertaining ourselves, making fun of some of the fashion disasters in the club, and basically having a great night.

On our last night in Atlanta we were walking along the street out of the village, dressed to kill, when we saw a limo in a petrol station. We all stopped and looked at it, thinking how cool it would be to drive around in a car like that. So we decided to try and negotiate a fee, hoping the driver would let us have it cheaply. He finally agreed to $80, only $10 each, so we took him up on the offer, and cruised around the streets of Atlanta in style.

One of the good things about having such close friends who know me very well is that, if it all ends tomorrow, they know the real me. I sometimes think that if I got injured and had to stop competing, or when I retire, I'll stay in the house anyway with the girls, just so it will be like old times. With them I can be myself – there are no high expectations, and I don't have to worry about being a little insecure or letting my feelings show. I can just be Denise Lewis.

Our return to England was all rather disappointing. Because the Olympics had been considered a disaster from a British point of view, it meant there was no big reception, no congratulations, and it opened up a debate as to why Britain had done so badly in the championships, finishing well down on the medals table and coming behind countries we would normally expect to do better than. Some individuals did quite well at the championships, but the elusive gold medals seemed to evade us. However, I do think that people forget how difficult it is to win gold medals, and sometimes going to the championships for some people is more about achieving a personal best and getting the best out of themselves as a competitor than coming home with a medal.

At the Atlanta Games, I think Britain felt the backlash of years of under-funding. The bottom line was that we hadn't put any real investment into athletes, sporting venues or equipment for years. At the time, grants were very small and were given very sparingly. As a consequence, the majority of British athletes were, and still are, working full time, and are therefore unable to devote as much to their sport as they would like. As with any sport, if you can't put the time in, you can't win. Only a very small percentage are lucky enough to get sponsored, and few athletes can say that it is their full-time career. Many spend year after year living at a financial loss, spending much more than they ever earn back.

Looking back, Britain needed to have that games. The country needed to experience real sporting disaster to appreciate how important it was for us to have winners. Things changed after that, mainly with grants from the National Lottery, allowing the various governing bodies of sport to improve on facilities, something which made a significant contribution to our improved performance at the Sydney Olympics in 2000.

*

1996 finished on a real high note for me, when I was bridesmaid at Denise's wedding in New York. It was my real opportunity to say thank you for spurring me on in Atlanta. It was a wonderful wedding, and it was great to see one of my oldest and dearest friends so happy.

On my return, I managed to get together with the group of guys who had formed themselves into the 'Magnificent Seven' to sponsor me. The group was made up of seven Birmingham businessmen, each of whom had paid £1000 to sponsor me through the Olympics, and I wanted to thank them for their support. We met at the Alexander Stadium in Birmingham, and I took my medal along to show them. It was lovely to prove to them that their faith in me had produced an Olympic medal. Their funding was one of the things that had allowed me to train full-time and thus be in the position to win at the games. Money does not produce winners, but it does give those with the ability and the determination to succeed the space and time in which to do so. I will be forever grateful to the Magnificent Seven who helped me along the way, and am thrilled that Britain was able to learn from Atlanta so quickly – to realise that there is a direct relationship between the support given to athletes and their ability to reach their full potential.

Chapter Twelve

'You Didn't Win the Silver, You Lost the Gold'

In June 1997 I agreed to be body painted for *Total Sport* magazine. This was something which my mum, along with a few other people, thought was a mistake, and I'm not sure why I agreed to do it, except that it sounded quite fun at the time. It sounded different, and when they showed me examples of other people who'd had it done, I thought it looked good. In particular, Jacqui Agyepong had been painted as a leopard in the past, and that looked fabulous. I thought it was a creative way of doing photography.

Adidas, my sponsors who organised the shoot, were keen for me to have the Adidas kit painted on to my body for the sports magazine, so when they approached me, raising the issue, I thought about it and decided to go for it. I took my boyfriend Jonathan with me on the shoot, so that I knew there would be someone there who could look at what was happening from the outside, and make sure I didn't do anything I might regret. I also made sure that I was happy with, and aware of, all the arrangements, and what would be expected of me.

I had already checked that it would be a woman doing the painting, and I knew that I would be able to wear a thin, flesh-coloured thong that wouldn't show under the paint.

I turned up for the photo shoot and the woman began painting. The whole thing took for ever because she used incredibly small strokes and paid enormous attention to detail. First, she painted over the thong to make the shorts, and then painted on a crop top. It wasn't embarrassing having it done, but it did feel odd being painted. It was a peculiar sensation and I had to hold lots of ridiculous poses while she worked – one arm in the air for half an hour, then the other arm, then waiting for it all to dry. It took ages to do, much longer than I had anticipated. I had been told by the magazine that the painting would take three hours, so I would be at the studio from 10am until 1pm, then the photographic work would take until 4pm. In the end, we didn't finish until around 9pm, and I had to go training afterwards.

When the painting was finished, they showed me myself in a mirror. I was horrified – all I could see was flesh with a bit of paint on. The photographer told me not to worry, that once the picture was taken it would look as if I was wearing my kit. Just to prove it, he took a Polaroid picture. Once I saw that, I was fine. You could hardly tell I was naked, it just looked as if I was dressed in a skin-tight strip. I realised it was going to look good – and I still maintain that you would need your face right up against the magazine in order to be able to see that I'm naked.

When the magazine came out it caused a sensation; everyone seemed to be talking about the pictures and I really wasn't prepared for the reaction they provoked. I was hardly the first person to be painted in that way, it had been done plenty of times before, yet it seemed to become a major talking point. The reason was because the *Sun* got hold of the pictures and ran them on page three with a headline implying that I had agreed to go topless for their readers. It said 'Denise gets her tits out for the lads' or something like that. It was awful and, ironically, exactly what we had tried to avoid. Darrell was annoyed and confused when he saw the pictures in the *Sun*. As far as he was concerned, it was intended to promote sport and my successful year, and we never imagined it would be seen as tacky.

Mum was deeply unimpressed by the pictures. She didn't make a fuss – she just looked down her nose at the magazine, then looked at me in that way that told me exactly how she felt, more clearly than she could ever have expressed in words. As far as she was concerned it was done, and there was no going back, but she knew I had learned a lot from the experience.

I always try to look on the bright side, and see the good in everything I do, and at least the mess with the pictures gave me added inspiration to succeed. I *had* to do well; I had no option, or I'd be seen as a bimbo, an insignificant athlete who had used the *Total Sport* shoot in an effort to promote herself. I wanted the shoot to be seen as something done by a talented and accomplished athlete because it seemed like fun, nothing more, nothing less. As a woman in sport you are always conscious of not wanting to be seen as 'a Kournikova' – a woman whose abilities on the sports field some feel are dwarfed by her ability to market herself off it. If you are an attractive woman, it is only by doing well that you can rid yourself of these accusations.

I was therefore extremely confident going into the World Championships, and encouraged by the fact that Jackie Joyner-Kersee wasn't entering, and Ghada Shouaa, the reigning world and Olympic champion from Syria, was out of action all summer with a back injury. This meant that Sabine Braun and I were being touted as the favourites to battle for the gold.

I had no problem with this, but was well aware that it was far from the whole story, as other heptathletes would challenge us for the honours as well. It was important that I didn't become too complacent, as Jane Flemming had in 1994. Unknown athletes have a habit of making themselves known when you least expect it.

When I discovered that Sabine had scored 6787 points to win the German championships in Ratingen, the same weekend I was at

Gotzis, I knew I was in for a tough competition. Sabine's result meant she led the world rankings, and I was in second place, 51 points behind.

When I thought about the competition, and how high my chances were of getting a medal, I realised just how much I had improved since 1995 when I went in hoping to finish in the top ten. In two years I had gone from being a possible top-ten finisher to being touted as a possible gold medal winner. It was a great feeling. I had finally become comfortable with the recognition of being one of the best heptathletes in the world. The way I had turned the competition around so dramatically at Atlanta the year before made me realise that I could still finish with a medal even when I was not competing at my best. But this time I was determined that I would not make as many mistakes as I had in the past.

In April, Darrell and our training group went back to warm-weather training in Tallahassee for the third year on the run. The group stayed there for around four weeks but I stayed for three, spending my fourth week training in Baton Rouge, Louisiana, with Charles van Commenee and Sharon Jaklovsky, who had been competing for Holland since 1994. I had decided to ask Charles if I could train with him for a week or so, because I knew he would push me harder than Darrell.

I had asked Darrell some weeks prior to departure if he would mind if I spent that last week with Charles in Lousiana, and he had reluctantly agreed, sensing perhaps that I wasn't really asking his permission.

I did some good work in Tallahassee in the first three weeks and enjoyed it, but it was during this time that the tension between Darrell and me really began. Since 1996 I had begun to notice that some things about him irritated me more than they had before. It was nothing I could particularly put my finger on, but significant none the less. We had also been arguing a little too much. Jonathan and I had spent a great deal of time discussing my concerns, as he knew Darrell well and could see how the situation was causing me problems. He had suggested I sit down and talk to Darrell at length, but I hadn't wanted to get involved in the inevitable argument that would result. I had therefore left it, thinking it was maybe a passing phase. However, these isolated feelings had increased throughout the year, despite my success at the Olympic Games.

I got a great deal out my week in Louisiana with Charles and enjoyed it very much. I had brought with me the programme Darrell had set and Charles added his own input. The week gave me a new perspective, which I found very refreshing. By this stage I felt much more confident when Charles was training me. It was the way in which he spoke that seemed to push me that little bit further every time, and I think we worked well together because I needed someone to be even stricter with me than Darrell. I needed someone who would be a leader, who would force me to get the work done whether I wanted to do it or not.

In Gotzis, at the end of May, I had again broken the British record with a consistent performance in all seven events. I had given the performance of my life. I was really on form, and had put on the best all-round display ever by a British heptathlete. Tucked away in the Austrian village, beneath blue skies and followed by big crowds from event to event, I had come alive, notching up a total score of 6736 points, a lifetime's best and a British and Commonwealth record that was 91 points better than my total the year before. In the process I had beaten Natalya Sazanovich – the Belarusian who won the silver in Atlanta – by nearly 300 points, and Urszula Wlodarczyk – the Polish girl who was just five points behind me in Atlanta – by more than 500.

I knew by this stage that as soon as the World Championships were over, whatever the outcome, I had to tell Darrell that I wanted to work with Charles full time. I knew it would upset him deeply, but I also knew I had put it off for too long. It wasn't fair to any of us, so I had to be strong, find some mental strength from somewhere, and tell him what I wanted to do.

But first, there was the small matter of a world championship for me to deal with.

*

On the first day in Athens, the weather was beautiful, the conditions perfect, and we all knew that this was the environment in which to get good points scored. As usual, the first event was the 100m hurdles – I was in lane four, with Sabine Braun next to me in lane five. I got a good start in the race and was going well, neck and neck with Braun, until I clattered heavily into the seventh hurdle. I don't know what happened, I just hit it with my left foot and was lucky not to fall over. It meant that I totally lost my stride pattern and rhythm. The momentary lack of concentration cost me dearly because it allowed Sabine to come past me on the line. I finished fourth in a race in which I had hoped for a top-two placing. My time was 13.43 seconds.

In the high jump, I had much to make up. Despite my historical difficulties with this event, having jumped 1.82m in Gotzis I was determined to get over 1.80m in these championships.

As we reached 1.81m it was looking as if I wouldn't do it. But I scraped over on my third attempt and watched the bar as it moved up to 1.84m. It would make such a difference if I could make this jump count. On my first attempt I hit the bar. Then came my second. The atmosphere was very exciting. There was a noticeable British and German rivalry in the crowd and the Germans were being particularly vocal. However, the British contingent was fantastic, doing claps of encouragement, which really helped fire me up. I took a deep breath and ran towards the jump, where I put every ounce of my energy into throwing myself over the bar.

As I cleared it I heard the roar of the crowd. I had done it. I had equalled my lifetime's best and had finished in fifth place. Not bad for someone who had always had such problems with the high jump in major competitions. But Sabine, whose nickname is La Grande Dame because she has been in the heptathlon for so long, went on to clear 1.9m – outstanding jumping for a heptathlete. She hadn't shown much form over the past two years, but this championship was very different. She had amassed a lot of points with her high jump and hurdles, making it difficult for me to contend for the gold. This was confirmed again in the shot put, in which she threw a personal best of 15.09m. But I also achieved a personal best, throwing 14.55m, which was an improvement of 19cm.

The next event was the 200m. I came in second place, in 24.13 seconds, just outside my personal best of 24.10 seconds. By the end of the day I had a total of 3888 points, a personal best first-day score. I was delighted.

I was lying in fourth place, behind Braun, Sazanovich and Remigija Nazaroviene. Since day two is always much better for me, I was not too concerned to be sitting outside the medals, and achieving a personal best score for the first day was a great result. So it was with some satisfaction that I went to sleep that night, and prepared myself for the next day.

Day two started extremely early, with the first event, the long jump, beginning at 8am. I was reasonably pleased with my jump of 6.47m, 5cm further than Braun's 6.42m. However, because of the early start, most of the jumping was under par. But it was sufficient to give me 997 points, lifting me into second position overall behind Braun. With only the javelin and 800m to go, the margin of error was decreasing with every event. Although I was better than Braun in the javelin, she was the faster 800m runner. So, if I could perform at my best in both events, I could win the competition. It was all getting extremely tense.

Because I was 107 points behind Braun, it was clear that the javelin was going to be absolutely crucial if I was to have any chance of getting the gold medal. I started slowly, not making much of an impression, then I threw 52.70m in my third attempt – not enough, I feared, to make any impression on Sabine's lead. Sabine then threw 51.48m, which practically confirmed that she would be taking away the gold medal.

Before the final event, the 800m, I had a deficit of six seconds. I would have to beat Braun by that much if I was going to win the gold. It was incredibly hot, not the perfect environment in which to run round the track twice, especially if you're a power-based athlete who hates running! So I was realistic with myself. I knew that the javelin had been my chance to pull back the deficit, and although I had thrown well, it just hadn't been enough. The deficit had lingered up to the last event, and I resigned myself to the fact that any chance of gold had gone. Darrell and I therefore decided that I should just run a sensible race.

In the end, Braun won the gold with 6739 points and I came second with 6654. It was the second time that Braun, who was thirty-two years old, had become world champion: I was just twenty-four so, even though Braun had dominated the championship from start to finish, I knew I had plenty of time left, and one day I would pull it all together.

Despite the disappointment of not winning, I was quite pleased with myself when I came back from Athens clutching my silver medal. I knew this meant that I was undeniably one of the best heptathletes in the world. However, Charles managed to put the dampeners on my excitement somewhat, by insisting that I could have won the gold. He said that clattering into the hurdle in the opening race cost me the medal I wanted. His way of putting it was that I hadn't won silver, I'd lost gold. That was one of the essential differences between Charles and Darrell – Charles always wanted more, always thought I could do better, whereas Darrell was pleased with me whatever I achieved.

When I came back to England after the competition, all the Midlands press were waiting for me at the airport, along with some fans who wanted autographs signed. Mum and I had travelled back together and we walked happily through the airport arm in arm, pleased to be home.

When we got back to the house, the neighbours were all out in the street, surrounded by lots of fans. They had decorated the house with balloons, banners and streamers and it looked fantastic. I was thrilled by the trouble they had gone to. Champagne and wine were in full flow and everyone was cheering and clapping as we drove up – it was a real celebration and looked like great fun. It was such an amazing feeling to see all these people there to celebrate my medal, all of them incredibly proud and delighted.

Just as I was getting out of the car I saw Nanny in the back of another car, just sitting there. My grandmother doesn't usually come to greet me when I get back from competitions, so I was surprised to see her. She was just staring ahead, lost in her own world. I assumed that she wanted to join in the celebrations, but thought it all rather odd. After all the initial madness had died down and I had told the story of winning a silver medal around fifty times, Nanny came into the house. Once everyone had gone, the three of us sat down. Suddenly I felt something peculiar, a cold rush went through me and Mum started babbling, she was becoming hysterical and I wasn't sure why. My grandmother still hadn't said anything.

Then my mum said, 'It's Nanny isn't it?'

The look on my grandmother's face said it all. It was a truly awful moment. Mum became hysterical, shouting at the top of her voice while I desperately tried to calm her down. She was making me nervous.

Nanny told us that her mother had passed away. Peacefully, she said. Her words wouldn't register properly at first. I just looked from Mum to Nanny then back again. Then my mum started screaming and Nan started crying. I just couldn't take it all in. It was all a big whirl, and I remember very little except that winning a silver medal for my athletics was suddenly put sharply into perspective. We had gone so quickly from celebrations to this. I really couldn't absorb the information, and didn't know what to do.

My own emotion then flooded in and I wandered around the room. I had never experienced anything like it; I just couldn't stand on one spot. Mum was on the floor, weak and sobbing. I didn't know what to do with myself. I just needed to get out of the room. I fled upstairs screaming and crying and ran into the bathroom, getting into the empty bath fully clothed. I lay on my side, kicking the bath and howling. The next thing I knew, Mum and Nanny were looking down at me with tear-stained faces, trying to calm me down. After a while I managed to pull myself together and that was when I knew I had to be strong. Mum needed me – they both needed me.

My great grandmother was like your archetypal grandmother. You could jump on her and sit there all day, cuddling her while she told you stories about her past and how different life had been for them. She was very jolly, and had a lovely, high-pitched, outrageous laugh, which would make her eyes water. She was incredibly tactile and always wanted to kiss and hug you. I met her on my first holiday to Jamaica when I was nine years old. The first time she saw me she gave me such a big, tight hug that I could hardly breathe, and I was incredibly struck by how wonderful it was to be loved so much by someone who didn't really know you. We became extremely close for two people who lived so far from each other and I loved her dearly. The phone calls we shared would be the highlight of any day, mainly on Mothering Sundays or birthdays, but also just random calls, usually on Sundays. I looked forward to those calls so much – and suddenly I knew I'd never have such a call again.

Great Gran died just before my uncle Jack's wedding, and the fact that she didn't see her beloved Jack get married was one of the things that upset me most about the timing of her death. We were all going over to Jamaica for the wedding, and I knew how much she was looking forward to having the whole family in the house together for the first time in three years. I had been looking forward to it, too. I had longed to tell Great Gran about my travels, about what I had been doing and how great life was. I knew she'd be happy to hear how well things were going. I knew she'd be proud, and I wanted that so much.

Once I had calmed down, my first thought was to get my mum and grandmother on to a plane to Jamaica as soon as possible. They needed to be out there to help my uncle. I rang around some contacts, dealt with BA and got them a flight in a couple of days. It was such a weird time for me. I was waiting for information about flights and organising transport for them, while at the same time I was getting congratulation cards and sympathy cards through the post – all arriving together. I was reading, 'Congratulations! Wonderful!' one moment, and 'So sorry, you must be devastated' the next. It was an incredibly bleak time.

When I eventually flew out to Montego Bay, I went alone. When we landed I didn't want to get off the plane. It was the first time someone so close to me had died, and I knew I was going to have to face the prospect of my first funeral. So I just sat there, crying in my seat. I was very scared.

As I walked out of arrivals I was met by my uncle Jack, my grandmother and Aunt Una, my grandmother's sister, who lives in Washington DC. There were no joyful hugs of greeting, just long embraces of support and comfort. We drove to the house almost in silence, and when we got to the gates I broke down. I couldn't face going in. I just couldn't bear the thought of walking into Great Gran's house, seeing her empty chair. Jack and I therefore had to drive round and round the area until finally I was calm enough to go through with it.

The funeral was extremely difficult to cope with. I was terrified to say goodbye, but, at the same time, I felt a small element of peace as I stood there. It was a hard service and you couldn't hear the singing through the crying and the wailing. It really broke my heart to see the people I loved most dearly in the world completely broken and shattered, and to know that there was nothing I could do about it.

The wedding which followed was, in a way, like a second funeral because Great Gran, the backbone of our family, was missing. There had been a lot of debate over whether the wedding should still take place, but Marcia, Jack's bride-to-be, was from Canada, and family had all bought their tickets, and many others were coming from different places round the world. The co-ordination of the whole affair had been very difficult, so it was decided that it would be best if the wedding still went ahead. But people weren't themselves. My grandmother had not made any real effort to dress up and just sat in a chair, staring blankly into space. My uncle looked tired; if you look at the wedding photos now, there's pain behind his eyes, behind his smile. He and Marcia were married in traditional African clothes, but even the bright colours couldn't liven things up, they just served to contrast dramatically with the sombre mood.

When it was time to leave, I couldn't bear to go. I refused to pack, refused to leave for the plane, and nearly missed my flight. I clung to the bread fruit tree I'd spent hours climbing when I was nine, visiting Jamaica – and Great Gran – for the first time. It was my special tree. Memories flooded back of her sitting next to it, watching me and laughing as I climbed, saying I was like a monkey. In the end, Uncle Jack had to peel my hands off the trunk to get me into the car and off to the airport.

Back in Britain I found everything hard. I completely lacked motivation for training, and simply couldn't face it. I was uncomfortable about working with Darrell, I just wanted to make a new start and try and live the life I wanted to live, and was trying to find the courage to tell him so. It was just time to move on, and I needed to find the guts to do it.

A big lesson I learned in 1997 was that the promotion and management of my career was getting too big for Darrell alone, and I needed to get an agent on board to manage my affairs properly. Darrell was trying his hardest, filtering out journalists and organising appearances and photo shoots between teaching lessons at school, but it seemed to me that it was increasingly becoming a full-time job.

Darrell thought he was the obvious choice to become my agent, because he knew my training diary, he knew when I was free, he understood what I wanted and what I was prepared to do. But something inside me said no. I knew deep down that it wasn't right – the athletic and the commercial roles were separate, and we needed an expert. Darrell had taken on more and more responsibility for my life, and it was starting to make me feel uncomfortable, I felt I wanted to loosen the ties with him and bring some experts on board.

Darrell dropped hints and I brushed them aside, which added to the tension between us. I felt selfish in a way, because I was at the stage where I could start to give him something in return, pay him back for all he'd given me; I could start to give him more responsibility and a real role in the management of my career. If he wants to be your manager, I thought, let him be your manager, he's done so much for you. But something stopped me. It just didn't feel right. Darrell felt like a tie to the past and I felt, instinctively, that I should try to move forward and build a future on a new footing.

I had received calls from various would-be agents, and decided to meet up with some of them. I took Darrell with me, so he wouldn't feel isolated, and Jonathan came too. It was very interesting to meet them all and we had quite a fun time. With many of them it was quickly apparent that a working relationship would be impossible; there were agents who promised me that I'd be a millionaire before the year was out, others who promised me a career in film and TV, but none of them seemed to demonstrate any real ability to fulfil their promise. For a time I thought I might be better off staying as I was, without some flash agent throwing his weight around. But in the end it was Sally Gunnell's agent, Jonathan Marks, whom I decided to talk to. When we met he seemed very good – unlike many of the others he didn't promise me the earth, but he did say he'd do his best for me, and I believed him.

As Darrell and I drove back to Wolverhampton after meeting Jonathan for the first time, I asked Darrell what he really thought. Inside he thought Jonathan seemed OK, but he was fighting against what he knew would be a huge change. An agent would mean that everything in my programme away from the track would be organised by somebody else, and Darrell was worried about where it would lead. For the first time he wouldn't be in charge of everything.

I signed with Jonathan in the summer of 1997, and made the first step towards a new, professional career. It was extremely hard, and all the way through the discussions with Jonathan I had begged him to treat Darrell with kid gloves. I explained to him how much Darrell had done for me, how much work he'd put in; it really wasn't fair if Darrell felt shoved to one side. He was still an important part of the team.

Initially I don't think Jonathan realised how close Darrell and I were, but he quickly saw how painful this new arrangement understandably was for Darrell, and did try to communicate with him on elements of my career that did not impact on my training. However, Darrell stepped back quite quickly, I think realising what a big job it was to manage my off-track career now I had very much moved from the amateur to the professional league.

The decision not to appoint Darrell as my full-time manager was the first step I made in loosening the bonds between us that had been there since I was a little girl. Darrell had seen me through my school years and my rebellious teenage years and had supported me as my career began to grow. The last thing I wanted to do now, as soon as I had some success, was to dump him. But it is extremely hard when someone has known you for a long time. There was so much emotional baggage tied up in every decision we made and every argument we had. I felt that the arguments, which on the surface, were about running, jumping and throwing, also reflected our changing relationship; the fact that he had invested so much time in me and now I was maturing, growing up, and mentally moving away from him.

I knew that I was still to tell him that I wanted Charles to be my coach – but how was I going to do that? After all Darrell had done for me, I didn't want to cruelly turn away from him now. But I knew, deep down, that if I didn't make the break soon, I'd never reach my full potential as an athlete. How could I make Darrell understand that without breaking his heart?

Chapter Thirteen
A New Coach

My relationship with Darrell had been deteriorating for a couple of years before I finally confronted him and told him that I no longer wished him to be my coach. There had been some pretty heated arguments, plus unspoken friction during training, which had a negative effect on our ability to communicate – all of which resulted in my final decision that enough was enough. We had to go our separate ways.

It would have been such a fairytale story if the coach-and-athlete partnership that had started when I was thirteen could have continued right through to Olympic Gold, but I know that the things I needed from a coach when I was a teenager were different to what was required as I reached Olympic standard.

It wasn't Darrell who had changed, it was me. I was growing, becoming more inquisitive, needing more answers and challenges. I travelled more, met other coaches and athletes, and wanted a more active role in the way my training was being structured, which I thought might give me the best chance of performing at the highest level. I needed a new stimulus. I felt I had outgrown Darrell's passive approach and needed someone more forceful, and I knew that to make the next few steps up the podium, something had to change. When I expressed these opinions, Darrell would sometimes take them as criticisms of what he was doing. I worried that everything might end up being reduced to a personal battle of power. Perhaps I was too outspoken, but I couldn't help myself. I realised that I challenged him in a way that no other athlete had. I knew that some of the things I said upset him, and I felt guilty because he'd invested so much time and energy in me. But you can't have an athlete who dominates their coach. I understood why he felt a little let down by me, and I understood why he thought I was being ungrateful when I criticised him after all the years he'd put in, but I also knew that this was not the way to progress as an athlete – forever feeling guilty and beholden.

Another problem was that he was also coaching some other, younger athletes. Although I am very aware of the importance of good coaching for younger children, I was becoming a world-class athlete, and having Darrell dividing his attention between me and the other groups became increasingly difficult. By then I was a heptathlete, and the group was trying to do several different events at the same time to suit everyone's needs, so it just wasn't working.

I'm sure it must have seemed as if I was trying to undermine Darrell or challenge his knowledge – I became aware that I was starting to get under his skin a little bit with my comments and back chat. A good example of this was one of our debates over my shot technique. Darrell was emphasising the active use of my arm at the release of shot, while I disagreed, wanting to know why it wasn't the right hip that should be focused on instead. Unfortunately this sort of debate could cause friction between us, so it got to the point where I'd not always say what I wanted to, just to keep the peace. That then resulted in feelings of annoyance and frustration because my training was being affected.

Darrell knew we were having problems but my perception was that he chose to ignore them. He thought things would be OK, that we'd stay together and survive. But every time I felt Darrell did not give sufficient weight to my views, it drove a wedge between us.

I also found it difficult because Darrell was a full-time teacher so couldn't train at the times I wanted to. I became less and less interested in training in the evenings, feeling I needed to train during the day when I would be fresher. I had also been told that it would be easier on my body if I could break up my routine a little instead of trying to fit so much into the evening sessions. But as Darrell's teaching was his main source of income, he couldn't devote his time to me on a full-time basis.

I had won Commonwealth gold, World silver and Olympic bronze, and I was increasingly competing against full-time athletes. But I was putting myself at a distinct disadvantage by not training for the same number of hours. That was another crucial point in my decision.

Added to that was the fact that I had worked with other coaches and seen what they could do. I'd seen how much harder I worked with Charles van Commenee, for example, and knew how much more thorough we could be if he was working with me full-time. Darrell had been very good at letting me work with other coaches in the past, such as John Trower, Steve Backley's coach who helped me with my javelin practice. But what I needed was someone who could commit more hours to my training, and could co-ordinate all the elements with the same burning desire to reach the highest level. Charles had those qualities.

When I look back at our time together I realise that the moment in 1997, when I pushed Darrell back from becoming my manager and employed Jonathan Marks instead, was a crucial point. I became increasingly analytical about the role that Darrell was playing, and found myself thinking about exactly what I wanted from him.

There were a few other factors that prompted me to act when I did, to pull away from Darrell in 1997 rather than any year previously. That was the year when I decided to move from Birmingham to London, as I felt it was time to change my environment

So it was the right time to start work with a new coach – but who? I thought of the options in the UK. There was Mike Holmes, a multi-events coach who would have been good, but he was working with Steve Smith who took up most of his time. If I was to move coaches, I needed to get it absolutely right, to work with someone who could dedicate themselves to me. So, I started to think outside Britain – and kept coming back to Charles von Commenee, with whom I had worked so successfully over the years.

I phoned Charles in March to have a chat about how my training was going and suggested that we do a session together during the warm-weather training in the US in April. He agreed. Eventually, I asked him if he might consider coaching me full-time. His first reaction was to burst out laughing.

'What's so funny?' I said. 'Why can't you coach me?'

'Well, Denise, you know I don't take any messing around. You wouldn't get away with things with me. I'm not as tolerant as Darrell. I'm more demanding.' Basically, he was saying that I would have to do as I was told and wouldn't be able to dictate the training according to the way I was feeling. Charles would decide the programme and I would have to obey – something that would be a new experience for me.

Charles thought I was a soft athlete who didn't train hard enough, and was doing just enough to get by. To move up to another level he said I would have to train much harder. That rang bells with something Daley Thompson had said to me after the Atlanta Olympics. He had told me I was talented, but talent would only take me so far; if I stepped up my training to a higher intensity I would get what I needed to give me those extra points. With Darrell, if I ever said I wasn't feeling too well he would be sympathetic, but with Charles I knew that if I said I wasn't feeling well he would shrug his shoulders or make me work harder. It was a completely different approach, and Charles wanted to be very sure that I was up to it.

It was at this point that I started questioning myself and wondering whether Charles was too tough for me. Maybe I would be better off staying with what I knew. But I was sure, deep down, that going with Charles was the right move. I also knew that training in Amsterdam, where he was based, could be fun and very different from what I was used to. A big bonus of Amsterdam was their small indoor facility that could be used throughout the winter, which meant I could practise my technique for different events all year round. It is invaluable for any athlete not to have to worry about rain or snow affecting the quality of one's workout.

By the end of October 1997 I knew it was time to sit down with Darrell and tell him that I wanted to work with Charles. It was one of the hardest things I have ever done.

I felt incredibly nervous the day I broke the news. My stomach was churning and I felt sick. I had carefully planned my speech but inevitably, it didn't come out exactly the way I had intended. I had to keep trying to think of words to soften the blow, to fill the silences. I explained that the time had really come for me to move on, and that I wanted Charles to take over my coaching. I tried to explain that it wasn't anything Darrell had done or not done, but that I simply had a feeling that I needed to make a change in my life.

Darrell just sat there, stunned. After an awkward moment he told me how disappointed he was that I had arrived at this decision without him, and then presented it to him as a fait accompli. He was quite tearful. But I had made up my mind, and I had to be strong. I tried to make him understand that I still wanted his input, that I didn't want to lose everything he had taught me, and that I hoped he would be able to find it in himself to communicate with Charles.

I felt awful, as if I was taking away his opportunity to become an elite coach – no longer just a club coach but the coach of an Olympic champion, a coach to stand out from his peers.

I know I hurt Darrell very deeply when I left him, but I tried so hard to keep him involved wherever I could. For a year or so Charles would call Darrell and give him a progress report and keep in touch, telling him how training was going and what we were working on. I was still coming back to Birmingham, and while I was there Darrell would oversee my training sessions. But I felt like the most selfish, ungrateful person in the world. I had thought many times that I was just making a change for the sake of it, but I knew this wasn't true. I needed a different coach. I felt I might not go any further with Darrell, and I needed to make it to the top, because I knew I would be betraying myself if I didn't.

CHAPTER FOURTEEN

AN AMAZING YEAR: 1998

1998 marked the start of the build-up to the Olympics. Although two years away, it was important that I began preparing myself psychologically, emotionally and physically. Two years may sound like a long time of preparation for just two days of competition, but it is absolutely necessary. In a way, it would be fairer to say that four years are spent building for the Olympic Games, as it is this single event that dominates all others throughout one's senior career.

There were three stepping stones on the way to the Sydney Olympics in 2000: the European and Commonwealth championships in 1998, and the World Championships in Seville in 1999. They were all very important tournaments in their own right, but combined they were the best possible preparation on my journey to the Olympics. My aims for the year were simple: retain my Commonwealth title, and win the European Championships. I went into 1998 ready for the challenge. Or at least that was the plan. Of course, injuries and lack of form can step in and thwart even the most ambitious, so I was also prepared to take one day at a time, work my hardest and hope that the victories came.

Charles was now my main coach, but I still intended to keep Darrell involved. Although Charles would be setting the programmes from now on, I thought Darrell could still be helpful as he had worked with me for so many years. He agreed, but I was aware that he might understandably find it difficult being usurped by Charles. But it all seemed to be working out; Charles was pleased that Darrell was still involved and could brief him on what I'd been doing in my sessions before he took over, and I think Darrell was pleased that he was a part of things.

It was only when all three of us went away on the warm-weather training camp to Lanzarote that any friction started to develop. Charles was very much in the driving seat in a way that was very akin to his character, and suddenly Darrell found himself being given things to do. I think he found that hard – he and I had been away on many training camps where we had worked together, but now someone else was giving the orders and calling the shots.

Darrell could see the potential that Charles and I had as coach and athlete, and how well I responded to his instruction. I think it was around this time that I felt he understandably began to feel less close to us, from a psychological point of view at least. I'm sure he thought his talent could be better used as the main coach of an up-and-coming young athlete who needed someone kind and nurturing. None the less, Darrell continued to support me throughout 1998, and attended the two major championships as part of the team.

As the months passed, it was obvious that 1998 was to be a transitional year for me. It became very much the hand-over period between Darrell and Charles, and at the end of the year Darrell would end his involvement with me altogether and go on to work with new athletes. But for 1998 he was a keen member of the team, having taken a seconded year from his school to dedicate his time to me during my preparations for the European and Commonwealth Championships. Because my focus had moved completely to Charles, I did feel guilty about his decision to some extent, wishing he hadn't done it. But it was a kind and generous thing to do, and showed how committed he was to me, and I very much appreciated the gesture. There was no animosity between the two men. They were both professionals and respected each other a great deal. They got on well, and no doubt exchanged information on how difficult I could be when I wasn't around to hear them!

The athletics season started with a series of small competitions around the country, to get back into the rhythm of competing. One of the tournaments I entered was the Staffordshire County Championships in Cannock in the second week of May, a competition in which I had been religiously competing since I was a child. This was the last chance for me to improve on a couple of individual events before Gotzis at the end of the month, where I intended to compete in my first heptathlon of the season. One of the events I was keen to get some practice on was my long jump, my main event before I took up the heptathlon. There is always a danger that you let your main event slip when you start heptathlon training, because you spend so much time focusing on your weaker events as you try to bring them up to the necessary standard.

As I ran up to jump for my first attempt I felt a sudden shock of pain through my ankle. It was not the agonising pain that tells you you're in for months of rehabilitation, but a pain none the less, an ache through the whole of my leg. I had to withdraw from the competition, a fact about which I wasn't particularly unhappy.

I assumed I would be off for a few days, a week at the most. With Gotzis just two weeks away it was far from ideal, but I saw it more as an inconvenience. I never thought for a minute that I would end up having to pull out. But my injury meant that I did have to miss out on Gotzis.

I went to watch the competition anyway, and was relieved to see that many of the other girls had pulled out too, including Shouaa, who was having problems with her back injury. At least I wasn't the only one experiencing difficulties.

My injury meant that I was unable to compete from mid-May through to July. For a couple of weeks I couldn't do anything at all; then, slowly, I was able to build up my training sessions, while still having to ensure that my ankle was well strapped up.

I had missed a lot of crucial running work during this period, and knew I wasn't as fit as I could have been. I therefore went into the two big championships of 1998 feeling under-prepared. The first competition was the European Championships at Budapest in August. Everyone had high expectations of me after winning my bronze medal in Atlanta and silver in the World Championships, which I found added to the pressure. They all believed I would simply turn up and win golds, whereas I knew that competition is intense and very unpredictable, and with an injury so fresh and training so hampered, I was extremely worried about how I would do.

By the time August came around my ankle was still sore. It was not consistently painful, but I did get twinges from it and enough discomfort for me to know that it was not fully recovered. I knew that this competition was going to be a battle of wills, a case of mind over matter as we all fought to see who was made of the sternest stuff. My battle plan was to try and make as much of a cushion for myself as I could before the 800m. You could say that that's always my battle plan because I don't enjoy the 800m, but it was especially true when I had done so little running preparation throughout the year. Without that buffer, I didn't believe I had what it took to win that final race. With it, I would know as I went into the 800m whether or not there was a chance for me to become the first British woman since Mary Peters to win a multi-event title at global or European level.

Mary Peters is my heroine. She was the Olympic pentathlon champion in the 1972 Games in Munich, where she defied the odds to beat her rivals to victory. She was a great ambassador for women in sport and, indeed, sport in general. Mary had taken a shine to me while watching me in the 1994 Commonwealth Games. Apparently my performance there reminded her of her own grit and determination during her 1972 competition. She is my sporting role model, and I admire her enormously.

So, to the beautiful city of Budapest on the banks of the Danube, the political, intellectual and cultural capital of Hungary. Unfortunately there was little time to enjoy the sights and sounds. I arrived two days before the competition began and immediately started to focus on the task ahead. I wasn't very fit, and I knew that this championship was going to be all about survival, and about minimising any huge mistakes I might make.

The 100m hurdles was an average start to the competition. The good news was that, for the first time that season, I cleared all ten barriers without touching them. The bad news was that I finished in 13.59 seconds, in fifth place. Natalya Sazanovich won, not too far ahead of me, but it did give her a 28-point lead leaving me trailing after just one event.

By contrast, the high jump was much better. Success in the high jump is always good news as this is where you can really pull the points in – each centimetre is worth 12 points. My final jump was 1.83m, my best jump of the year.

The good results continued in the shot put, which was situated in the corner where all the British support was gathered. The atmosphere was incredibly personal and positive, and I received an extraordinary reception that really spurred me on. Because it was the only event that didn't exacerbate my injury during my rehabilitation period, Charles and I had put many hours of time and effort into working on my shot technique. As a result, I was not particularly surprised when I achieved a personal best of 15.27m on my first throw of the competition. It meant that after three events I was in the lead with 2923 points.

The final event of day one, the 200m, was a disaster. The first problem was the way in which the lanes were drawn: I was in lane one, with no athlete in lane two. This is particularly difficult in an event in which competitors run at the same time in direct competition with each other, unlike events such as shot and javelin where you compete in turn. When you are drawn next to an empty lane in a sprint you feel out on a limb and away from the main action of the race. I was very aware of this, and ran a very poor race, looking almost pedestrian. As a result, as we went into day two, I dropped back into second place behind Sazanovich.

When I got back to the hotel that night my muscles were sore and tired. In an attempt to relieve them I had my legs massaged, then took an ice bath. As I contemplated the next day I knew that every event had to be performed to the best of my ability. Sazanovich was hot on my tail, and we were both strong in the long jump; there was no room for any mistakes.

The long jump is always the event at which I hope to pull back any deficit from day one. But Sazanovich was not going to let me off the hook too easily. She jumped 6.50m with her first leap while I had a first-round disaster. I ran through the board because I misjudged my take-off. There was a big gasp from the crowd, and I felt a huge amount of tension and nervousness creep swiftly into my body. The long jump's conditions were difficult because the wind was swirling around the pit. I therefore had to trust in Charles's good judgement and advice over how to approach my run-up. At least things could only get better.

The next jump was my best for a long time and felt right from the start. My run-up was powerful, the take-off accurate, and the jump was technically about as perfect as I ever hope one can be. I landed at 6.59m and was back at the top of the leader board. Sazanovich didn't improve on my distance, so as we went into the javelin, only one point separated us. There was much work to be done in this event if I was going to go into the 800m with the points cushion I so desperately wanted.

So, once again, the javelin had to rescue me from a high-pressure 800m. My throw had to be good, and sufficiently further than that of Sazanovich to ensure that I had the best possible advantage going into the final event. The atmosphere was tense. I threw 50.16m – not my best throw ever, but at least it was over the 50m mark, and put me 121 points ahead of Sazanovich, whose javelin was below par.

The aim in the 800m was now to keep as close as I could to her. I had an 8.5-second advantage, so I simply had to make sure I stayed close enough to prevent her from winning back enough points to steal the gold. Happily, the race was one of the most comfortable of my career; at no point was I under any great pressure. I finished in 2:20.38 seconds, and Sazanovich came in behind me at 2:22.51. I had won the gold medal with 6559 points, 99 points clear at the top of the table.

Receiving my gold medal was a fantastic experience, and I couldn't stop smiling and waving to the crowds. It was made doubly special when Mary Peters presented me with my flowers afterwards. I was thrilled. Having her involved in my medal presentation was the perfect end to two solid days of competition and my first European title.

Our return to Wolverhampton was just amazing. I must admit to being slightly apprehensive, having returned in 1997 to the dreadful news that my great grandmother had passed away. However, this time it was pure delight – a civic reception at which all sorts of dignitaries and old friends and colleagues had gathered, a street party, and more letters and cards than I had ever seen before. It was a very special time and incredibly exciting.

But it also heightened the sense of expectation that surrounded me. With the Commonwealth Games in Kuala Lumpur just a few weeks away, I knew that the world was expecting me to win easily. As defending Commonwealth champion and newly crowned European champion, I knew I would be the firm favourite.

*

As I flew off to Kuala Lumpur I felt nervous. In the couple of weeks since the European Championships my injury had prevented me from doing as much training as I would have liked. As a result, I was concerned about how I would cope in the hot, humid conditions. But I needn't have worried: after two days of competition I retained my title.

It had been a steady build to gold. Unlike previous competitions when I've put myself under so much pressure that I've had to produce a huge throw, a massive jump or a fast race to get myself out of trouble, this was a much more gentle approach. I slowly built up a lead which, in the end, couldn't be beaten, and I ran a lap of honour at the end of the 800m, which was thoroughly appreciated by the crowd. When you win and you have fantastic support from everyone in the stadium, you feel the need to say thank you in some way, and a lap of honour round the track always seems the most appropriate thing to do.

By the end of 1998, I was able to look back upon an interesting year. It had been extremely difficult because of my injury just before the start, but ultimately I had been triumphant. I had won two out of the three championships on the road to Sydney and my confidence was high. All this was capped when I heard I had been nominated for the title of BBC Sports Personality of the Year. The other main contender was Michael Owen. We had a wonderful evening, and at the end of the night it was Michael who won. Some people have said that I deserved to win, but when a girl from athletics is up against an England striker, what chance has she got?!

Chapter Fifteen
Struggle in Seville

It was a strange set of circumstances that led to what I think was the best modelling job in the world. It all began with a man called Mike Buswell who, with his wife Angie, had settled himself down in front of the TV over Christmas 1998 and seen me in an interview on the screen. Apparently he wasn't looking to sponsor anyone at any time, but after seeing me, realising how determined I was, he decided he wanted to help me.

When I met Mike in his Leicestershire offices it was immediately apparent that he wanted little in return for his support, which is very unusual. I warmed to him immediately, and we talked for hours about his company, and my goals and aspirations. One of the companies owned by Mike's business, Dower Green Holdings, was Praxis, which supplies clothes to Next. So when we moved on to the topic of my interest in fashion, he suggested having some photos taken of me wearing some outfits from some of his lines of clothing. I thought this was a fantastic idea, and was doubly excited by the prospect when Terry O'Neill's name was mentioned as a possible photographer for the shoot. Mike's friend Doug Haywood was friendly with Terry O'Neill, and eventually, through Doug, Mike persuaded Terry to photograph me.

The shoot was held at a studio in Parsons Green, south-west London. I arrived early and walked tentatively into the building feeling rather nervous. I was greeted by the PR girl, along with the hair and make-up girl, the stylist and Terry's assistant.

The famous photographer was there too, and looked up from his crossword. He stared at me rather uncompromisingly and greeted me in a rather underwhelmed sort of way, then continued trying to solve the clues. I wasn't really sure how to react. Obviously I hadn't expected him to jump up and embrace me like a long-lost cousin, but I did expect a handshake or a smile. Instead, I was led quickly away by the girls so they could get me ready for the shoot. They suggested the idea of me wearing a wig, so I tried on a selection as they created a wide range of looks.

When the hairdressers and make-up artists had finished with me I went back into the studio, hoping and praying that the great man would be happy.

I know I am usually confident in front of the camera, but Terry O'Neill's lens was a different matter entirely. I was aware that he had photographed some of the most beautiful women in the world, and that to him I was probably just an athlete he'd really rather not have been bothered with. I also knew he was doing this shoot as a favour to friends, rather than from any personal desire to work with me.

As I walked into the studio, Terry was behind his camera, so I sauntered up and stood brazenly in front of it, staring into the lens. Suddenly the atmosphere changed. Terry came alive, started communicating with me and the shoot really took off. It was fantastic.

I was to learn later that Terry had found some of the sports people he had previously worked with to be slightly wooden and unnatural, but I'm delighted to say that he was pleased with the way our shoot went. The final pictures were excellent and I loved them. Apparently

Terry thought I was a natural, comparing me to Naomi Campbell at the beginning of her career, saying that as a model I could definitely make it. It was amazing to hear such praise from such a brilliant photographer, and I was incredibly flattered.

I do find that modelling comes quite naturally to me, but it's not all instinct. I do have to practice. Perhaps it's understanding the value of training through athletics, but I make sure that I am confident and know what I'm doing in shoots. I'm conscious of how certain poses come across in print, so I practise different poses in front of the mirror at home, and work out which one looks the best.

I love doing modelling shoots and seeing the results they bring. It's great to be pampered for the day, to wear beautifully tailored garments and have my make-up and hair done by real experts. It's a great privilege and a fantastic bonus to the wonderful world of athletics I live in. I am very aware that without the successes of my career I wouldn't have the opportunity to do the other things that are seen to be glamorous such as modelling shoots and attending awards ceremonies. But my philosophy is very much athletics first, the rest second.

In 1999 the main competition was the World Championships in Seville. It was the last big stepping stone before the Olympics, and an event I was keen to win, particularly as I had finished second in the previous World Championships in 1997.

Before the season started, Charles, Lieja Koeman – one of the Dutch shot put athletes and my training partner in Holland – and I went to Martinique for an intensive pre-season training camp. Martinique is beautiful and I was incredibly impressed with the place. It was much more developed than I had expected it to be, and there were far too many cars for such a small island! The training facilities were outstanding: we had a choice of six tracks and the Stade de Dillion at Forte de France was very impressive, outshining much of what we have in the UK. It is when you go to other countries, even

The hurdles, day one of the heptathlon at the Olympic Games in Sydney, 2000.

The high jump, Olympic Games, Sydney, 2000.

The shot put, Olympic Games, Sydney, 2000.

The long jump, day two of the heptathlon at the Olympic Games, Sydney, 2000.

A very subdued me during the javelin competition, wondering whether or not I could hold everything together, Olympic Games, Sydney, 2000.

The javelin, Olympic Games, Sydney, 2000.

Before the 800m, Olympic
Games, Sydney, 2000.

After the 800m, when
I realised I had won
the Olympic Gold.

My lap of honour, Olympic Games, Sydney, 2000.

Relief! A hug with Mum after the competition.

The press conference. Me with silver-medal winner, Yelena Prokhorova (right) and bronze-medal winner, Natalya Sazanovich (left).

At the closing ceremony for the Sydney Olympics: me with my coach, Charles van Commenee, and Dutch training partner, Lieja Koeman.

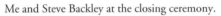

Me and Steve Backley at the closing ceremony.

At the closing ceremony with one of my all-time favourite athletes, long jumper Heike Dreschler. We both won gold medals in Sydney.

Me with my Olympic Gold Medal, Sydney, September 2000.

Me with Nanny in the courtyard at Buckingham Palace, just after receiving my MBE, 1999.

Me and Lord Lichfield at his studios after our photo shoot, 1999.

Brian Welsby, Mum, me, the Dean of Wolverhampton University, Darrell and Brian's wife, Blanka, on the day I received my fellowship, 1999.

At the Mencap/Transco
charity day at London
Zoo, October 2000.

Proudly wearing my t-shirt
for the 'Kiss Goodbye to
Breast Cancer' campaign,
organised by
Breakthrough Breast
Cancer.

A day with a group of very enthusiastic schoolgirls involved with the very worthwhile Youth in Sport/Nike campaign to encourage girls into sport, 2001.

Steve Redgrave, me and Audley Harrison at the England v. Germany Game at Wembley, October 2000.

Me with my runner-up award at the BBC Sports Personality of the Year, December 2000.

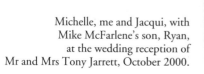

Michelle, me and Jacqui, with Mike McFarlene's son, Ryan, at the wedding reception of Mr and Mrs Tony Jarrett, October 2000.

What a fun night with Frank Skinner on his show! October, 2000.

You can't see how nervous I am, but I thoroughly enjoyed my experience on *Parkinson*, with the legendary chat-show host, February 2001.

A very excited Michelle and I at the Brits, February 2001.

Off with the tracksuit and stepping into style at the BAFTAs, February 2001.

A photoshoot for Powergen, with the photographer Bob Carlos Clarke.

A wonderful shoot with Stefano Massimo for *Harpers and Queen*.

a little island such as Martinique, that you realise just how bad British sporting facilities are, and realise how disgraceful it is that we can't even pull together a decent stadium in our nation's capital. I know I received a lot of publicity earlier on this year when I condemned the state of Britain's facilities on *Parkinson*, but I do stand by what I said.

Michael Parkinson and I talked at length on the show about the state of British sport. I conceded that we have a lot of talent in the country and that, as a whole, most sports manage to do well – but emphasised that there is not enough government support or funding for sport in Britain, and that the facilities around the country are in dire need of improvement. For me, sports facilities should not simply be functional amenities or profit-making initiatives, but should also be landmarks of inspiration for future generations.

My season began with the Staffordshire County Championships again, which this time was held at the Northwood Stadium in Stoke-on-Trent. Upon my arrival, the stadium was already full. Athletes of every age, with an array of talents and abilities were there. Some would have been hoping to qualify there for the English Schools Championships or the under-20s team, while dress would have seen it as a way of moving on to the AAA Championships and maybe, ultimately, a place on the Great Britain team in the future.

For me, the championships represented the beginning of a busy competition schedule after seven months of training. As we went into the competition I was a little on edge following the injury I had incurred at the same competition in 1998, which seriously disrupted my preparation for the European Championships and Commonwealth Games. The ankle injury had continued to bother me throughout the season, and even into the start of the winter training in October. My Dutch doctor, Peter Vergouwen, had suggested that if we were to save further damage I should seriously consider a change in my jumping leg, so I would not be long jumping and high jumping off the same foot.

So yet again I was faced with the need to change my style. It was decided that I should stop long jumping off my left foot and revert to using my right, as I had done before my knee injury in Italy in 1988. I would then be able to continue high jumping off my left foot as usual.

It was at this point that I thought my doctor and coach had lost their minds. This was not as simple a prospect as they made it sound. Didn't they realise that the World Championships were only ten months away and that this change would take a good few months to perfect? How could they possibly want to take such a big risk knowing that your long jump distance equals precious points in the heptathlon? I knew I would be seriously jeopardising my chances of winning; it would be like handing points to my competitors. So I refused. But Peter stressed how my ankle could potentially break down at any stage, forcing me to have surgery. After Peter had played that card, I said I would give the change a try, as surgery was something I wanted to avoid at all costs.

So, it was at the Staffs Championships, after seven stressful months, that I was finally in a position to test the effectiveness of my latest change.

As well as the long jump, I had entered two other events: the 100m hurdles and the shot. I was very aware that the hurdles could be tricky, because a minor hamstring injury I had sustained in Martinique had prevented me from training properly for the event. By contrast, I had put a lot of time into working on my shot put, and it had been going well.

I was thrilled to get through the competition comfortably. My long jump, although not as good as I'd have wanted it, went OK, the 100m hurdles was a smooth and satisfactory race, and the shot put went well. Everything was looking good, but I felt I needed one more competition in preparation for the annual Gotzis championships, which were two weeks away. I had missed Gotzis through injury the year before, so I desperately wanted to compete this time. I loved the venue and had a good rapport with the crowd – and in addition, this year was a special anniversary and some of the legends from the past had been invited to share in the memories, including Daley Thompson and Jürgen Hingsen.

But my long jump needed further work before I competed, as I was nowhere near the reasonable standard for an international champion-ship. On my left foot I was a competent jumper to 6.5m and above, but now I was only managing to jump just over 6.15m, which was a long way off the distances I needed to be achieving on a regular basis. Charles and I therefore decided that I needed to enter one more competition, so I selected one taking place in Holland.

There must be something about the small, friendly competitions that occur just before Gotzis – because for the second year in a row I injured myself badly. At first I thought nothing of it, but within two hours I couldn't weight-bear through my leg. The next morning it was much worse and I was in agony. I went to see Rick Menick, one of my physios in Holland, who did some tests on the joint of my tibia/fibula head, which was where I was getting the pain. I appeared to be experiencing some of the classic signs of a stress fracture – which would mean that my season was effectively over. I rang Kevin in London to talk to him about it and we all agreed that the next thing to do was to get some scans taken of the affected area.

My next job was to talk to Charles. He could not believe his ears when I saw him later that afternoon and updated him on the situation.

It was important that we acted quickly, so scans were organised for early the next morning. I prayed that they would not show any signs of a stress fracture – I needed a lifeline.

As I waited anxiously for the results to come back, I wondered why I was having such bad luck. I had now experienced two consecutive years of injury. Last year I had managed to get away with it – but would I be that lucky again? I also felt sorry for Charles. Since he had started working with me we had done some really good training, but it seemed as if all this good work had been overshadowed by months of injury.

Thankfully the results came back clear. Although there were no signs of a stress fracture, I was told not to do anything that would cause me any pain for at least two to three weeks. It seemed I had disrupted the joint and it needed time to settle down. Yet again I would not be competing at Gotzis. I was devastated.

I think the worst thing for me was once again knowing that my competitors were all out there, improving themselves and challenging one another, while I was at home, desperately trying to find the Gotzis results on the internet, feeling myself slipping further and further behind them.

I went to see Peter so he could examine the injury himself and talk everything through with me in more detail. He is a ruthless and uncompromising doctor, always thoroughly professional in his diagnosis. He also has a quality that I have not come across before in a doctor – he is frank and honest about his findings, even if it hurts you to hear it. Although he is quite aggressive in his approach I adore him and respect his work immensely.

Peter worked out a rehabilitation programme that was to last for about two-and-a-half to three weeks, and I began to follow it to the letter. Charles and I hoped that I would be much better by the end of the rehab period, ready to start working towards our new goals: to compete in the Europa Cup for combined events in mid-July, and to finish the season with Seville.

To my surprise, rehab went much better than I had expected. Because I spent half my time in Holland and the other half in London it was essential that I had good medical back-up in both. London was easy – I had Kevin there who had been my physio since 1994, and now I had Rick and Peter in the Netherlands. Both physios have a superb knowledge of the body and have strong beliefs in the values of manual therapy, working very much with the hands. During my rehab period they spent a lot of time liaising with each other, comparing notes on how each of them felt I was progressing.

I felt very fortunate to have two such super guys on my team.

Finally I was back on track and happy. I had slowly built up training as instructed, and had another two-and-a-half weeks before my next scheduled competition – the Europa Cup.

Javelin was one of the events I had been unable to practise during rehab as it gave me a lot of pain in my leg. But as soon as I thought I could handle it, Charles arranged for us to do a session. As I warmed up tentatively on the grass my leg felt good, so I progressed on to the javelin run-up. On the last stride of my approach, before I released the javelin, I felt a sharp, searing pain down my leg. I couldn't believe it. I had aggravated my injury again!

I was back to square one, and back to rehab.

Time was not on my side as I had just ten weeks before the World Championships in Seville. I therefore decided to cancel the Europa Cup – and it was then that I realised that, if I was fit enough to make it to Seville, I would be going without having had the benefit of participating in any heptathlons in the run-up. It was a scary thought.

I confess that I lost a lot of heart and spirit at that time. I found it impossible to see any way in which I could get in shape in time to do myself justice at the championships. But Charles was a tower of strength. He reminded me that I was made of sterner stuff, and told me that I had much more drive than a lot of the athletes he had worked with in the past. He said that I shouldn't give up before the race had begun – but at this I reminded him of a certain Eunice Barber of France, who had made a reappearance in heptathlon and was having a fantastic year. Barber had won at Gotzis in May and later in June, clearing seven metres in the long jump, which is an outstanding achievement. She had gone on to win the French national championships. It was clear that I would need to be in very good shape to have a chance of doing well against her – much better shape than I had been the previous year.

So, for the five weeks that remained, Charles set about making me tougher mentally than I had ever been before. Every session was like a psychological rehearsal for competition; he probed into my consciousness, tested and challenged me, then pushed me as far as my physical limitations would take me. By the end of the five weeks, what I lacked in physical preparation I had certainly made up for in mental strength.

As the championship approached I thought through the task in front of me in a logical manner, weighing up my chances and thinking about what I would need to do if I was going to win a medal. I realised I needed to get close to 13 seconds for the 100m hurdles and around 1.8m in the high jump. I was hoping to throw further than 15m in the shot, and achieve about 24 seconds in the 200m. The long jump was more difficult to analyse because of changing legs, but I hoped to jump around 6.5m. I thought I could clear 50m in the javelin and maybe get near my best for the 800m. I had worked so hard and finally, both mentally and physically, I felt ready.

Charles, Lieja and I went off to Madrid to do some pre-competition training. Seville began on a Saturday, so Charles and I got the train from Madrid on the Thursday. We decided to wait until the last possible moment before entering Seville, so I could make the most of the much-needed training camp.

I was tired from the training and the journey, so when I arrived in Seville I just wanted to rest and focus on my competition, but the UK Athletics press officer told me that the media wanted to do a press conference. No one had told me anything about this before my arrival, and it was the last thing I wanted to do. I just wanted to rest in my room and get a good night's sleep so I could begin to focus on the mammoth task that lay before me. Because the press officers were so insistent, I finally agreed that if the journalists sent questions up to my room, I would answer them from there – it seemed like a fair enough compromise to me.

Unfortunately, the response I got back was that they wanted to see me in the press conference – answering questions from my room was not good enough. I decided to repeat my earlier suggestion. As far as I was concerned, I'd explained my position, offered a solution, and that was the end of it.

The next morning I was woken by the phone. It was Jonathan, my boyfriend, asking me if everything was OK. I told him everything was fine, but I was aware of a peculiar edge to his voice, and I couldn't quite work out what the problem was. He kept asking me if I was sure I was all right, and each time I told him nothing was wrong.

When I went down to breakfast a bit later on, everyone seemed to be looking at me a little strangely, again asking if I was all right. By now I definitely sensed something was up, but because I had no idea what it could be, I forgot about it and headed over to the track.

After my first session I went into what's known as the mixed zone, the area in which the players and the press mingle. This is where you always get stopped by journalists and asked to comment on the competition. However, this time I walked straight through without anyone saying a word to me. I thought it strange – but even stranger was the way my agent, Jonathan Marks, was hovering around, again asking me if I was OK and smoothing my path through the media.

I spent the rest of the day with this slightly strange atmosphere hanging over me, and it was only in the evening that I found out that the papers had completely laid into me that morning. Everyone had been worried about whether or not I'd seen them, and thought that by asking me carefully if I was OK they would find out whether I had read the report. Of course I hadn't, so I knew nothing about the controversy until I was told about it.

I felt so upset; it all seemed so unfair. I couldn't believe that the one occasion I didn't play ball I was criticised in the press. The *Daily Mail* reproduced one of the pictures of me from the *Total Sport* photo shoot, with my back turned to the camera. The headline read something along the lines of 'Denise is becoming a right pain in the rear' – it was awful.

As an athlete, you give of yourself all the time, non-stop, all year round, leaving yourself open and vulnerable to the media. I do comment and talk to the press whenever I can, but when I've got an important event coming up and I'm struggling to overcome an injury, I would hope that they'd consider how awful I must be feeling.

The really childish thing was that after the tournament they didn't turn up to my press conference. How stupid was that? There were only a few journalists sitting there, looking around nervously, sensing the atmosphere. I refused to let it bother me unduly, so I answered their questions and continued with the rest of my day. However, it did make me realise how much of a power game the whole relationship with the media can be. I didn't acquiesce to just one of their many demands, and they reacted by turning on me.

I had come into this competition as one of the favourites alongside Eunice Barber, so on the first morning I was quite nervous. A lot of people were not familiar with Barber's name, but that had certainly changed by the end of the first event.

As usual, the 100m hurdles was first. The gun signalled the start of the race and Barber left everyone in the blocks. She was running in the lane outside me, and I was dismayed to see she was a clear hurdle ahead of me. She sliced 0.05 seconds off her personal best to win by five metres in 12.89 seconds – unbelievable. I finished in fourth place with 13.60 seconds. I was shocked by how slowly I had run, but also by how quickly Barber had run. I was temporarily mesmerised by what I had seen, but knew I had to really focus on my next event, the high jump. Charles and I had worked hard through the previous winter to perfect my technique, so I entered the event ready and optimistic.

The high jump competition was electrifying. There was a huge British contingent and a huge French contingent, both of which were confident their respective girls would win. I cleared my personal best of 1.84m, and although I was pleased, Charles told me not to celebrate until I had got every last cent out of my jumping. When I cleared 1.87m I put both my hands aloft and the crowd went crazy. However, Barber also cleared it – with room to spare. The bar was raised to 1.9m. There were three of us left in the competition: me, Barber and another French girl. It was incredibly exciting. Barber cleared 1.9m with apparent ease; the other French girl failed three times at 1.9m and was out. As I started my approach and gathered speed towards the take-off the British crowd were on their feet. I climbed up and up, over the bar, but unfortunately my heel clipped it. I thought for a split second that the bar would stay on, but it came down.

I stood up and thanked the crowd because they had been such fantastic support. I wasn't disappointed because I had done more than my best – I just had to wait and see what Eunice could do. She soared to 1.93m, a 10cm improvement on her best.

There was already talk of Lewis, the European champion and favourite, being cut down by the 'Barber of Seville'. But I didn't worry. I was lying in second place after the first two events. There was a long way to go, and I had not given up the fight.

In the shot, I improved on my two-year-old best by almost a metre and went into the lead for the first time. The fight for the gold medal had begun. After achieving 15.41m on my first attempt, I topped that with a new personal best of 15.95m in my second throw, and then went over 16m for the first time in my life in the third. Three throws, and three personal bests. I was thrilled, and the result sent me to the top of the table.

But in the 200m, Eunice Barber stole first place back by winning the event in 24.14 seconds. I finished third in 24.26 seconds.

As we went into day two, traditionally my strongest day, Barber was in the lead by just one point.

That night I felt good, and ready for the next day. However, I knew Barber had her best event to come, the long jump, and that this event would be about damage limitation for me. I had to stay as close as I could to her, but I also knew that my lack of experience jumping on my right leg might prove to be my downfall.

The long jump event proved to be controversial. Initially I had a no jump. I then jumped 6.20m, which was far from good – and I wondered if this was the point at which I would be kissing the medals goodbye. I needed something special. My third jump looked good and I breathed a sigh of relief. But then I saw the red flag go up to mark another no jump. I was astounded, as you usually know whether or not you've jumped a no jump. I walked up to the board to see if there was a mark in the soft material beyond it. There wasn't. I tried in my best Spanish to explain to the man that the jump was good, but he just shrugged. The crowd watched the action replay on the big screen and let out a huge groan as they saw that the jump looked good.

At this point I called for the match referee, just as the jump was shown a second time on the large screen. You could see clearly that my foot was in a perfectly legal position, and again the crowd reacted in support with a huge boo. They realised that the official had made a mistake and was refusing to budge.

Suddenly Charles leaped over the fence out of nowhere, determined to ensure that the sandpit was not raked over. If this happened, all would be lost. Eventually, after much fuss and a British protest to the Jury of Appeal, the decision was overturned. They measured the jump: 6.64m. The protest had rescued me 141 crucial points.

To my surprise, the French and German officials then put in counter-protests. Thankfully these were overturned, but not before I had spent a large part of the afternoon with no idea where my fate lay. Then, just before the javelin it was confirmed again; my 6.64m jump stood, and I was still in contention.

Unfortunately, I did not throw my best in the javelin. I tend to judge myself as having made a successful throw if it goes over a distance of 50m. This time my throw went to 47.44m. It wasn't enough. I had simply left myself too much to do in the 800m, which meant that Barber walked away with the gold.

It was incredibly disappointing, but I knew I had made too many mistakes. You can't let anything slip at this level. Barber had been consistent, and had therefore triumphed at the end of the day.

A huge consolation was the chance to see Uncle Jack, who had come over to Seville to watch me compete in the championship. It was the first time he had ever been to Europe, and it was fantastic to see him – cheered me up no end.

Off-track, Seville had been really disappointing as a result of the attitude of some journalists and an isolated rumour linking my name to drugs. I do not know where it came from, but it did disappear quite quickly. I was furious though. It was claimed that the reason I was being so cagey with the press was because I had tested positive for drugs.

Of course, this was complete nonsense. The newspaper article was complete rubbish and was probably trying to damage me in advance of the competition. I now believe that all results of drug testing should be published in a regular bulletin showing how frequently athletes are tested and what the results are. It would end all the speculation immediately. I am tested regularly – in and out of competition. I have testers arriving unannounced at all times of day. Those who are tested are chosen randomly, so you never know when you'll get a call. I thoroughly approve of this, and I think if they published the results the whole process would be more transparent, less open to Chinese whispers, rumours and lies.

The lasting feeling from Seville 1999 was one of frustration and anger with myself. After winning two gold medals in 1998, it felt like a let-down to come away with silver. It seemed as if my Olympic plans had come temporarily off the rails, and I needed plenty of reassurance when we got back to England. I think Charles needed some too; he knew that his coaching skills were as much in the spotlight as all my performances. I therefore went to see the sports psychologist, Alma Thomas, with whom I had done some very successful work in the past. During the championship I had felt that I was missing the knife-at-the-throat feeling – when you know it's now or never and you *have* to perform – particularly in the javelin. So I thought it important that I talked my thoughts and feelings through with her.

In those darker moments I had to keep reminding myself how much I had improved in some of the events in which I had previously struggled. I had achieved three personal bests in the shot – an event that I had not looked forward to at all in the past, and I had also done well in the high jump and the long jump off my new take-off leg. Things were definitely improving, I just needed to ensure that they all came together on the same day – preferably in Sydney in a year's time.

Chapter Sixteen
Countdown to the Games

Every year there is one goal, one dream that you're working towards. Then, every four years, there is the Olympic Games, which is bigger and more important than any other competition. Once in a lifetime – for a precious few – there is an Olympic Games at which you actually think you might be able to win. At the beginning of 2000, with party poppers and champagne corks popping around me, I knew that such a competition lay ahead.

It was going to be a long, hard road. At the end of 1999 I had suffered a real crisis of confidence. I was still in pain, and an end-of-season scan had found the culprit to be a small, bony nodule that had formed on my tibia/fibula head. I had no choice but to undergo surgery, which took place on 4 December and left me on crutches for four weeks. In addition to that, whenever I looked at Eunice Barber I would wonder how on earth I'd be able to beat her. I spent a lot of time looking at both our strengths and weaknesses and, on the whole, she seemed to be far superior.

Charles would tell me not to be so ridiculous, reminding me that I had to focus on myself, not worry about the opposition, as that would not help me. I knew he was right, but my surgery was going to mean a twelve- to fifteen-week rehabilitation period before I even began what I knew was going to be the most intensive time of training I had ever undertaken. Before I hung up my calendar for the year, I drew a big ring around 23 and 24 September – the dates of the heptathlon at the Olympic Games in Sydney. My life could start again once I'd got past that second day – but until then it was to be entirely devoted to athletics.

I felt both excitement and fear as I looked at the calendar. It was as though all my life I had been thinking about those two days. This was probably the closest I would ever come to achieving my dream: winning Olympic gold. Watching the great champions on television during the 1980s, they had seemed almost unreal and untouchable. I had never thought that I was of that calibre; but now here I was, poised and ready for my biggest challenge to date. I secretly wondered whether or not I really had what it takes to be a champion, but somehow, I really did believe that it was my destiny to win at these games.

My rehabilitation period posed a number of dilemmas for me, particularly when it became clear from a very early stage that competing at Gotzis at the end of May was not going to be possible for the third year in a row. Sadly, I just wasn't ready. After ten weeks in rehab, my comeback had to be gentle. I needed to get a couple more weeks of training under my belt before making my first appearance of the year.

I knew that all my main competitors would be in Gotzis, most notably Eunice Barber and Ghada Shouaa, who had made a remarkable comeback to finish third in Seville the year before, and was still the reigning Olympic champion. It worried me that they would be working hard towards Sydney, testing their boundaries, while I was doing nothing more than light rehabilitation work, trying to recover from the surgery. But what could I do?

Although the physical training had to wait, I was determined that my mental preparation didn't. I therefore began to read some books about self-confidence and self-belief. One of the books I found the most inspiring was by an American author called Iyanla Vanzant, called *One Day My Soul Just Opened Up*, a forty-day appraisal about how to become self-fulfilled. I had actually bought the book for other areas of my life, unrelated to athletics – but one has only one mind, and if it is healthy it has a knock-on effect on everything one does. Thus I saw no reason why this book couldn't relate to all aspects of my life.

It was just when I was feeling more on top of things that I heard the results from the competition at Gotzis: Eunice Barber had set a world-leading score of 6842 points. I couldn't believe it, and went straight back to my books to reassure myself and motivate myself further!

I was relieved to hear that my successes in recent competitions meant that I didn't have the pressure of having to qualify for the Olympics. This was good, because it meant that I could make a slow and steady build-up to my first heptathlon of the year, at the Decastar 2000 competition at the Stade de Touarstakes in Talence at the end of July. Naturally I was slightly concerned about the standard of competition because I hadn't competed in a heptathlon since the previous August. However, I had done some good training in the six weeks prior to my departure for France which came to fruition when, in the warm French sunshine, I achieved four personal bests and smashed my own British and Commonwealth record. It gave me a total of 6831, an improvement on my previous record by 95 points. The competition was mine from start to finish. I made an excellent start in the 100m hurdles, achieving a personal best with a time of 13.13 seconds. Less than two hours later I had cleared 1.84m in the high jump and thrown the shot a distance of 15.07m. The first day finished with another personal best in the 200m.

Day two saw yet another personal best, this time in the long jump, with a distance of 6.69m. I then added another 849 points to my score with a throw of 49.42m in the javelin. Then came the biggest shock of the day: a great run in the 800m. It was the best two laps I had ever run, and I finished in 2 minutes 12.20 seconds, three seconds faster than my personal best.

The result took me to within 11 points of Barber's Gotzis total (injury had kept her away from Talence), and gave me very positive feelings as I prepared for the Olympic Games, only eight weeks away. I was left with a strong sense of confidence, very pleased with how I had overcome the effects of my surgery through my rehabilitation period. I had managed barely five weeks of uninterrupted training since the beginning of the year, but still I had triumphed.

I was delighted to find that even Charles was happy, and to the press he was saying things like; 'It may sound a bit cocky, but we expect her to be better in Sydney. Her body has not been very co-operative in the last couple of years, but Denise's goal has always been to win two Olympic gold medals and you don't easily give up on a dream like that.'

But the key thing for me was the feeling that my performance in Talence proved Eunice Barber was beatable. I had certainly experi-enced doubts about whether or not this was really the case, but as far as I was now concerned, the result meant that the person who performed best over the two days in Sydney would be the one to win the honours. Eunice had her strong events, but I did too.

On top of this, my performance in the 800m was proof that I could really run this race. Although the 800m is my least favourite event, it was the one into which I had put the most work before I got injured. Charles had made it clear that if I didn't improve on my 800m, any chance of a medal in Sydney would be lost. After Talence, he was pleased but not elated, and we both knew that while my victory and the new record were fantastic, we still had quite a distance to go before I had a strong chance of winning the Olympic gold medal.

Talence signalled the start of my real build-up for Sydney 2000. It was when I started to see the event getting closer on the calendar – but more importantly, I actually started to 'feel' it. Mentally, I was completely focused. All thoughts of injuries and recovery were out of my mind, and I was very much focusing on the championship ahead. Nothing else mattered; I felt strong, powerful and ready. I felt as if I was living and breathing the Olympics, which was exactly the way I had aimed to feel. The thought of Sydney, and of making good my hopes, were overriding all other thoughts.

The months before the Olympics saw me adhering to a very strict routine to ensure I was 100 per cent ready to compete. In the mornings I would wake up and have breakfast – which was always nutritionally precise, everything counted and measured as directed by Brian Welsby. During the months before a championship it is particularly important to ensure that your nutrition is right, because there is no room for error at this stage, everything has to be spot on. Although I can decide to have a little treat or slack off a little bit six months or so prior to competition, when I'm in the final few months I have to be the epitome of the perfect athlete – everything I put into my body, and everything I get my body to do, has to be absolutely right. I also make sure that I get the right amount of sleep: I know that I need eight hours, so I endeavour to achieve this.

I started doing a lot of mental rehearsal as the games approached, more or less every night before going to bed, or before my daily afternoon sleep. This involves visualising the actual event. For example, I mentally run the 100m hurdles, seeing the race and feeling the adrenaline. It's as if all my senses are alive: I get the sensations and I'm convinced I'm on the track. I try to set the scene in my mind – the arena, the effect of the crowd on me. I try to anticipate it. Sometimes, when I'm really zoned in, relaxed and focused, I can feel a physical contraction in my muscles. When this happens, when the sensation is very real, I know that my frame of mind is right, that it and my body are in total harmony. I can see and feel myself there in the middle of my performance, and I always see myself winning.

In these last, precious couple of months, time is crucial because training has to be precise. The long, drawn-out sessions are gone; they are shorter now and more focused, almost mirroring competition conditions. Whereas my high jump session could last fifty minutes in the pre-season phase, in the two months before a championship the session is more likely to be around twenty-five minutes – I set the bar pretty much where I'd like to come in, and give myself eight or so jumps in which to achieve it. Shot put sessions are similar. I'll take long pauses between my throws, which mirrors the timing of a championship. I'll go and lie down after throwing, get off my feet, think about the technique, positioning and feeling, and enter the circle as I would in a competition. I don't know if it is the same with my competitors, but Charles says he sees the discipline in me. He once told me that he never goes into an athletics arena fearing that I'm going to fail or make a mistake, because he knows that I have a mental capacity to reproduce what I need to reproduce. I do believe that this talent comes from that specific rehearsal.

Charles also helps with setting the scene and pressures of a competition. He will say things like, 'Eunice Barber has just thrown forty-eight metres in the javelin, and you have to throw forty-nine to maintain the lead in the competition – now respond.' I therefore have to set myself up in the training sessions as if my life depends on success, inspiring me because it keeps me alert. Training is supposed to be preparation for competition, and I believe that part of the mental process is considering every worst-case scenario, everything that could possibly happen in the competition, so that nothing is a surprise. Which is why we also practise best-case scenarios: Charles will say that everything is going well, and ask, 'How are you feeling now? What are you thinking now?' He provokes me to comment and gives me feedback all the time.

But, no matter how careful the preparation, things don't always go according to plan. With just seven weeks to go, after coming back from injury, having scored a string of personal bests and started building towards the Olympic Games, things started to wrong. I was in Holland with Charles, doing my usual warm-up jog when suddenly I felt shooting pains through the back of my heel – in the Achilles' tendon, where every athlete dreads feeling pain. I made a mental note of it, and told Charles that my Achilles felt a bit tight that day, so he revised my training programme. The next day was the same, followed by the next. Although I thought this was strange, I still didn't think it was serious, as I did not have a previous history of Achilles' tendon problems. However, after a week had gone by and the pain hadn't really subsided, I knew something wasn't right.

I went back to England as I was due to take part in a competition for my club. As soon as I got back I began to get treatment from Kevin. Because of the pain I was experiencing, I told my team manager that I was going to have to withdraw from the long jump and hurdles, but that I thought I would be able to manage the shot put and the javelin. I didn't want to admit to myself that my Achilles injury was as bad as it was; I even continued to suffer pain during the shot put, and while I was doing the javelin it nearly broke down. Charles told me I had to withdraw from the competition, but I was so frustrated by my lack of training and the need to compete that I ignored him. On top of that, I had set my own personal goal to throw the javelin over 50m. Charles was not impressed by this blatant act of defiance, though I did succeed in throwing over 50m – but at what cost to my Achilles' tendon?

I returned to Amsterdam on the Monday, and as soon as I told Peter, my doctor, about the problem he rushed me into the hospital for scans. As I lay on the bed while they looked at the scan results, they were all speaking in Dutch. Although I can understand some of the language, I couldn't follow exactly what they were saying, which was very frustrating. Those minutes seemed to last for ever, and my heart beat loudly in my chest as I waited for their diagnosis.

Finally, the senior radiographer came over and told me that he thought he could see a tear in the sheath of the Achilles. I was devastated and burst into tears, as I knew that any tear at this stage would mean the certain end of my dream. But they were awaiting another scan – which, when it arrived, confirmed that what they could actually see was a line of degeneration in the tendon. I was hugely relieved, especially when Peter reassured me that all was not lost.

Peter had had some experience with this type of injury in the past and said it could be treated, but stressed that he was uncertain whether or not time was on my side. I would have to begin an intensive programme that would include physiotherapy three times a day every day, and I would have to administer treatment myself in between these sessions to reduce the inflammation around the tendon. That was fine with me; I was prepared to try anything and everything if I just had a chance.

I rang Mum when I got home from the hospital that night. I wanted to tell her everything, but was scared of worrying her. It was around 1.30am, Amsterdam time, and I was fairly quiet with her when she first picked up the phone. When she asked why I was calling so late I told her I had been out and had just got back. But Mum knows me so well and knew that I was beating around the bush, so I finally told her what had happened. I told her that the injury was bad and that she should cancel her ticket because we probably wouldn't be going to Australia. I wasn't crying, but by now I was in a pretty bad way, so she advised me to try and get some sleep and said she would call me the next day.

In the morning she called Charles, who told her what was going on and how we were not to give up hope.

Mum said, 'I know this is your dream and I know it's Denise's dream, but at the end of the day she's my daughter, and I don't want you to push her into the Olympics to hurt herself.'

'Don't worry, Joan,' Charles said reassuringly, 'you know I wouldn't do anything like that. But this is the Olympics, and if we can get her there, we will.' Charles was great with Mum, and called her every day for the first two weeks to tell her what was happening and keep her informed about the developments. It made a big difference to her, and she knew I was being well looked after.

From that moment on I entered into intensive physiotherapy. Because all the machines I needed were in Holland I had to stay there for the whole period. Peter recommended that I see a physio called Mark Haark who worked near to where I was staying. The therapy was hard work, and involved special movement and manipulation of the ankle, massage on and around the soft tissue of the Achilles, massage of the calf, strengthening exercises for the calf, ankle and Achilles, plus treatment with a special machine that would help regenerate healthy cells in the tendon. When all that finished I was strapped up with tape from the top of my calf down to my mid-foot to prevent the Achilles' tendon from moving and causing the pain, and allow the inflammation to settle down. It was not a pretty sight – the strapping looked like a cast around my leg.

I saw Mark for three-and-a-half weeks, at 7.30am, 3pm and 7.30pm every day. In between these sessions I would try to train, keeping fit in the gym, doing a little bit here and there, lifting some body weights. Although I was deeply upset and worried, I was determined to get myself well again; I hadn't come this far to let my Achilles interfere with what I felt was my destiny. Charles was equally relentless – he would make me do anything that didn't cause me pain. When the time came that I was ready to do bike riding and rowing in the gym, he made sure the sessions were hard and that I came away pouring with sweat.

Naturally there were bad days, during which I asked myself what

I was doing. The negative voice inside me would try to convince me that I was incapable of recovering in time, and that I must have done something pretty wicked for fate to be so cruel. How could I expect to go to the Olympics with only one Achilles' tendon intact? How could I even think that I would be able to complete two days of competition in one of the most difficult events in athletics? Even if I did make a miraculous recovery, surely all this time spent in physio and rehab would mean that I wouldn't be fit enough anyway. Yes, that was it, I told myself: I would pull out of the Olympics, one of Britain's gold-medal hopes gone. The British public would understand – after all, I was injured. But would I be able to look myself in the mirror if I didn't keep trying right up to the last second to get into those starting blocks in Sydney?

It's at times like these that you really need to draw strength from your friends, family, and the people you trust. I had made sure that only a few people knew of my predicament because I didn't want word to get out to the British press – I felt they would have added to the pressure I was already feeling. Nor did I want my opponents to get wind of just how bad my injury was. Instead, my mum, Kevin, and Jonathan, my boyfriend, called me constantly in an attempt to keep my spirits up. I wouldn't be seeing them until Sydney, but in Holland I had Charles and his family, to whom I had become very close over the past three-and-a-half years, and I knew they would look after me and take my mind off the situation.

After the three-and-a-half weeks came the first ray of hope. I went for another scan to check on my progress, and was relieved to see that it showed a reduction in the area of inflammation in the tendon. I clung desperately to the hope that I might have a chance of getting fit enough to compete after all, but I was very aware that time was running out: I had just ten days until my scheduled departure to Sydney, and was yet to start running. I wasn't too worried about the technical events at this point, but without real running one's fitness levels can drop considerably.

Charles and I went to see Peter for his final analysis. He looked at the new scans, checked the tendon, and gave me the all clear to start jogging. He warned Charles to ensure that my training was increased slowly and carefully, as another breakdown in the tendon would definitely mean the end of my hopes for the championship. He gave us strict instructions on how to build up from here, and made it clear that I had to maintain my discipline with regards to rehab and recovery, even though I could begin my running. Technical work was forbidden until I reached Australia.

The ten days progressed far better than I had imagined. I had built up from gentle jogging to striding on the grass – a pace quicker than jogging, but slower than sprinting – to being able to sprint at about eighty per cent of my top speed.

I was so grateful to the medical team who had brought me to this stage, but now there was nothing they could do or say – the rest was up to me and Charles. I flew back to London for one day to pack up and get myself organised. The next stop was Australia.

The plan was to head to Brisbane to train for two weeks with the Dutch team before flying to Sydney for the games. Because Charles was a key part of the Dutch team, and they had already based their training camp in Brisbane, I was unable to stay with the British team. But as far as I was concerned, if Brisbane was where Charles had to be, then I would be there too.

I had always told myself that if I was selected for Sydney I would fly out to Australia in business class. I had therefore asked the British team management to ensure that they booked me a business class ticket, and told them I would pay the extra, as athletes normally fly to championships and competitions in economy.

I arrived at Terminal 4 of London's Heathrow airport. The rest of the British team were flying out that evening, and a handful of other athletes from different sports were also on my flight. Our bags were checked, tagged and taped with the special Olympic identification, and the check-in staff were buzzing around with excitement – I could feel that they were proud to be doing their bit for the Olympic team.

We finally boarded the plane and I was shown to my seat. I settled myself in and put Egbert – my teddy bear of sixteen years who goes to every major championship with me – on my lap ready for take-off. As the 747 climbed over the city I looked out of the window at the lights below. It was a slightly melancholy moment; I felt lonely, and fearful of what might take place in the coming weeks. The next time I saw the lights of London would my life be the same? Would I be a hero? Was I ready for the emotions that success or failure might bring? Only time would tell. I closed my eyes for a few moments, lost in my thoughts.

Although there wasn't much else for us to do in Brisbane, being situated there was perfect from a training point of view, as athletes need to be somewhere where they can really focus. In addition the weather was good and the apartment complex only seven minutes away from the stadium, which was great.

For the first couple of days I just relaxed so I could recover from the jet lag and make myself comfortable in the temporary lodgings. My apartment had one bedroom and a kitchen-diner. It was comfortable and quiet and just seconds away from Charles's and Lieja's apartments. The other Dutch athletes were dotted in their own lodgings around the complex. Everyone had their own privacy, which is important just before a major competition. As the pressure starts to mount, people tend to get quieter and start going to bed earlier. The time for fun and games is past. It's a time for visualising what is about to happen.

After two days it was time to start training, and I knew that every day would be a test. Charles had prepared a provisional training programme, which also acted as a checklist: yes, Denise can shot put; she can jog and sprint in her trainers; she can do low hurdles in her trainers; no, she can't high jump yet, or throw the javelin, but maybe she can do easy take-offs for the long jump. Everything I *could* do was a bonus – Charles always tried to be positive – but there were moments when I could see in his eyes that he feared I was losing time and fitness.

My legs was still being strapped every morning by Rick Menick, the Dutch team's physio. We managed to perfect the routine to twenty minutes, which was important to know because I needed to have a clear idea how much I would have to add on to my regular warm-up period during the competition.

The training continued to make steady progress, and a breakthrough came when I was successful in my attempt to do the hurdles at the normal height of 2'6", with the correct spacing and the regular three strides in between. It was the first time in eight weeks that I had really looked like an athlete. I screamed with delight, and Charles clapped his hands in triumph. At last! Still, it wasn't until I managed to high jump that I felt I was completely over the worst, even though I wasn't totally confident at taking off because I didn't trust my Achilles. The fear that it might tear during take-off meant that I was starting my jumps cautiously and softly, rather than the powerful leaps I knew I needed. I was very frustrated, but I couldn't help it. A good high jump is very important to the heptathlete: for every centimetre you jump you win twelve points – so if your jumping ability is significantly poorer than your competitiors', you can lose a lot of points and your position on the leader board. But generally I had made very good progress, and now, with five days to the start of the heptathlon, I felt I was pretty much back in business.

When the time came for the Olympic opening ceremony I was still in Brisbane. The British athletes had been advised against it, and I had deliberately said that I wouldn't attend because I didn't want to get my arousal levels too high too early. But I couldn't resist watching it on TV. That was when I realised how big this whole event was going to be. Suddenly I felt goosebumps all over me and the hairs on the back of my neck stood on end. I was watching in my room. The Dutch group were gathered upstairs, but I wanted to see it on my own. I was doing a jigsaw puzzle I had bought to keep me occupied in the evenings after training, and I sat there with the TV blaring, waiting for the different countries to come on. I stood up and gave a clap when I saw the Jamaicans, and I knew that my mum would be doing the same thing back at home as she watched. I then clapped at everyone else I knew. When the Ireland team came up I gave a little clap for Jonathan and a couple of other friends of mine. I stood again when the British flag came up, trying to see who was carrying it this time round, as I didn't know who had been chosen.

It was strange to watch it in many ways – principally because I was a part of it, but not actually there. Events such as the Olympics are excellent at unifying a nation – I'm sure that British nationals all over the world will have watched that ceremony and felt a part of it.

I remember checking out the kit the Great Britain team was dressed in. The outfit wasn't that nice, and contrasted greatly to that of countries such as Tonga, who had these fabulous multi-coloured garments in glorious, rich colours. Ours are rarely like that – maybe we'll brighten things up for 2004!

It was a shame that the other members of the athletics team and I were unable to take part in the ceremony, but we had been told that it would be a very long evening, and it was therefore decided that we would be better off spending the time preparing for our events in our training camps, rather than flying in to Sydney a week before we were due to compete. I've never taken part in an opening ceremony, but I would certainly like to one day.

On Wednesday 20 September I flew from Brisbane to Sydney. I was competing in three days' time, and felt I had done all I could in my training. I was not in pain, and was proud that I had given myself the opportunity to get this far under the circumstances. I was confident that I would start the competition, and believed that I could get through all the events, with the only question mark hanging over the high jump.

Charles was with me on the flight, and on our arrival we were met by Mum, who had flown in a couple of days earlier. I hadn't seen her for about twelve weeks, because I had stayed in Amsterdam longer than expected while getting my treatment, and I hadn't had the chance to go home to Wolverhampton when I'd gone back to England. It was wonderful to see her; we spent about forty-five minutes together before I had to take a bus into the village with the chaperone from the British team management.

I couldn't wait to see what the village was like. At this stage I wasn't sure whether or not I was going to stay there. I didn't want to be a prima donna, but villages can be very lively places and very distracting, so I had planned to stay on my own a little distance from the hub of activity. I wanted to stay focused, especially as I already felt at a slight disadvantage because of my injury. So I had made enquiries about staying elsewhere, just to get my head down for a few days and get some personal attention from Kevin – who hadn't been in Brisbane, but who was coming to Sydney to be with me for my biggest challenge to date.

I knew my friends Marcia and Donna were really keen for us to stay together in one of the apartments. They assured me that they had organised a really good apartment for us and I had promised them I'd come and have a look. Once we got into the village and I saw a few people I knew well, I started to think how nice it was to be surrounded by all these fellow athletes and a great sense of camaraderie.

The village was a short bus ride from the Olympic stadium, and as I entered the British section it was great to see the Union Jacks hanging from bedroom windows. As I entered the two-storey apartment where the girls were staying they came running over excitedly, shouting, 'At last! You took your time!' They had heard I was injured – that had gone round like wild fire – and they were desperate for me to stay in the apartment with them. 'You've got to stay,' they kept saying. 'Look at this apartment, it's really good, you have to stay here. Look how close it is to the dining hall – there's not much walking, and the transport to the track is just there.' I went to have a look at my proposed bedroom and liked it. They wanted to put me in what they called 'the penthouse', the top level that overlooked the street. If I craned my neck I could just see the Olympic flame from my bedroom window, which made me tingle with excitement and anticipation. My mind was made up. Although the room had two single beds in it, I had it to myself. It was spacious, warm and my friends were there – so I told the team management I was happy to stay in the village.

The first thing I had to do was get my bearings, because with so many teams being there, the village covers a big area. It's full of bus routes that you have to learn – which you have to take to the track, or the warm-up track, or any of the other competition venues. You also have to make sure you know where all the key areas are, such as the gym, the restaurants, and the international mixed zone where you can e-mail or send post and meet people who have day passes into the village. There's a lot to take in, and I only had three days in which to do it!

I had been watching Britain's early achievements in Brisbane, so by the time I arrived at the camp there was already a real buzz and lots of talk of us having a successful games – in the first week we had won three medals. However, of all the races I saw, I managed to miss our coxless four win their golds because I was in my own personal zone time, focusing on my own competition and what I needed to do. But I certainly heard about it from everyone else. People were coming up all the time saying, 'Steve's done it!' It was wonderful and I was thrilled for him and the other members of the rowing team.

My first big task when I arrived in Sydney was the press conference. I had managed successfully to keep my injury out of the limelight, but now I was over the worst and felt it was time to talk about the problems I had faced. I reassured the media of my confidence and told them I felt I had as good a chance as anyone to come home with a gold medal. They asked other questions about what score I thought I could achieve and what I thought it would take to win – pretty much the same ones they ask year in, year out – but I thought I had given them plenty of information with which to fill their columns and write their pieces. I also think I created a sense of anticipation for the heptathlon, and hoped that it was now regarded as one of the premier events for Britain.

The last training session I underwent was the day before the heptathlon began. I had jogged and stretched to get the flight out of my legs and I felt good. While I was on the track I saw Cathy Freeman doing a session with some of her training partners. Cathy was Australia's favourite for the 400m title, and as I watched her I thought to myself, if I've got pressure, that girl's got the weight of a nation on her shoulders. She was an Aborigine competing for Australia, and her pre-eminent role seemed to be as some kind of figurehead for the joining of two cultures through sport. She was on home soil and her face was all over the city on big billboards. In a way, it was almost as if her success would stand as a symbol of Australia's success in race equality and integration. That was real pressure to succeed, and I didn't envy her.

Before I left I gave Charles a big hug, and it felt as if I was preparing for battle. He told me that no matter what happened tomorrow, he was proud of the way I had coped with everything thus far, and I thanked him for all his help and support in getting me to this stage.

Everything was about to begin, and the tension was building. This was what we had been waiting for over the past three-and-a-half years. This was it. I was looking forward to the moment when it all started, but inside I also felt fear. I can remember thinking to myself, come Monday morning it's all going to be over. In the blink of an eye, that will be it – and how will you feel? But Charles just told me to enjoy it.

Check-in time for the heptathlon was around nine o'clock the next morning. By then I was to have had my breakfast, done my bandaging, be wide awake and on the track, ready and warmed up. It would mean getting up very early.

The night before a big competition I always lay my kit out, and this Friday night was no exception. What was I going to wear? Was it to be the leotard or the crop top and shorts? The long-sleeved T-shirt or the short-sleeved? I laid the clothes out fully from the top to the bottom including my socks and shoes at the end. I always place my shoes at the end of the layout so I can see exactly what the whole thing's going to look like. I do that with my clothes when I'm going out as well – my friends think I'm nuts. Before I got into bed I gave each of the girls a long embrace but told them that once I was in bed I didn't want to hear any noise. I told them I would be coming in and out during the competition, and that, after the first morning session I'd be in my room and sleeping all afternoon. I warned them that if I woke up I wouldn't be very nice, and apologised for that in advance!

After that I read a little to centre myself, and listened to some music, a song I had nominated as my own theme tune – Whitney Houston's duet with Mariah Carey from *The Prince of Egypt*, 'There Can Be Miracles If You Believe'. I was reading Iyanla Vanzant's book to uplift me and give me focus. I remember one paragraph that seemed to convey what I was feeling and what I needed. It was on willingness:

Willingness is an active declaration that life is a divine game, but it is your move! When you move, you want to be able to make it through difficulties and challenges. Be willing to be wrong. Be willing to walk that extra mile. Be willing to fall down, get up and fall down again . . . when

we are willing to give up everything we have, the Divine
will replace it with ten times more!

I was willing to take myself beyond the realms of pain – I had proved
that. I was prepared to commit myself fully to the task ahead. The
only question that remained was whether it would be good enough.

Chapter Seventeen
Sydney 2000: Day One

Even though I had placed three alarm clocks around the room, by the time the first of them went off at 5am, I was wide awake. My body instinctively knew it was time – even at this early hour when I would normally be struggling to wake up – as if it were somehow independently aware that I was about to embark on the two most important days of my life.

As I watched the hands move on the clock-face I lay still, thoughtful, taking in the enormity of what was to come. This was the moment I had been waiting for all my life. I had come a long way to get here, and I resolved to give it my best shot, no matter what. I felt my inner strength, and I knew I was ready. I did another stretch, and got out of bed.

I'd organised a little routine to go through before leaving for the track. Kevin Lidlow, my physiotherapist, friend and hero all tied up into one, had put together a checklist of what needed to be done as soon as I woke. The first thing was to massage my Achilles' tendon with heat. So I boiled up some water and poured it into the bathroom sink, adding a little cold, but trying to keep it as hot as I could tolerate. This procedure helped to loosen the Achilles' tendon, as it was often tight and stiff first thing in the morning since the injury. After ten minutes of perching over the sink I hopped into a luke-warm shower, which I knew would ensure I was sharper and brighter than I would have been following a stream of hot water. After that I changed into my kit and put on my ankle warmers, which would keep my Achilles warm until I was ready to be strapped up later on.

Once I had gone through the first preparations to protect my Achilles, I switched on to autopilot – my standard pre-competition routine. This involved making sure I had my four official numbers – two for my kit, one for my rucksack and one for my track-suit – safety pins with which to attach them, bottles of water, my towel, sunglasses, and my spikes for the hurdles and high jump. I also had some food to nibble on – a yoghurt, a banana and some raisins – and, most importantly of all, Egbert my teddy bear. In addition to this I took music to listen to on the journey to the track. It all went into my rucksack, and I was ready to face the world.

Kevin came to my apartment at six o'clock to check that I was all right. He wanted to ensure that I had done my treatment, and to see whether I needed any further work done on my body. I told him I was fine, but he still insisted on looking at my calf and ankle to make sure they were moving freely.

At 6.30am we went to the dining hall for breakfast, where Charles was waiting for us. He wanted to make sure that we were on time – he doesn't like me to be even a minute late. But he seemed quite happy that everything was running to plan. He gave me a warm smile and asked if I was OK and had slept well.

We had breakfast in the big communal restaurant where I spotted a few other heptathletes, obviously on similar schedules. I always have a quick examination of my competitors to see if they look awake and alert, and that morning they seemed to look fine. But I was perfectly happy with that, because I felt very much in control.

Breakfast is always an effort on competition day – eating is one of the biggest hurdles: you know you have to, but your throat is dry from nervous tension and doesn't want to take anything in. But that morning I was able to eat – which I immediately took as a good sign. I had some cereal, raisin bread and herbal tea while Charles, Kevin and I made small talk, trying to keep the mood light. I ate as much as I could before it was time to catch the 7.10am bus to the warm-up track.

We were joined by Tudor Bidder, the technical director of combined events at the time. He was there to make sure everything was OK, but in our case he kept in the background because he knew I had a very experienced team around me and would be well looked after.

The four of us got on the shuttle bus that runs between the residential area and the stadium, and headed off to do battle.

On the short journey to the stadium, I sat alone listening to my music while the adrenaline stirred in my body. I was beginning to feel a little nervous, but it was more than two hours until the start of the competition and I knew I needed to relax, so I focused on the R&B tunes playing on my personal stereo.

I was one of the first athletes to arrive at the warm-up track. Charles and my medical team went off to set up a room for us, while I spent a few minutes on my own. I usually like to be on my own for ten minutes or so just to gather my thoughts, so I walked slowly around the track a couple of times. The morning was fresh; the dew was still on the grass and the air was crisp and clear. I could tell that when the sun rose a little more it would be a beautiful day.

I drew a lot from those few moments, enjoying what seemed to be the calm before the storm. Finally I felt composed, and I went off to find Kevin and the others so we could begin the taping session and my treatment.

While I had been in Brisbane I'd slightly aggravated my right ankle during long jump practices – so not only was my left leg taped up from ankle to calf, but my right leg also had strapping on. So far I had successfully managed to avoid many people seeing all this, as I didn't want my competitors to think I was disadvantaged, giving them a psychological edge over me. We therefore taped pieces of paper over the windows of the medical room so that people couldn't look in. Pretty soon, though, we were told to take some of them down so that the medical supervisors could keep an eye on what was happening and ensure that everything was above board.

It was now around 8.15 and, after taping, I found a little corner in which to stretch. Outside on the track the temperature was beginning to rise and a few other athletes had started to arrive, including some of the heptathletes.

After my stretching I felt quite loose, so I went out on to the track and did some easy drills, some practice runs and a couple of starts from the blocks. All the heptathletes had to share the hurdles that were available, but we tried not to get in each other's way. There were a few other British athletes on the track too, and the occasional shouts of 'Come on, Denise' helped, as they reminded me that I was a part of a team, which was a great feeling.

The first heat for the hurdles was then called. There were to be three heats, the participants in each allocated according to their seeding, which had been calculated on recent performance as well as personal best. I was in the third and fastest heat, so I had a while to wait. Before the first heat we all had to go to call room number one, which contained a few tables and chairs and some TV monitors so one could watch what was happening on the track. This was where the officials checked spike length, numbers, accreditation and which brand we were going to be competing in, such as Nike or Adidas, for example.

Before I went in, Charles gave me a knowing look, then that was it – he was gone and I was on my own.

As I sat down, feeling calm and ready to focus on what lay ahead, I put on my sunglasses. Heptathletes are very friendly with one another, but before the first race we all tend to avoid eye contact. I especially try to avoid any contact with my closest rivals, and I know that Eunice Barber certainly avoids looking in my direction.

This was the first time I had seen Ghada Shouaa, who was widely regarded as the dark horse of the pack. None of us was sure what she was capable of because of a recent lack of form following a bad injury she had sustained. But I was wary – once you're that talented you're always a threat – so I avoided eye contact with her altogether.

From behind the protection of my sunglasses I glanced around, looking at the other girls and wondering who was feeling nervous and who was feeling confident. Everyone always tries to look calm, focused and ready, to show how much in control they are, when all you really want to do is get out there on to the track.

Finally my heat was called, and we were called in lane order and escorted to the stadium.

The walk down the endless tunnels to the arena was an intense psychological period. I wished, as I often do, that the call room could have been just a little bit closer to the track. (The worst such walk I ever had to do was at the 1994 European Championships in Helsinki, where the journey took at least ten minutes and was up an incline. Every athlete will remember that, as we were exhausted by the time we arrived at the track, trying to catch our breath. Thankfully, Sydney wasn't quite that bad, but it still took almost ten minutes.) As we paced along I found myself playing little mind games. Who's walking in front? Who's behind? Is it significant? I looked to see who was leading the group and thought, does she think she's going to lead in the race as well? Is Barber walking ahead of me? Is she doing it deliberately? Then I stopped myself and rationalised – let her walk ahead, it means nothing.

We were still under the stadium, but as we approached the track we stopped, put on our spikes, and while some people went to the loo we were issued with number badges for our hips, corresponding with our lane numbers. Because my warm-up had gone well, I felt confident that I was going to have a good race. From where we were,

I could see the sun on a small corner of the track, and I desperately wanted to get out there and get the competition under way.

Then suddenly we were there – in the arena. As we emerged into the sunshine there was a big round of applause from the packed stadium. The sheer size of the place was startling, and all 112,000 seats were occupied.

Never have I been in a stadium at that time of the morning and seen so many people who have come to see the heptathlon. Normally, people look at the programme and pick out the 'highlights'. They might decide to get down there early to see the warm-up for the men's 100m, for example – but for the heptathlon . . . ? It was fantastic. The atmosphere was electric, and there was a hum of expectation from the crowd. They seemed to be as ready and keen to watch us as we were to compete. I couldn't believe it – I had never experienced anything quite like it.

I concentrated on drills and on warming up properly. I set up my blocks and did a couple of starts over the first two hurdles, as I had on the warm-up track some forty minutes earlier. I then sat down behind my blocks to catch my breath. Get a good start, I told myself, think speed between the hurdles. My heart was pumping, and somewhere in the distance I heard a few shouts and people calling my name, willing me on.

Then, 'Track-suits off, ladies.' The third and final heat was announced, and it was time to perform. I took off my long tights to reveal my strapping, almost waiting for a gasp from the crowd as I did so. It may have looked terrible, but I knew I was fine.

I vaguely recall my name being announced, and I think I nodded instinctively, but I don't remember completely. I usually acknowledge the crowd, but sometimes I feel I can't – it's as if I'm indulging myself too much by smiling and waving when I should be focusing completely on what I'm doing. It's a very difficult time – on the one hand I want to thank the crowd, to say 'I hear you, I feel you,' to let them know I'm ready, but the other part of me wants to shut everything out, concentrate on the race ahead and what I'm hoping to do.

There are games that athletes play with one another – more so the males, who have big psychological battles, strutting past one another, puffing out their chests. It's all about showmanship and gamesmanship. Eunice Barber makes noises when she's competing, particularly just before a race, but it doesn't irritate or annoy me, as I understand she needs to prepare for the event in whatever way she feels fit. But I can just be me, I can be charged from within. I don't have to let anyone else see what's going on. At the end of the day, if you've got a Ferrari you don't have to keep lifting up the bonnet to see how good the engine is – it just is good. I have an inner confidence, so I don't need to show off. I don't need to flaunt it.

We were called to our marks. I knew I had to be focused and aware, ready to be out of my blocks like lightning. Barber was next to me, on the inside. I could feel her presence and hear her noises, but I kept my tunnel vision and focused on my preparation. I was very aware of my breathing and my heart was pounding in my chest. It was tense and quiet, and there was a stillness in the crowd. We were poised, waiting for the command from the starter. My fingers were just behind the line and my head was down, my eyes focusing on the bit of track just in front of me. My muscles were tensed and ready. We were called to our set position, then we were off – but almost immediately a second shot was fired as the recall gun went off. Someone had made a false start. I had no idea who it was, but I knew it wasn't me as my start had been disappointing. I was therefore grateful for the reprieve, and was determined to get a better start next time.

As we waited behind our blocks for a second time I was determined to be aggressive out of them and to be the first to the first hurdle. We were called to our marks. I shook out my legs and put my feet in the blocks and my fingers behind the line, waiting for the start. As soon as the gun went I was gone. The race was under way.

I had a good start, and although I tried to focus on my own race, I was very aware that I was just behind Barber. Hold on to her, Denise, hold on, I was saying to myself. This was good – it meant the race was going well for me. I knew I wouldn't pass her because she's a better athlete than me over the hurdles, but I had to stay with her. My last two hurdles were not brilliant because of fatigue and lack of training, but I sprinted off the last hurdle and threw myself over the line in a time of 13.23 seconds. Barber had won, I had come second. Although my last two hurdles were disappointing, I was really pleased with my time. 13.23 seconds was the best I had run in a championship by a long way, and this was an excellent start to my two-day campaign for Olympic gold. The competition had begun.

I felt good and nodded to the crowd. As I looked over to the BBC commentary team they gave me the thumbs up. One of the BBC commentators came over and asked if I was happy with my time. I said yes, but walked away without saying much more than that I thought it was a good start to the competition. Sometimes I don't mind giving interviews straight afterwards, but this time I didn't want to. I didn't want to indulge in the fact that it was a good beginning, as everything can change so quickly in a heptathlon competition.

I quickly retrieved my kit. There were no more than forty-five minutes to the start of the high jump, so I was keen to collect my things and make my way over to the high jump area. But the organisers had other ideas for us. They wanted us all to go to a designated meeting place then walk together over to the high jump area. My group were not at all happy about this; there was nearly a mutiny as we were all up in arms. We wanted to stay on the track and begin our preparation. Although we were all of different nationalities and spoke different languages, there was a real sense of solidarity and unity over the issue. But despite our protests the organisers wouldn't budge, saying it was unfair that some athletes were at the other meeting point while we were on the track. We therefore reluctantly picked up our bags and began to follow the officials to the meeting place. But we hadn't even got half-way there when the other girls were led out on to the track anyway, and we had to turn round and head off to the high jump area after all. It was all a bit of a farce really.

The high jump requires a different type of aggression from that needed for running – it needs to be much more controlled. It's all about consistency and the rhythm of your approach, and you need to feel light and bouncy in your actions. I did have reservations about this event because of my injuries, but as I performed my practice run-up and jumps I was surprised by how bouncy and explosive I was off the floor. My strapping was holding up and I was still without pain – it all seemed to be going well.

My opening height went OK, and the bar quickly moved up to 1.75m. I cleared that with relative ease and was relieved by how well it had gone. I therefore decided that I would miss the next height of 1.78m and come in again at 1.81m, which is what I normally do when I'm feeling good about myself and my jumping. Perfectly happy with my decision, I notified the officials accordingly and went off to the bathroom.

I wasn't feeling at all tense or nervous, I was just pleased that my jumping was going better than expected. In hindsight I think I was slightly over-confident, and considering what I had been through over the past eight weeks I should probably have been more cautious. I should have acknowledged that because I hadn't done much jumping throughout the year, let alone the last few months, I ought to have made as many jumps as possible to get me into a good rhythm. However, I had made my decision and I happily stuck with it.

When I got back to the track the girls were just finishing their attempts at 1.78m. Barber had knocked off the bar on her first attempt, then did the same on her second. I was shocked; this was so unlike her. I had mixed feelings – surely she couldn't go out of the competition like this? On her third and final attempt the crowd really got behind her and started to clap as she prepared for her jump. Some of the other heptathletes started doing the same. I paused – what was I going to do? The competitor in me was saying this is her problem, not yours, but the other side of me wanted to give her support. In the end I joined in, encouraging her over the bar. She sailed over this time, leaving plenty of daylight between the bar and her body.

Although I was pleased for her, I realised an opportunity had gone.

The bar went up to 1.81m and it was my turn. My first attempt was poor – my positioning was all wrong and I was nowhere near clearing it. Barber cleared the bar with ease on her first attempt – but this didn't worry me, as I was still convinced I would do the same. I looked to Charles for some feedback and noticed that he seemed to be agitated, but didn't think any more of it. He gave me instructions to attack the bar and keep my shoulders up.

On my second attempt I was still not close. As I landed on the high jump bed it was as if a bolt of lightning had hit me – two failures at 1.81m, this was unbelievable. I had made 1.75m look easy, and now I was struggling at a height that was only 6cm more – what was wrong with me?

I was in shock, as I knew I had to get over this height. I gathered myself and tried to focus, but my legs felt like jelly. Before I knew it, my name was called for a third and final attempt. The crowd was clapping me, and was very much behind me as I looked at the jump, willing myself to get over it.

I took my run-up, but as soon as I took off I knew that I hadn't done enough. To my utter dismay, the bar came crashing down and I lay on the bed, thinking about the consequences of what had just happened. My heart sank, and I realised I had probably just kissed goodbye to the gold medal.

I got off the bed and walked away, disappointed and angry with myself inside, but blank on the outside. I gathered my gear together, changed my spikes and put on my sunglasses – I didn't want anyone to be able to read my expression. In the past, other athletes have burst into tears or made public displays of frustration when faced with a similar situation. However, I didn't feel like having any public tantrums. I wasn't anywhere near as expressive in my emotions. I felt numb. But despite my deep disappointment, I felt a calmness inside. Perhaps something deep within told me that it was only by holding it all together that I would still have a chance of winning gold. Perhaps I realised that tantrums would be pointless. Or perhaps it's just that I have learned over the years that this event is thoroughly unpredictable. Everyone has to go through seven events – seven chances to excel and seven chances to mess up.

But it was time to get some lunch and prepare for the afternoon session. Kevin didn't know what to say to me, but asked me if I was all right and put his arm around me. I was surprised that I didn't see Charles as I went to pick up a bus back to the athletes' village, but Kevin told me that he'd said he would see me there later. I had a feeling that Charles was annoyed and disappointed with me, but I wasn't going to let it worry me. I just decided to see what he had to say to me when we met.

We saw each other just as I was about to go into the dining hall. He started to say something to me but I quickly said, 'Look, I don't need to hear any attitude right now. I don't want you to get annoyed with me here because I don't feel too good myself. I'm going to have lunch with one of my friends and we can talk afterwards.'

He wasn't pleased, as he thought that it was a perfect time for the two of us to sit down and talk about what we were going to do next. But I wasn't quite ready to discuss the afternoon session, and I certainly didn't want to face a telling-off for the decision I had made in the high jump competition. I needed some distance between the event and an analysis of it, and I knew that if we sat down together there and then I would probably end up feeling worse than I did already. We therefore agreed to meet later on.

Colin Jackson and Robert Wagner – who organises my races and Colin's in Europe – were in the dining room, and asked me how it was going.

'I just lost the gold medal,' I told them unhappily.

'Rubbish,' replied Robert, 'you're too pretty to lose.'

Colin gave me a big hug, saying, 'It's simple – there's a long way to go yet – just kill 'em in the shot.' They both made me laugh, and Colin's words did make me realise that the competition was far from over. There was still time for me to pull back.

I had five hours before the next event, so after lunch I went to get some treatment from Kevin, then slept for a bit. When I woke I felt refreshed and ready for the shot. I knew I needed to achieve some good throws in order to make up the points deficit I was now facing. Because I had left before the high jump had finished I wasn't sure exactly where I stood, but I desperately hoped that no one had managed a really good height. Shouaa had had a first-round fail, and when I found out that Barber and Sazanovich had only gone on to jump 1.84m I began to feel more positive. It was a lifeline, and I grabbed hold of it with both hands. I was back in eighth place, but there was a chance that I could still do it.

When I got back to the warm-up track my ankles were restrapped. Because my body was still quite loose from the morning's activities, my warm-up was much more gentle than the morning's session. I put the disappointment of the high jump behind me and focused on what lay ahead.

I was very aware that I needed a good result in the shot put to bring me back into contention for the gold, and was totally determined to do it.

On the track I was aware that Barber wasn't around, and I wondered why she wasn't warming up with the rest of us. But the next thing I knew, we were being asked to make our way to the heptathletes' call room. This was different to the place in which we had waited that morning – this was call room two, and was situated on the far side of the arena. It was a big, windowless area lit with electric strip lights and empty except for a few chairs and tables and some water. The atmosphere was more relaxed than it had been earlier, but everyone was still very focused on the next event. Barber had appeared, and I was interested to see that she was being quite chatty with some of the other girls. However, I kept to myself, feeling calm, determined to stay that way and do a good throw.

As we were led out, the sun was still shining and I saw that the stadium was still full. There was a lot more activity on the track now than there had been earlier – other events were taking place and there was much more noise.

We warmed up in our competition order, and my two practice attempts were fine. I now had a real eagerness to throw – my shot had improved a lot over the previous couple of years, and I knew I needed something close to my personal best to make up the points I had lost that morning. I was ninth or tenth to throw – which was agonising, as I wanted to take my turn while I was still fresh. As I watched the others I was relieved to see that no one was throwing in a particularly exceptional way – especially Barber. But I was keen to focus more on myself, and trying not to get agitated that it all seemed to be taking so long.

Finally it was my turn. My first attempt was technically quite poor and was well below my capabilities. I was exasperated, but I still had two chances to improve on it. I needed to think more about where my hips were and ensure that my right foot worked better. On my second attempt I made a slight improvement, but it still wasn't enough. I was now very annoyed because I had expected so much more. But I was too keen, too eager, and was rushing myself. It was very frustrating, but I was reassured to see that my nearest rivals were still not improving on their throws either. I had one throw left, and it had to be good. On my third attempt I tried to slow my thinking down. As I launched the shot it felt much better than the previous throws. It measured just over 15.5m – slightly down on my personal best – and although I wasn't overly happy I was satisfied. I had wanted to get the maximum out of myself in each event and I didn't feel I had achieved that here, so I hoped that the 200m would be better.

There were just over two hours before the 200m so I went back to the warm-up track to have a massage and try to relax. I needed some time to be on my own and gather my thoughts. Although I didn't feel that I had totally got to grips with the 200m, I knew I could run a better race than I had managed in the past. I had seen a glimmer of potential in my performances recently, but had still been finishing in over twenty-four seconds. Now I wanted to achieve a faster time. Although I wasn't sure I would be able to do it today, I wanted to give it my best shot. With an hour to go I completed my warm-up, then went back to the stadium.

I felt optimistic. I had been drawn in the lane next to Barber again – which was good, as it meant that I had a good target. I was ready. By now it was dark, but the bright lights of the stadium illuminated the arena as if it were day. The stadium was still full and the atmosphere was charged. I went to my marks thinking, OK Denise, this is the end of day one, let's finish it well.

The gun went and Barber was out of her blocks quickly – but she didn't seem to be pulling away, which surprised me. Prokhorova and her Russian team-mate Natalya Roshchupkina were well in the lead as we went round the bend, but I tried to concentrate on my form and give it everything I had. Barber and I were battling it out down the home straight when suddenly I was ahead of her, amazed that I might be about to beat her for the first time in the 200m. As the line drew nearer I waited for her to pass me, but she didn't. I finished with a time of 24.34 seconds, and ended the day in the top three.

I had been so focused on my own battle with Barber that I hadn't been watching my time, which wasn't that good. It was a solid enough performance, but I was sure it could have been better. Barber finished in 24.47 seconds and slipped down into seventh place overall. She obviously wasn't as fit as she had appeared to be.

I was relieved to find that I wasn't in any pain and that there didn't seem to be any problems with my Achilles. However, I was glad the day was over. I had a quick interview with the BBC, and then headed back to the athletes' village to meet Charles and get something to eat.

Charles and I had dinner together, and he told me that although he didn't want to dwell on the past, he felt he needed to say something about the high jump. He was very angry with me, and said he couldn't understand why I hadn't taken my jump at 1.78m. He said it was the behaviour of a novice, that he had expected better of me, and that it wasn't the kind of thing I would usually do. I tried to explain that I had felt confident I would clear 1.81m, but he interrupted me, saying that with all the problems I'd had this confidence was misguided and over-ambitious. I conceded that he was probably right, but told him that I can only ever act on how I'm feeling at the time. Normally we signal to each other, but in this case he hadn't given me any indication that I should do something different. I think he had wanted me to jump 1.72m, miss 1.75m, then attempt 1.78m. It was clearly a misunderstanding, but Charles made it very plain that I was to follow his instructions to the letter from now on, as he couldn't trust me to make decisions on my own.

I could see that it made sense in his eyes – I hadn't done what he had wanted me to do in the high jump and had made a mistake as a result – but there are times in an athlete's career when you have to make decisions for yourself. Sometimes it will work out, sometimes it won't. Charles knew I wasn't a reckless performer, so I felt he shouldn't underestimate my ability to do what I judge is best for me in a certain situation.

But then again, he is my coach, and he is there to give instruction. It's a complicated relationship.

When I got back to the apartment it was around eleven o'clock and some of the girls were already in bed. I was tired, but I had a quick chat with Marcia and Donna before going to my room. I set my alarm clocks for five again and got into bed. If I could get six hours of sleep, I would be happy.

I fell asleep, picturing myself achieving a great result in the long jump the next morning.

CHAPTER EIGHTEEN

SYDNEY 2000: DAY TWO

A new day, and in the morning I went through exactly the same routine as I had for day one.

Before we got to the long jump Charles was on my back, determined to exert his authority. He didn't want a repeat of the situation the day before, so he gave me strict instructions: 'When you run up, if I tell you to move it back a foot, then you move it. If I say forward a foot, you move it. We can't afford any mistakes or miscommunication.' I knew he was right, so I just bit my tongue and nodded.

When we entered the stadium to a big round of applause, I was thrilled to see that once again the British crowd was out in force. They seemed to have congregated as close as they could to the back straight of the track where the long jump was to take place. All their banners were out, the Union Jacks were flying and I heard lots of shouts of encouragement, just for me. I gave them a little wave to show I had heard them, but I had to focus on what I was about to do. It was vital that I got my run-up exactly right.

As the crowd settled down to watch us take our warm-up jumps I spotted Mum, who was sitting near Charles, Kevin and Rick, waiting for her daughter to perform. I gave her a wave. I hadn't seen either Jonathan Marks or Jonathan my boyfriend at that point, but I knew they would be sitting together somewhere.

I had a good warm-up and felt optimistic and confident with how I would perform in this event.

Unfortunately, for the first jump my run-up wasn't quick enough. I also made mistakes, but only those a technician would notice: the flexion in the knee joint was wrong, my hips were too low and I was sinking. The deceleration of my hips meant that I wasn't able to utilise the board properly, and the jump was therefore not as good as it should have been. I made the necessary improvements on my second attempt, and managed to jump 6.48m.

Eunice Barber had only made a few practice run-ups and she was already way down in sixth place. I was surprised, as the long jump is usually her event – she's jumped 7m in the past, whereas my personal best is 6.69m. Barber took one jump as I sat there watching, hidden behind my sunglasses, but seeing everything that was going on. It was nowhere near the standard of which she was capable, and she made only 5.96m. I had never seen her jump so badly. I thought it was strange, but I didn't really register what was happening, and could never have predicted what was about to follow. On the outside she didn't look injured, then, in the second round, I saw her with her trainers on and a rucksack on her back. I didn't notice at first that she hadn't taken her second round jump, but as I glanced at her she gave me a knowing look. 'It's all over,' were her unspoken words. I gave her a look to show her how sorry I was. She put out her hand and we shook – there were no words.

I felt sad as she left. I just thought how easily that could have been me. She must have thought that the Olympics would be easy for her after her performances in 1999 – but this was incredibly unfortunate and she must have been devastated.

While Barber was leaving the long jump area, and I was lost in my musings about her premature departure, I stood up to stretch off and felt an intense pain in my foot. At first I assumed I must be imagining it – brought on by the thoughts I'd just had. But I soon realised that the pain was very real, and I felt a sharp jolt across my foot every time I put pressure on it. Because I am flat footed I have experienced problems in the past; however they had never been quite like this.

I took off my shoes and started to manipulate my feet, grabbing my toes in an attempt to free my foot from the pain that was becoming increasingly worse. I tried to stand so I could jog, but I couldn't even walk. Then I started to panic and looked for Charles, though I didn't want to inform anyone else about what was going on because I still had one jump left. Stubborness made me continue. The competitor in me took over and somehow, stupidly, I carried on. On my third jump I had to bite my lip against the pain in my foot and, unsurprisingly, I made no further distance. I managed to walk out of the pit and back to the rest of my kit.

By now the competiton had finished. I loosened some of the straps on my shoe, which gave me partial relief, and I signalled to Charles and Kevin to meet me by the buses to the athletes' village. Before I left I saw Sazanovich jump 2cm further than I had, maintaining her lead overall. She had come back from having a baby in 1999, and this was her big competition. As I walked away I could see the competitor in her eyes. With two events to go, she was ready for a fight – and I could hardly walk.

I saw Kevin first and told him my foot was in agony, that it wasn't my Achilles, but a bone in my foot. Despite the excruciating pain, it had come on so suddenly that I was convinced that once Kevin looked at it he would be able to fix it. Charles met us at the bus and I told him about it. I was sure that in an hour or so it would be fine. I knew I needed to rest it, but that was not a problem because the javelin competition was six hours away. So, back in the village, I had some lunch and went to my room to sleep.

When I woke I was shocked to discover that my foot was still hurting enormously. Kevin went to work on it remorselessly and, though his attentions certainly helped, the pain was only marginally lessened. I couldn't believe it – it hadn't gone.

As the time approached for us to leave for the warm-up track, I had to decide what to wear. I felt compelled to wear my one-armed suit to make myself perform at the highest level. I had been involved in the garment's concept and design, so I felt very much a part of it. This was the outfit that had to be worn. The only reason I had deliberated about it at all was because it's not the most practical kit – you can't get the zip undone yourself, so have to take someone to the ladies' with you, and getting into it isn't easy either!

At the warm-up track I was desperately trying to control the pain. I tried to jog, but couldn't. Kevin was strapping and unstrapping my foot, trying to get it right, to ease the pain. He tried three or four types of strapping, and all the while my warm-up period was getting shorter and shorter. I was getting more and more anxious – nothing Kevin was doing was alleviating the pain. Normally I look to him to solve all my problems – he fixes everything, including my pain – but this time, nothing was working. I could see him and Rick glancing at each other, wondering what else they could possibly try. Why wasn't this pain easing up? I desperately needed to start my warm-up for the javelin, but I was in agony, and putting pressure on my foot was simply not possible. The other girls were all around me on the track, and I was trying so hard not to let them see what was happening.

We had already lost about forty minutes – what was I going to do? My whole Olympic challenge was in jeopardy.

I hobbled gingerly over to Charles, the pain now so intense that there were tears in my eyes. 'Charles, I'm in agony. I really don't know if I can do this. It's impossible for me to convey to you just how much pain I'm in. I know I won't be able to do the run-up before my throw.'

'Denise,' he replied, 'you've come so far, you can't give up now. You've got to work through the pain, put it in a box and carry on with the competition.'

He just didn't seem to understand how much pain I was in. He was determined that I should throw, and I could see the desperation in his eyes. I understood his anxiety, but right at that moment, there was no way I could work through the pain. I needed a doctor.

There were talks of injections in my foot to numb the pain, but I just wanted to see Peter. However, because Peter was the Dutch team's doctor there was a lot of protocol that had to be followed, and the British doctor had to be consulted at every stage. A maelstrom of mobile phone and walkie-talkie calls then began as Tudor and Rick tried to locate the British and Dutch doctors. Kevin and Charles stood above me, not knowing what they could do to help. It was at that point that it started to rain – could things get any worse?

Eventually, Kevin decided to put a piece of felt under the middle of my foot to push the bones upwards, open them out slightly and hopefully ease the pain. It gave me some temporary relief and I could put some pressure on my foot, but I didn't know how long it would last, or even if it would be enough to enable me to compete. I therefore took some painkillers – ibuprofen – the maximum dosage I was allowed.

Suddenly Charles looked at his watch. 'Look, we've got to go or she's going to miss the competition anyway.' The last call for all competitors had been made fifteen minutes before and we were still at the warm-up area – a good ten minutes from the stadium. We had to get moving.

There was a mad and frantic rush. Because there was no way I would be able to walk to the stadium, Tudor went off to find me a buggy. My bags were then thrown in on top of me, Charles ran off to return our javelins, and Kevin rushed around gathering up his equipment. By now I was extremely upset, tense and stressed. Everything hinged on this javelin competition. Sazanovich was still in the lead so I had to put some distance between us in the javelin as I needed buffer points going into the 800m, otherwise all would be lost. As it was, I couldn't see any light at the end of the tunnel, I couldn't see any way in which I would be able to throw far enough to secure those points. It seemed pointless to even try. I sat on the buggy thinking, why is this happening? Why have I gone through so much to lose it all now? I was in second place by a couple of points – why was this happening to me? I felt so sad, I just couldn't believe what a mess this was. I just kept saying to myself, 'I can't believe it, I can't believe it.'

I eventually got to the call room where the other heptathletes were waiting to see whether or not I was going to show up. I was very late, and everyone was looking at me. I had held up the whole group and all the girls were sitting there, looking at each other, desperate to know what was happening. The officials were not happy about the situation, so I told them to take the others out. I wasn't at all ready to go out myself – I was surrounded by my bags and must have looked so disorganised. So they left me there with Kevin, who tried to calm me down.

Before Charles had left to go on to the arena, he had told me to do one big throw, to give it all I had, and as Kevin helped me into my suit and pinned on my number, he reiterated Charles' advice. We had agreed that as soon as I had finished my throw I would leave the arena and we would head back to the medical room to decide whether or not I needed the injection.

I didn't feel at all confident. On the contrary, I was in despair – I just couldn't believe that I had come through everything to be caught out at the last minute by this strange injury. If it had been my Achilles it would have been easier to take, but this was just cruel. As I stood there I thought, well, maybe this is how it's meant to be – it was just one thing after another – maybe I wasn't destined to win after all. I was on the verge of giving up trying to fight what was going on. I felt powerless.

Eventually I made my way towards the arena. I had gained some temporary relief from the painkillers and the felt under my foot seemed to be helping, so the injection had been postponed and we had agreed to see how things went during the javelin. The rain had eased off a little, but the wind had picked up. I was still cold, so I put on my fleece and walked out on to the track on my own.

The spectators had protected themselves from the cold and the rain, but they had stayed, and the stadium was still full. The girls had started their warm-up and there was a real buzz in the stadium. I heard shouts of encouragement from the British crowd and closed my eyes. If only they knew what was happening – they sounded so hopeful. I must have seemed only a whisker away from securing the gold medal, but the reality was very different.

The rain stopped as I marked out my run-up. I picked up the javelin for my practice throw, feeling nervous and very tentative. I was terrified that I was going to collapse in front of everyone, so I only did half my run-up. Every time my left foot came into contact with the ground I was expecting it to give; but it didn't, and it didn't seem to be too painful either.

I searched the crowd for Charles and saw him waving to me. Then I saw everybody – Kevin, Rick, Peter, Mum, Jonathan, all sitting together. They could tell that something wasn't right, but were giving me encouraging smiles and signs. I was still OK, but I didn't know how long it was going to last. Charles shouted to me to just do one throw. I had no idea then that they had spotted something was amiss. I felt completely on my own.

The crowd was getting more and more excited, but I was mentally detached from everything that was going on. I felt alone and stayed alone – I didn't have anything to share with anyone there. There were shelters to protect us in case the weather turned again, so I went over to one on the far side, away from the other girls. I lay on my back, looking up at the dark sky, thinking please, just let me get through this one event without any pain. Just one throw, that's all I'm asking for – just one throw. I wanted to use every nerve, sinew and fibre to draw on to make myself strong; I wanted to pull on all the strength in my body to make myself throw well. Just one throw.

I was one of the last to take my first throw, so I sat there for a while, looking at the crowd, at my mum and my team, thinking how sad and miserable this whole situation was.

I felt tears welling up in my eyes as I looked around the stadium.

They just don't know, I thought. They just don't know, and they're so full of elation while I'm so full of fear.

Then I was called. I took off my kit and picked up the javelin – as I did so, the crowd went berserk. As I walked towards the runway the announcer called my name and said I was in second place. I drew long, deep breaths. I was now standing on the runway, looking at the grass before me. I tried to focus solely on my technique, nothing else. All I could feel was the javelin and my arm – all I could think about was what they had to do.

I took another deep breath and ran, trying to put all thoughts of failure from my mind as I launched the javelin. It flew up into the dark sky and I felt surprised as I watched it – it seemed to be a good throw.

As I walked back I looked at Charles, who was nodding encouragingly. I had thrown 48.49m – much better than I ever thought I would achieve. He was putting his bag on his shoulder, getting ready to get back to our medical room. But I decided to carry on. He shrugged as if to say OK – if I was sure. But I knew I needed to improve on that first throw, and I had a feeling I could. I needed as many points as I could get.

On my second throw I didn't even think about any damage I might be doing to myself. All I was thinking about was points, and getting a good distance from the others. This time I threw 50.19m, but I was still convinced that I could throw a bigger one. My competitors were watching, and they looked from one to another – they were waiting to see if I had anything left. My second-round throw had moved me in to first position.

My third and final throw was technically very sound. I expected it to be further than my second, but was surprised to discover that it wasn't. Because Sazanovich hadn't thrown as far as me, and because there had only been a few points between us as we went into the javelin event, I knew I was now in first place. But I wasn't out of the woods yet. I knew that when I got back to the medical room I was going to have to decide whether to have the injection – something I was not looking forward to.

If I was going to have the injection I had to get back to the medical room as soon as possible, as there was only a small window of opportunity in which it could be administered to ensure its full effectiveness. But when I ran to the edge of the stadium and tried to leave, the official wouldn't let me. The competition was still going on, and I was told that I had to wait until it was over so all the heptathletes could leave together. Despite my pleas I had to stay. Charles was fuming. Kevin and Peter had already left to get everything ready back in the medical room. It was incredibly stressful.

Eventually I managed to get through to the warm-up track where everyone was poised, ready to inject me. Peter looked at my foot and moved it around. Having loosened the tape, it seemed to be OK. There was a possibility that it was a stress fracture – we weren't sure, but there was definitely severe bruising. Peter reminded me that, although this was a very difficult situation, I was a fighter – and very close to winning my Olympic gold medal. He also reminded me that the 800m was only two laps.

I thought long and hard about it. Other athletes had had these injections, but it was not something I had envisaged for myself. Peter, Charles and Kevin were worried that the local anaesthetic to numb the pain might make me feel nauseous, and I wasn't too happy because I didn't know what the effect on my performance would be if I ran on a numb foot. Usually one has to consider all the adverse effects that an injection could have on one's performance, but at this stage there really wasn't time to make such a decision. I had complete faith in my team, though, and was willing to take their advice. Finally, having gone through all the pros and cons, we decided I could probably manage without it.

So they loosened the strapping and adjusted it from the top of my calf to the bottom. I was going to have to run the 800m and cope with the pain. We had just under an hour and a half until the race began, and I had to start thinking about my warm-up.

It was at this point that I asked where my 800m spikes were. Neither Kevin, Charles nor Rick knew where they were. I knew I hadn't left them at the javelin area because I hadn't taken any bags with me. The guys had been the last ones with my bags when we were all at the warm-up track together before the throws. This was crazy – wasn't this torture ever going to end? How could I possibly run without my spikes? The bag also contained my orthotics, the in-shoe correctors specially shaped for my foot.

Suddenly the second mad frenzy of the day took place. Everyone was rushing around – it was as if someone had shaken a beehive. What a series of events. What was I going to do now? For the moment I had got rid of my pain, but now I was without my spikes. It became very tense, and nerves were frayed. Kevin went off to the warm-up track to see if they were there, while Charles went off in the other direction to check the call rooms and other places they might be.

Peter told me to lie on the bed, close my eyes and try and get some sleep. As he left he turned off the light. I lay there thinking about everything. This couldn't be real. This was not what an Olympic experience was meant to be about. It wasn't right. I was past tears and just felt exhausted. I felt that this was another sign, that someone was saying, 'Denise, you really should have been out of this competition a long time ago – you should not be here.' I tried to relax and listen to some music, and somehow I managed to drift off to sleep for fifteen or twenty minutes.

Rick then came in and gently woke me up. Charles sat down with me and went through my race plan and talked to me about my competitors. It seemed that the gold was out of Sazanovich's grasp, and Prokhorova was therefore my closest rival. However, there was a ten-second differential between us, so as long as I kept within that, everything would be OK. As I was digesting this news, Kevin burst into the room, breathing heavily and dripping with a mixture of rain and sweat from his run over to the warm-up track – but he had my spikes. I was so thankful, and the heavy atmosphere dispelled almost immediately. I was back on track again.

I put on my spikes and headed outside for some easy jogging, where Peter came out to check that everything was all right. I seemed to be fine despite the problems we had experienced, and the relief was overwhelming. None the less I was still worried that my foot would collapse at any moment during the race because it was so unpredictable. I didn't trust it at all.

As I sat on the buggy back to the arena I was subdued and pensive – but this was normal as I don't like the 800m at the best of times. Now I felt, more than ever, that I was completely in the hands of fate and destiny. I just wanted this race to be over. But I was going to do my best.

We walked out into the brightly lit arena to a huge round of applause. Mentally I was very tired, but I was going to run. I was going to run to the best of my ability, and I was going to finish this race . . .

* * *

It is very hard to describe the feelings that rushed through my body after my Olympic victory. It felt as if life had somehow speeded up, was more vibrant and colourful than before. The clapping was so loud I could barely catch my breath with excitement, and everything seemed bigger and more real than ever before. But at the same time, I was left feeling somehow lost and slightly confused. For a few moments I felt as if I were moving in slow motion while everything else was rushing past. It was quite a bewildering experience.

I suppose it was because of the size of the achievement. I am not saying that what I did was 'important' in any real sense – I know I didn't save lives or end wars – but for me it was a huge personal triumph. It was the realisation of a lifetime's ambitions, something that takes a quite considerable amount of getting used to.

As I stood there in my moment of glory, a small person in a huge stadium, watched by millions of people there and on the television, I remembered how, as a child, I had hoped that one day, maybe, I would make it to the Olympic Games and be a success. I had always thought Olympic champions were special, superhuman beings, not simple, ordinary people like everyone else. But now, suddenly, it was me. I was the champion.

I wanted to do a lap of honour, of course, but after that I wanted to see Mum and my friends, knowing that would allow me some of the space I needed. But instead I was immediately led on a whirlwind tour of publicity and post-event administration and analysis.

Almost as soon as I had finished competing, the BBC took me to the trackside where they had arranged a link-up with Mary Peters. It was a very special surprise, and I was thrilled to be able to talk to her. As I watched her on the monitor I was overcome by a sea of emotions. I had just been through a day that had gone from utter despair and crashing disappointment to hope and ultimate triumph; I had experienced dreadful physical pain and was also extremely tired after two days of competing at the highest level. As I heard Mary's soft voice and all the kind things she said to me, I felt like crying. She told the world how she had watched me in 1994, and had kept an eye on my progress ever since. I could tell that she was genuinely pleased for me and thrilled at what I had done.

After I had spoken with Mary I was escorted by the British doctor to doping control where I signed in and they took my accreditation details. We then began to make our way to the press conference, but were intercepted and told that we had to go to the arena for the medal ceremony. This was a shock: it was very late, spitting with rain and people had started to leave; when events finish this late the medal ceremony usually takes place the next day. I was told I could refuse, but apparently all the TV people wanted it, and when I found out that the other two girls – Sazanovich and Prokhorova – were down there, it was clear I didn't have much choice. But it was a wonderful experience and as I stood on the podium as the national anthem played and the Union Jack was raised, my feelings of elation and joy were overwhelming.

At about 11pm, following the medal ceremony, we headed downstairs to the press conference. The press were delighted, and I was amazed by how much they already knew. They asked me how I felt when my shoes went missing. I thought only three or so people had known about that – how on earth had they found out? But I just smiled and told them about the nightmare that had gone on, and how thrilled and delighted I was that I had won.

After the press conference I went back to doping control where I gave my urine sample and completed all the necessary paperwork. Then, finally, my time was my own – or so I thought until I was told that the BBC wanted to do a live interview with me in the studio. So, at about 1am, I said goodbye to Mum and Jonathan, who headed off to their hotels in town, then Jonathan Marks, Charles and I got into a van and headed over to the media centre. Although I was incredibly tired, a feeling of peace had started to settle over me. After the interview, which took about an hour, the three of us spent ages trying to find some transport to get Charles and I back to the athletes' village, and Jonathan back to his hotel. Apparently there was a car waiting for us, but we couldn't find it, so we waited for what seemed like ages before we found a bus that would get us home. I was on my last legs and just wanted to go to bed.

On the journey back I woke up a bit, and suddenly felt starving – I had an urge to eat anything that was greasy. So Charles and I went straight to the dining area as soon as we got into the village. I wanted a McDonald's – Big Mac, fries, apple pie, the works. And I must admit every bite was heaven. It was great to eat whatever I wanted, and to have it covered in cheese, mayonnaise, thousand island dressing and salt. As Charles and I sat there we chatted away, laughing and joking – but also, finally we had the chance to take stock of all the dramas that had taken place. I felt revived; life was good. Surprisingly for the hour, there were quite a few people milling around, and a couple of them came over and congratulated me. Then I saw Robert Weir – one of our discus throwers, a fellow Birchfield club member and British team mate. He came over and gave me a big hug. He asked me how I felt, and I found that I didn't really know how to answer him. I was tired, but awake, and felt as though I was in a strange limbo wherein I didn't really know what to do with myself. I suddenly started to wonder what was going to happen now – what would tomorrow bring? Robert grinned at my confusion and told me just to enjoy it and make as much money as I could while it lasted!

An hour or so later I was exhausted again, so we all got up to leave. I gave Charles a hug and he went off to the Dutch section, while Robert and I headed off to the British section. Robert walked me back to my apartment and we said goodnight.

It was now about 3.30am and the apartment was quiet and dark – all the girls had gone to bed. As I crept in and switched on the downstairs light I was thrilled to see that they had decorated the place with banners and posters congratulating me and saying some really lovely things. I smiled to myself as I crept up the stairs – what a lovely welcome to come back to. I tiptoed into my room and closed the door quietly, then threw my medal and all my stuff on to the spare bed and collapsed into mine, completely worn out. Although I was exhausted, I lay there for a while in a state of exhilaration, delirious and high on all the adrenaline that was still pumping through my body. But finally, I drifted off to sleep.

The next morning I was woken up by Marcia and Donna who flung open my bedroom door and came bounding in.

'Denise, Denise, well done! We couldn't stay up any longer because it was so late, you took ages to come back.' They gave me big hugs and were thrilled. 'So where is it? Where's the medal?'

I pointed over in the general direction of the other bed, which was covered in junk – my medal wasn't immediately apparent, and I wasn't sure exactly where it was. 'It's over there somewhere. I was so exhausted when I came in last night—'

'What? You don't know where your gold medal is?'

I clambered out of bed and started rummaging around wearily for my medal. I couldn't find it.

'Oh my God!' said Marcia. 'She's won an Olympic gold medal and doesn't even know where she's put it. Denise!'

Eventually we found it under my clothes and bags. They admired it and told me how thrilled they were, and throughout the course of the morning the other girls came in to offer their congratulations and to look at it. It was great fun and they were all so proud.

When I walked into the dining room for breakfast I felt different – elevated. It was a strange feeling, but very special. It is at this stage that many athletes report feeling a come-down after all the exertions, as the process of the body coming back to earth can leave one feeling slightly hollow and empty inside. If you think about it, it's quite natural. You spend all your adult life with one goal in mind – it preoccupies you, dominates your thoughts and monopolises almost every waking hour. Then suddenly it's gone, you've achieved it. You feel a bit lost, because as well as being the goal that you were striving towards, your Olympic dream has also defined the parameters by which you have led your life. Now it's over – what happens next?

Thankfully I didn't get a chance to experience this, as the few days between the end of the heptathlon and the closing ceremony were packed full with a seemingly endless run of media interviews. By the end of the week I was worn out. I hadn't had much of a chance to do any real celebrating, and I had found it very difficult to sleep in the nights that followed my victory. I think I was still on a high after all the excitement. I was also really looking forward to getting back to Britain and the opportunity to relax and spend some time with my family and friends.

The closing ceremony was a fantastic event, but I very nearly missed the bus to get there! I had been doing an interview with the *Telegraph* when I realised how late it had got, so I limped back to our apartment, hoping that the girls hadn't gone without me – and thankfully they had waited. I didn't have time to do my hair, so I shoved my cap on, threw on some make-up and headed out to the bus.

The event was so colourful. We were all dressed in our red track-suit tops and blue bottoms, so we made our own contribution to the riot of colour. It was so exciting. I couldn't believe we were here – the weeks had flown by so quickly. I had never really envisaged this point, standing here at the closing ceremony of the Olympics, proudly wearing my gold medal. I had come here, struggled against countless problems along the way, but I had realised my dream. It was wonderful and I felt totally elated.

After the speeches all the athletes went on to the inner field, where the fun started and we really began to celebrate. The British team were really upbeat because we had done so well. Audley Harrison had won us another gold medal that day, and our two pentathletes, Kate Allenby and Stephanie Cook had won bronze and gold medals respectively. The atmosphere was great and there was a real buzz at how successful the competition had been for Britain.

Fireworks were going off everywhere as we ran round trying to see everyone we knew, catching up and taking photos of each other. The rowers had found a big sheet from somewhere and held it between them as a trampoline, launching the gymnasts up into the air. It was a wonderful impromptu display – but I was convinced someone was going to get hurt, especially when a lot of the guys started clamouring for their turn!

Finally it was time to mark the end of Sydney 2000 and extinguish the Olympic flame. It was a sad moment in a way, but suitably dramatic. One moment it was burning, the next, out of nowhere, a plane flew over the stadium with a thunderous roar and the flame was put out. It made the hairs on the back of my neck stand on end and I felt goosebumps all over my body. It was a truly spectacular finale to what had been the best time of my life.

We left the stadium on a total high. A lot of the athletes went on to big parties, but I was exhausted so headed back to the athletes' village for drinks in someone's apartment. We drank and danced for a while, enjoying the last moments of our Sydney experience, then I headed off to bed, worn out but deeply happy, thrilled beyond words with my Olympic adventure.

Chapter Nineteen
Life After Sydney

When I got back to Britain after the games my foot was still in a lot of pain. I was mentally and physically tired from the week's activity, and now I needed regular physiotherapy and lots of rest. Before going out to Sydney we had decided that after the games I would take four months off from sport and have a total break, giving myself some time to relax, recover, and spend time with family and friends whom I don't usually get time to see. Charles had reluctantly agreed, but now this decision seemed to be the right one because of the possibility of surgery, for which I would definitely need time off.

I was stunned by the amount of attention I got on my return, from both the media and the general public. There were so many different types of people who would stop and talk to me in the street, ranging from little old ladies who had stayed up to listen to the event on the radio, to young guys who would tell me how they came home from a night out and watched it half drunk! They had all celebrated my victory and felt proud when they saw how I'd had to battle against injury.

One of the things I hope will happen as a result of my success is that more children, having seen me on the TV, will want to take up athletics and give the heptathlon or the decathlon a try. I want more kids to be aware that you don't have to be simply a runner, a jumper or a thrower – you can do them all in one event. I think that doing combined events in schools is a fantastic way for kids to learn a variety of disciplines and skills, thus identifying exactly where their strengths and weaknesses lie. I hope that I have done my part for the promotion of the event, bringing home medals and showing that persistence can bring results. I believe that if the media can do its part in trying to raise the profile of all aspects of track and field events, we can keep athletics interesting and fashionable for kids to participate in and follow.

I was certainly very much in demand from the media when I got back to Britain. It seemed as if everyone wanted me on their shows, from Trevor McDonald to *SM:tv*. The first major television appearance I made on my return was on Frank Skinner's show. I don't like a lot of comedians but I do think he's funny and I was very excited about being a guest. I love his Midlands accent, and I was curious to see what he was like in real life. When I arrived at the studio the rehearsal for the final sketch was under way. Frank was there, as was Jamie Oliver who was also appearing on the show. Frank greeted me as I walked in and explained to me what they were doing. It was a very relaxed and friendly atmosphere, and I immediately felt at ease. The final sketch for the show was to be a rendition of Spandau Ballet's number-one hit, 'Gold'. Frank was singing the main part of the song, Jamie was accompanying him on the drums, and I was to sing the word 'gold' at the beginning of each chorus. Singing is not one of my specialities, so I was relieved not to have much to do!

When the shooting began Jamie was on first. When he and Frank moved on to the subject of Jamie's younger days, Frank brought up the subject of a wardrobe door that Jamie would scribble on when he was an adolescent – diagrams on the sort of subjects boys begin to find fascinating at that age. The next thing we knew the actual door was brought on to the set! Jamie was mortified and sat there with his head in his hands, saying how his mother was going to kill him. And I was horrified – what did Frank have lined up for me?

Not long after that, Jamie came off stage, muttering something about needing a beer. It was my turn.

I went on stage feeling some trepidation, but Frank was actually very sweet to me. We did a scene involving my medal, which was funny: Frank was wearing a replica, which the audience didn't know was fake. I had to do a sort of role play, telling him how precious it was to me. He went to touch it and 'accidentally' broke it, to a huge gasp of horror from the audience. But then we took out the real one and I got a big round of applause from everyone. We talked about a lot of things: my childhood, the Midlands, the heptathlon, Sydney, and my infamous abs. That was when Frank lifted up his shirt to display the six-pack he had drawn across his belly, which had everybody laughing. We then did the closing scene – the Spandau Ballet song – which was great fun, although I did get teased for weeks after it, by lots of people telling me not to give up my day job!

I also got an invitation to go on *Parkinson*. When I found out about that I reacted with a mixture of excitement and terror. Michael Parkinson is a legendary chat show host who is watched by millions; I was amazed that that he was interested in me and thought I had something worthwhile to say. I was also fascinated to discover that the other guests on the show that night would be Tracey Ullman and Dolly Parton. Mum was beside herself, as she's a great Parkinson fan and always listens to him on the radio as well as watching his shows. I was accompanied to the studio by Mum, my boyfriend Jonathan, my friend Ashley, and Emily from my management company, MTC. We were all very excited, and even more so when we were told that Michael wanted to say hello before the show started. We met him in the green room; he has an incredible presence, but he was very friendly and warm and managed to make me feel a bit more relaxed. However, I was still terrified, especially as I was still trying to work out exactly where I fitted into this star line-up. The other two women had such established careers, had been round the world and met so many people, I felt intimidated just by the thought of them.

I met Dolly and Tracey backstage, before the show started. My first impression of Dolly was how attractive she was. She was a tiny packet but had so much presence – enhanced by her blonde, big hair, her big red lips, a short, tight red dress and red high heels. She looked perfect, flawless. She was very friendly and chatty, interested and interesting, and she instantly put me at my ease.

After a few minutes Tracey came through, and the contrast between the two women was immediately apparent. Tracey was wearing a smart black fitted 'power' suit, and walked and spoke with determination and control. She was the first on, and we watched her from backstage on the monitor. She dominated the set and was so funny. Everyone was listening to her intently and she seemed to talk for ages. How was I going to do the same? What did I have to talk about?

Then it was my turn, and I took a deep breath before walking out into the studio. The interview seemed to go very well, and I relaxed quite quickly. Michael is a big sports fan and it is always nice to talk to someone who is aware of sporting issues and interested in your world. However, I spent the duration of the interview wondering how it was going. Was I being interesting enough? How much time did I have left?

But it wasn't long before Dolly came on. She started with a song, and then came and sat on the set. She was very funny, and I really admire her for her ability to laugh at herself and her image. But it was also very obvious that inside was a very sweet and caring woman – I was very struck by her. She finished the show by singing 'I Will Always Love You', the song that was made famous by Whitney Houston. She told the audience she didn't have a voice like Whitney's, but said that she would do it her way, and she certainly did. It was very moving, and brought tears to my eyes.

After the show Dolly rushed off, but the rest of us went back to the green room. I had a great time chatting to Michael Parkinson's mother, while Mum chatted to Michael. Mrs Parkinson is a very lovely lady who has gone to every one of her son's shows since he started on TV – I was very impressed!

Some time later I sat down to watch a tape of the show at home. I tend not to like seeing myself on TV and am always very critical of what I say and do, so I went behind the sofa and watched it through my fingers – but eventually I did manage to relax into it, and came out of hiding. It wasn't so bad after all; in fact I thought it went quite well, and that the all-woman line-up was incredibly effective. On top of that, Mum had fulfilled one of her dreams and met Michael Parkinson!

But one of the invitations that caused me the most excitement was for me to attend the Brits music awards. Not only that, but I was to present an award, the first of the evening; for the best British music video. I took Emily from MTC with me, and Michelle Griffith, one of my best friends. I knew she would be in her element as she rubbed shoulders with the stars and listened to her favourite artists and music. I had decided to wear a long, red fitted dress that I had borrowed from Ghost. Because I was up first, I wanted to make doubly sure that I looked just right.

When we arrived we were taken to wait in the VIP lounge. We were so in awe of everything that was going on, seeing starts roll in and out as if being there was the most natural thing in the world. It was a real evening of people-watching, and was fantastic. At one point, Eminem and his bodyguards were sitting behind us, Robbie Williams and Geri Halliwell were to one side of us, and Westlife were to the other. I was amazed by just how tiny Geri was, and Michelle, who was forward enough to ask her, spent a while chatting with her about all the training and the running she was doing. The Westlife boys were lovely – Cat Deeley was also chatting to them. I had met her before on the Saturday morning kids' TV show *SM:tv*, so it was nice to see her again and say hello. I also met Chris Martin, the lead singer of Coldplay. He came over and introduced himself (although I knew who he was) and told me he thought I was fantastic in the

Olympics and that I'd put on a great performance. I was delighted and told him how great I thought his group was, and he replied by simply saying that there was only one champion there that night. I was touched.

Then the show started. I was presenting the award with Audley Harrison, and as we stood backstage waiting to go on I was rather nervous. Then we were announced, and as we walked down the stairs I was very aware of where I was putting my feet – I had very high heels on and had visions of taking a tumble down the steps – but I kept smiling. The atmosphere out there was fantastic, and although I couldn't see much of the auditorium I could definitely feel it – the audience were revved up and eager for the evening to get under way. Once we had made our entrance I felt more relaxed and we got a great reception as we came on. Ant and Dec were hosting the show, and the fact that I had met them before on their own show definitely put me more at ease. Also, Audley was there, which certainly took the pressure off a bit. We chatted easily and even made a few jokes – it was a lot of fun. The award went to Fatboy Slim for 'Praise You', and as he, Audley and I walked off stage together we chatted about his wife Zoë Ball and the new baby.

After the show I met Samuel L Jackson. We chatted easily, but all the while a little voice inside my head kept reminding me that I was there having a conversation with *the* Samuel L Jackson, who had starred in some of my favourite movies of the previous few years, such as *Shaft*, *Pulp Fiction* and *The Negotiator*. I was thrilled; it really was the highlight of my night.

The night before the Brits I had been lucky enough to attend the BAFTAs. The Brits and the BAFTAs were equally exciting, but very different in atmosphere. When I'd opened the invitation to the BAFTAs I'd been truly amazed – surely it couldn't mean *the* BAFTAs? For that event I'd worn a golden gown by Maria Grachvogel, and felt like a star. It was a very glitzy night full of evening gowns, beautiful accessories, and photographers lining the entry into the Odeon, Leicester Square, where the event took place.

All I could see as I walked down the red carpet – which must have been about thirty metres long – was the constant flash of camera lights. I felt very exposed – this was certainly no place for a wallflower! Hugh Grant was behind me and I was very aware of all the fans calling his name. For a moment I even stopped and contemplated asking him for his autograph or saying hello! But instead, I carried on walking. There were so many other big stars there that night and I had a wonderful time, but I was particularly taken with Annette Bening, with whom I was lucky enough to have a fascinating conversation.

I was thrilled to have had the opportunity to attend these wonderful events, as they gave me a real insight into a big, glamorous world for which there is not usually much room in the life of an athlete.

But it hasn't all been fun and games on talk shows and at award ceremonies and parties – my sporting success has also allowed me to promote and get involved with some causes very close to my heart. For some time I have been working with the charity Breakthrough Breast Cancer, who established the first dedicated breast cancer research centre in partnership with the Institute of Cancer Research, and are committed to fighting breast cancer through research and awareness. The promotion of a wider understanding and awareness of breast cancer is where I can help, as I can use my 'fame' to help make Breakthrough's work and campaigns more high-profile, thus attracting more media attention – which in turn means they have a better chance of making an impact on the public and ensuring that the issue remains a top priority for the government. One such project I have been involved in this year is the 'Kiss Goodbye to Breast Cancer' campaign, which has also attracted the support of other faces in the media such as Melinda Messenger, Gloria Hunniford, Helen Baxendale and Claire Richardson from Steps. The campaign encourages people to give their lipstick prints, hoping to highlight the level of public commitment to rid society of breast cancer through funding for further research.

Breast cancer is the single biggest health concern for women today, and almost everybody knows someone who has suffered from it. It is therefore vital that if Breakthrough is to achieve its ultimate goal to free the future from the fear of this disease, its fundraising and constant promotion need to be as successful as possible – and I will do my best to help them achieve this.

Being able to work with and do something for children is also something that is incredibly important to me, as children need all the help and support they can get. Of all the things I have done since Sydney, the most rewarding was spending a few hours with a group of kids with learning disabilities at London Zoo, to promote Transco's Safety Charity Challenge. Through encouraging employees to spot and remove potential hazards in the workplace, Transco makes payments to Mencap to support its nationwide network of community support teams and family advisors, who provide vital everyday help and advice to people with learning difficulties and their families. It's such a brilliant idea, and raises money for a truly excellent cause. The day itself was so incredibly special, and having contact with the children was especially moving. I firmly believe that everyone needs a chance in life, and if I can play a small role in helping a child with any sort of problem to get a moment of happiness, then I really can say I feel worthwhile and purposeful, that I have achieved something special.

When I got back from Sydney, all the papers were saying how my gold medal was my entrance to the VIP club, that a vast number of companies would be beating down my door to get me to work with them, and that I would easily be able to achieve seven-figure sums every year from sponsorship and advertising deals. Well, that wasn't the case at all – which was fine – but what really did surprise me was the level of the offer I got from Adidas to continue working with them. I had expected that my value to them would have risen after what I achieved in the Olympics, but that didn't appear to be the case. Jonathan Marks, my commercial agent, therefore made some enquiries and got a more encompassing deal with Nike.

One of the biggest pulling factors was that Nike were on the verge of launching projects that struck a chord with me, such as the Girls in Sport campaign.

It is so important that children take part in sports, and over the years I have been increasingly concerned about their levels of participation, particularly among girls. Girls have always had a problem with the teaching of sports in schools. The main stumbling blocks are that they don't like some of the sports they are made to do, that they don't enjoy the way they are taught, and the fact that some of the clothes they are made to wear are not at all flattering – and this is a big problem, especially when girls are maturing at different rates and are very aware of the changes that are taking place in their bodies. All this leads to girls having a bad experience of sport, and tends to mean that they opt out very early on – much more so than boys. Additionally, boys tend to have many more sporting role models than girls, particularly as the media tend to be dominated by coverage of male-oriented sports such as football, rugby, cricket, motor racing and golf. There are not nearly as many sporting heroines for girls, and the magazines aimed at young women tend to focus on boys, sex and make-up. But there should always be room for sport, and if girls think smartly they will realise that the art to looking good is through health awareness and exercise. It is a very good idea for a girl to find an interest in sports in order to keep fit. I'm not saying that everyone should be the next budding Olympian like me – but how do you think I got my six-pack, girls?

That is one of the great things about Nike's commitment to women in sport, and I'm very pleased to be with a brand that takes this issue so seriously. The Girls in Sport initiative has been set up in conjunction with Youth in Sport, and represents everything I believe in concerning schoolgirls and sport. It enables girls across the country to actively take part in, or at least have an opinion on how they feel they would like sport to be conducted in their schools. This ranges from exactly what they want to do, why and how they want to do it, through to what clothes they would like to wear. It gives them an invaluable voice in controlling how their sport is organised, and I think it is a brilliant idea.

I recently visited a school in east London which is participating in the programme, where I was very encouraged to see just how many girls took their sport seriously – and how many of them had aspirations to take it all the way and become international sports stars. While I was there, I got involved in one of their indoor PE lessons, which really brought back memories, and took part in a question-and-answer session during which I got to ask the girls questions too.

I very much hope that my involvement in such initiatives, and my own success in sport has shown young people that you can get to the top and have a lot of fun in the process. I also hope that I have shown that sport can be attractive and lead to a wide range of opportunities – if you are prepared to put in the time and the effort.

At the end of 2000 and the beginning of 2001 I won a lot of awards for my sporting achievements at Sydney, which was a great honour. I won the UK Athletics Sportswoman of the Year, the Sportswriters' Association Sportswoman of the Year, the Sunday Times Sportswoman of the Year, the British Athletics Writers' Sportswoman of the Year, the Leah Wright trophy at Birchfield Harriers for overall performance of the year, and I was runner-up again in the BBC Sports Personality of the Year – this time to Steve Redgrave, who I can say wholeheartedly deserved the honour. I also attended two civic receptions, one in Wolverhampton and the other in Birmingham. At the Wolverhampton occasion I was made a freeman of the city, which as well as being a great honour means that I can apparently drive a herd of cattle through the town at midnight! Although I'm not sure just how useful that is going to be, what I am hoping is that I'll get free parking.

But it wasn't all fun. One rather sad occurrence was the way in which I was linked to a court case involving Chris Cotter. Dealing with the media is something that a lot of people don't get trained for particularly well, and this can sometimes lead to problems. Luckily, on the whole, I think I have managed to deal with the press reasonably well – and sometimes not taking them too seriously when they do print negative articles is important. But on one occasion I did have my tolerance pushed to its utmost: in the case of Ashia Hansen and Chris Cotter.

Chris Cotter is now serving a prison sentence after being convicted of staging a race attack on himself in order to win back the affections of fellow athlete Ashia Hansen. Apparently, something was said in court about how he dumped another leading athlete to go out with Hansen when they first met in 1994 or 1995. The immediate conclusion drawn by a lot of the press was that I must be the athlete in question, as previous news articles have referred to a rivalry between us. I was furious to read that the papers had dragged my name into a relationship that I had nothing to do with.

But the press often try to draw on any indication of a rivalry, however slight. As a child I saw them play on the relationship between Tessa Sanderson and Fatima Whitbread in the javelin. However, from my point of view, the world of athletics is a big enough arena for everyone to have his or her share of the limelight when they deserve it, so it should not be a problem. In the end, I just let the story go, and it was soon dropped when journalists found that it could not be corroborated. I had more important things to do, such as concentrate on my athletics.

I had had some fun and much-needed rest during my time off, but it was also a time for thinking and planning. I needed the four months to recover from the injury I had sustained to my left foot while in Sydney, and as that and my other injuries began to clear up and the new year dawned, I was beginning to miss training and my athletic way of life. Although it seemed punishing, I wanted to achieve more. A gold medal in the World Championships had always eluded me, and I knew that there was another Olympic gold in me – but could I keep it going for another four years? I therefore sat and thought carefully about the future. I had received a lot of offers – I could go into modelling, try to train as a TV presenter, or pursue some of my other interests such as promoting girls' sport. But no matter how appealing all these options were, my drive to carry on as an athlete was greater. I wanted a World Championship gold, I wanted to compete in the Commonwealth Games in Manchester in 2002, and I really fancied having a crack at another Olympic Games.

I felt, more than anything else, that my main desire was to beat the best at their best. I found myself wondering how I would have fared in Sydney if all the competitors had been at their peak. What then? Which of us was really the greatest heptathlete?

There was only one way to find out. So, in the second week of January, I put on my athletics gear and prepared myself for the next chapter.

CHAPTER TWENTY
THE REAL WORLD

Training had to begin slowly in the New Year because I had not undergone any physical activity since the moment I crossed the 800m line in Sydney, four months earlier. All my energy, every waking moment of the previous four years had been about the Sydney Olympics. I had given everything I had, and really needed that break from training to have a rest, to spend time with the people close to me. Even if I had wanted to start training earlier, I would have had to wait for the bone bruising to settle down in my foot. Only then could we establish if it was a stress fracture and whether or not it would need surgery. But by the time I got back on the track in the second week of January, I knew this was where I wanted to be.

The period of time I had before the World Championships in Edmonton was tight. The heptathlon was scheduled to take place over the first weekend of the competition, on the third and fourth of August. As a result, not only was I short of training time, but there were just a few competitions in which I would be able to compete before the championships began.

Charles and I had decided I would enter three heptathlons over the season, starting with Gotzis at the end of May, followed by the World Championships in August, and finishing with the Goodwill Games in Brisbane in September. I was slightly nervous at the thought of this, as my usual number of heptathlons per year was two, a number that had dropped to one in 1999 and 2000 as a result of my injuries. But despite this apprehension I was optimistic: I wanted to throw myself back into my training, prepare myself, as much as possible, and see what I could do. In contrast, Charles was anxious from the start. He was uncomfortable about the amount of time I had taken off and was aware that Gotzis would be tight.

February and March rolled by incredibly quickly. I was doing a lot of general fitness in my early sessions, getting my body back into reasonable shape before I could start the more specific training relevant to heptathlon preparation. Then, before I knew it, it was April and time to go to Los Angeles for my month of warm-weather training. It had come by so quickly that I didn't feel ready to go, but I looked at it positively, hoping it might be exactly what I needed – that four weeks of focused training in the warmth would raise my training to a higher level.

Warm-weather training is a key element for an athlete and LA was no different. Unfortunately, by the end of my month out there it was clear that it had not been successful. I was very disappointed, and could see that Charles was really beginning to worry about my form. Most athletes rely on that concentrated time away to give them the core information they need in relation to the standard they are at and how well their training is going. But the results of my time in LA gave us little constructive information to go on. I was a little concerned and had to face the fact that I wasn't as fit as I would have liked to be at that stage. However, I was able to recognise that I had taken quite a lot of time off, and that I shouldn't compare the results I was attaining with those from the training camps of previous years. I therefore remained optimistic, knowing that a simple re-evaluation of my programme was what was needed. We had done this whenever I had injured myself in the past – particularly in the May of both 1998 and 1999, when our plans for the whole season had been turned upside-down – so I didn't panic.

It was clear I was not going to be ready for Gotzis – which meant I would enter the World Championships without having competed in a heptathlon since Sydney – but I felt quite calm about this; the key was to ensure that I was mentally prepared. I therefore increased my focus and, as the next few weeks went by, my level of training picked up.

It was only when Charles and I sat down to work out my competition programme for the approach to Edmonton that I realised just how little time there was left. I had got back from warm-weather training during the first week of May, and my first competition had been for my club at the beginning of June. That had gone well, and I had really enjoyed the feeling of being back in the competitive field once again. But now I had only eight weeks before the World Championships and I was worried about how few competitions I had left to compete in.

Although training was better, this was the first time I started to feel concerned. In an ideal season I would do one full heptathlon six to eight weeks prior to the main event and back this up with a number of quality competitions in individual events, as this would really sharpen me up. It is necessary to enter as many competitions as you can before a major championship, because it takes a while for an athlete to reach their peak in a season. In the past we had compensated for any lack of competition with very high-quality training levels, but this time I didn't appear to have either opportunity. Of the competitions I did finally enter, some were rained off, most were conducted in the cold – so the optimum conditions just weren't there – and in the competitions where I was entering more than one discipline, the timetabling was such that I didn't get to focus on any one event completely. One example of this was at Luzern in Switzerland in mid-June, where I competed in the long jump and hurdles in torrential rain. The two events took place within about five minutes of each other, so I was forced to run from one to the other, getting soaking wet – and consequently getting very little out of either of them.

I hadn't managed to enter a high jump competition by this stage because I had developed patella tendonitis, an inflammation in the knee tendon which I had first suffered in 2000. Eight weeks before Edmonton, at the start of June, it came back with a vengeance, preventing me from doing much jumping. This was closely followed by a hamstring problem which was neural – almost like sciatica. I was getting treatment for this and had expected it to clear up quickly, but it was persistent, inhibiting my range of movement and my ability to practise the events that required a certain amount of power. As a result of these two problems my high jumping standard was lower than I could ever remember it. It seemed as if everything was going against me.

However, over the first two days of July I entered the hurdles and long jump competitions at the Norwich Union Challenge in Glasgow. I finished with a jump of around 6.53m, and ran a good hurdles time of 13.29 seconds – about a tenth of a second outside my personal best. Although I didn't win, I was very happy with the result.

Heptathletes rarely win competitions when they are competing against single-event athletes, so I was quite surprised when I saw that the papers were quite negative the following day. I think this was when the media began discussing the degree of my motivation, and the 'real' reasons why I got back into training late. I hadn't given a lot of interviews since the beginning of the year because I didn't feel that I had anything to say. Other athletes were competing on a regular basis, and some doing very well, so I wanted to keep in the background and prepare myself quietly. This had clearly caused a lot of speculation, as people wanted to find out if I was still interested in competing after winning at the Olympics. After all, I had won the biggest prize you can as an athlete, so I wasn't surprised that there were some questions. But I have given my life to this sport, and since starting in January 2001 I had been on the track, day in, day out, just as before. Thus I had no reason to query my own motivation at that point – and I answered accordingly when faced with searching questions from the press.

Unfortunately, it was not long after this that everything began to get yet more difficult. A week later, at the Dutch Nationals, I suddenly felt as if a firecracker had gone off in my head. Something inside me clicked, and I realised that I wasn't in very good shape – or at least not attaining my usual standard this close to a major championship. I just couldn't high jump properly, which was a huge concern, especially as I couldn't find a real explanation for it. I was taking anti-inflammatory pills for my knee, and it was well strapped up. This situation gave me good days and bad days, but I had been in pain before and had still managed to get the best out of myself. I had jumped in 1998 and 1999 while my ankles were in excruciating pain – every time I planted my foot it was as if a bolt of lightning was shooting through my body – but I had got through it. So I couldn't understand why I couldn't pull it together now.

It was just this one event that was causing me problems. I don't think it was a psychological block, but I guess there comes a point at which, despite constantly working on something and trying your best, it still doesn't work out, and you do have to ask yourself if there is something else behind the problem. So maybe it did become psychological, as it certainly wasn't physical.

In the week before the AAA Championships in Birmingham on the weekend of 14 and 15 July, my concerns deepened. I had continued to hope for the miracle session during which everything would come right, hoping that I would somehow salvage everything. But all my high jump sessions were a disaster, each one mentally setting me back by a few paces.

I was experiencing feelings I had never known before. I was trying to beat the demons in my mind, the ones that tell you you're not good enough, the ones that focus on the negatives rather than the positives. My performance in Birmingham reflected these emotions, where my performance in the three events I had entered – the javelin, 200m and high jump – were all below par. I couldn't believe it.

I was due to fly to Edmonton on the Friday after the AAA Championships, to give myself two weeks to adjust to the time change and altitude, and familiarise myself with the accommodation and training tracks. When we had made these plans a few weeks before the idea was to make sure I was relaxed and well prepared. But in those few days between competing in Birmingham and leaving for Edmonton I felt as far from relaxed and well prepared as I could possibly be. I had felt low before Birmingham, but afterwards I felt worse because it was then that the realisation really hit hard. Could I really do myself justice in Edmonton and contest a gold medal with so many apparent weaknesses? I knew something was missing, and I didn't know what I could do to get it back.

Charles had watched my buoyant optimism descend into pessimism, and voiced the question I had been silently asking myself – did I think I could go out there and perform well? I had to reply that I really wasn't sure, and that I had doubts about going at all. So many people had said to me 'don't worry, you'll be fine'; they had reassured me that Denise the competitor, who had achieved so much in the past, would shine through and come to the rescue. I had believed them – I had needed to believe them. But I was finally admitting my doubts and uncertainties.

Charles gave me a couple of days to think seriously about whether or not I wanted to go to Edmonton and the World Championships. I came up with a long list of reasons to go, and a long list of reasons not to go, all of them equally valid in my eyes.

I began to reflect on the year, analysing everything that had taken place, and decided that my driving force seemed to be missing. Something inside me was saying, 'Denise, I don't think you can do this,' and my head swam constantly. I had so many questions and at least two answers to each one. I had been through a patch during which everything was going well, but one by one the problems seemed to have found me.

But something inside me – probably in my head rather than my heart – said that even if there was only a one per cent chance that I might be able to go out there and win, then it was worth getting on that plane.

So I ignored my gut feeling, and on Friday 20 July, I stepped on the plane to Canada.

On the flight I thought, OK, I'm here, I'm on my way to Edmonton and the World Championships. I'm going to train for two weeks, and I expect things to get better. All the feelings I've had, all the mixed emotions are no more. I will do this and I will do well. I thought that once I got away from the UK, I would be able to focus wholly on my athletics and the difference would be immediate. It had worked in the past, so why not this time?

Once in Edmonton I went through some really good training sessions, even though for most of the first week it poured with rain and the temperature wasn't as warm as we had expected it to be. This did not do a great deal to raise my spirits, but I went into the second week – the week of the heptathlon – hoping that things would get better.

Charles had decided that I should work with a high jump specialist on the Monday and the Wednesday of that week, which I was unsure about. I told him that I had reservations, because if they both went badly it wouldn't help me mentally. I would have preferred to take my chances and go for the single Monday session, because I knew that if that did not go well I would have almost forgotten about it by the time Saturday morning came around. But he slotted them both into my schedule anyway.

The Monday session was unproductive, and afterwards my spirits sank lower. I was not seeing any sign of improvement – what was wrong with me? I couldn't work out why I wasn't pulling everything together. Everyone was still saying, 'Don't worry, you'll be fine.' I knew they were trying to boost me up, trying to help me be optimistic, but I felt as if they weren't hearing me or seeing the signs.

My stomach problems started later on that Monday. I had been having problems with my stomach for a long time. I think it was stress-induced, and it is the sort of condition that manifests itself in the whole of the digestive system – from the stomach, through to the intestines and beyond. It was very uncomfortable, and gave me quite a lot of pain. I had brought some medication with me as I always did, just in case, but it didn't seem to help. I called Mum the next day and suggested that maybe I shouldn't compete, and yet again I heard those words: 'Don't be silly, you'll be fine.' She said once I got out there in the arena everything would be OK, as it was my place, where I belonged.

On the Wednesday I went through the second high jump session with the specialist. It was one of the worst sessions I have ever had. I was supposed to try and forget as much of the technical preparation as possible and just go for it, but it didn't work. Charles knew it wasn't happening and so did the coach, and I ended up storming off the track angry, frustrated, disappointed and hurt. I didn't talk to anyone about it properly, but Charles knew how I was feeling.

Everyone – and probably myself to some extent – thought that once I got into the arena everything would be different, that it had some magical power over me that could transcend every problem I was experiencing. But the problems had rooted themselves deep within my spirit, and that mental ability on which I pride myself so much had evaporated. When I spoke to Charles, he was trying to be sympathetic, but I felt that he didn't quite understand. I could see him really trying to follow my reasoning and feelings, but something appeared to prohibit his comprehension of what I was saying.

As a result of all this, by the Wednesday night I was feeling very depressed, and by Thursday morning my stomach was even worse and I didn't even get out of bed for most of the day. Going to the bathroom was painful, and I didn't feel at all well. I felt totally out of sync – everything was upside down and inside out.

A press conference had been arranged about three weeks previously, and we decided that it was best if Charles went to it alone. Because we honestly didn't know exactly what was going to happen, we thought it best to say that it was not yet decided whether I was going to compete. Charles kept it reasonably brief, explaining that I had a stomach condition and that we were waiting to see how I felt nearer the competition. I had decided not to face the press because I felt that sometimes the media forget the fact that behind the competitor an athlete is a human being with spirit and soul. I didn't think I could explain how I was feeling and be confident that an accurate representation of what I had to say would be relayed in the papers the next day. But I knew that the moment I didn't turn up I would get bad press anyway and, as I expected, the articles that resulted were not sympathetic.

On Friday I lay on my bed all day while a stream of people came in and out. A doctor visited me, as did Charles and Max Jones, the team manager and performance director of UK Athletics. I had a long talk with Charles, trying to give him an insight into my feelings physical and mental – both very low. I was simply not my usual self, the person one would expect to see going into a major championship. So, after speaking with Charles, he and Max Jones recommended I see the team psychologist. I wasn't opposed to the idea, to the prospect of talking things over with him, as I was still hoping for a flicker of light somewhere inside. I have always had a very positive attitude towards the work sports psychologists do, and was prepared to try anything. But despite all he said during our conversation, it was unlikely I would compete.

Late on Friday afternoon, after I had seen everyone, I made my final decision official: I was not going to enter the competition. I had been through too much turmoil, too many sleepless nights. As I uttered the words I felt relieved and so much better. My stomach was still causing me problems, but at least I had mental peace – I knew I had made the right decision.

*

I had wanted to be out of Edmonton before the heptathlon began on Saturday morning but because it had all taken so long, the next flight I could get was on Saturday evening. I couldn't have done what Katherine Merry did and stayed on in Edmonton until the end of the championships. I couldn't integrate and pretend that nothing was wrong. I think there was a perception that I should feel guilty about my decision, but I didn't. I wished everyone well, but I just wanted to go home, get some treatment and relax. I didn't leave my bed all day and was looked after by Mum, who had arrived on Friday.

I was interested to see what was happening in the heptathlon, so I turned on the TV at around 10am, expecting to watch the second event get under way. However, there was very little coverage until later that morning, and it was only in a review of the day's events so far that I actually saw what had been happening. Charles came to see me at the end of the morning session to fill me in on what was going on in the competition. Obviously, under different circumstances I would have loved to be out there in the arena with the other girls – but I had to come to terms with what had happened and was now interested to find out what was going on.

As usual, the afternoon session consisted of the shot then the 200m. Frustratingly, the TV seemed to be running around two hours behind the actual events, so I wasn't aware of what was happening in the shot until I got a text message from Michelle Griffith, who was back in England, telling me that Eunice Barber had had two no throws. I was shocked. Moments later the phone in my room rang. It was Charles, telling me that Barber had had three no throws. He was very upset and went on about how unpredictable the heptathlon can be – something I know and have always said myself.

I tried to explain to him that it hadn't been the fear of losing that had prompted my withdrawal. I'm not afraid of losing. I've lost before; it is part of a career in sport and you have to accept that. What I couldn't tolerate was the fact that I wasn't mentally ready or strong enough to compete to the best of my ability through two days of tough competition. If I had gone ahead, one of two things would have happened: by sheer luck (and it would have been by luck alone) I might have got from the beginning to the end relatively unscathed; or I could have crashed and hurt myself even more – a risk that did not make sense.

I was surprised that Barber had had three no throws though, as the shot is probably the hardest event in which to make such big mistakes. I thought perhaps she felt she had something to prove. She had had to pull out of the Olympics the year before and I had won the title – maybe she had thought it should have been hers. Going into 2001 she had kept the leading score and was the reigning world champion – and I wondered if she had decided that, with me out of the running she could forget about the competitive element and simply go for the 7000 points. Maybe, as a result, she overdid it.

When I found out she had withdrawn from the competition I wasn't surprised – you can't recover enough to win if you fail to score in one of the events. She was obviously devastated, and I really felt for her.

But even that didn't make me regret my decision not to compete. It had nothing to do with Barber; the fact she was partaking was irrelevant to the choice I made. Even when I found out that she was being coached by Bobby Kersee, the husband and coach of Jackie Joyner Kersee, I wasn't too perturbed. Obviously I had had my apprehensions – as he had coached the most prolific heptathlete ever and certainly knew what he was doing. Barber's raw talent and his enthusiasm and ability were certainly a good combination. But I didn't think that it made her unbeatable – I still don't. I believed, and still believe, in the team Charles and I have – that together we can really make waves.

Life always seems to be about peaks, plateaus and troughs, and you have to keep running with them all. You have to try to understand where you can make your changes and what you can do next. You have to make decisions to survive. If you don't, you give up – and what do you do then? Nothing. That's not me. It may take me a while to reach a decision, but once I'm there I'm pretty confident that it's right.

I believe that before I can move on, I have to find some form of acceptance of what happened in Edmonton. I had found it very difficult to accept that I wasn't ready to compete; I was fighting against it, telling myself that it would all work out. Looking back with hindsight, I would probably have done some things differently: not put myself under so much pressure. Entering a championship, you immediately give yourself a time restraint and the pressure is really on – especially if you are not on form.

Before I left, Charles, Mum and I went for dinner. Charles kept talking about what had happened that day, and his disbelief that we had sacrificed so much of our time on the track only for me not to compete. I think he thought I had let him down and let myself down at the same time. The conversation was rather heated, but Mum managed to keep the peace.

Afterwards, Mum took me to the airport. There were a couple of cameras there, and she was worried that there would be more at Heathrow and that I would have to face them alone. But I told her I would be fine, gave her a hug and walked through the gate. We were delayed by an hour and a half, but once I got on the plane I settled down to sleep. I slept for most of the flight, and it was probably the first decent sleep I had had in days.

When I got home on the Sunday, Michelle and Jacqui came round to make sure I was all right, as they knew I had just made one of the hardest decisions I'd faced in a long time. It was great to have them there, and we settled down and watched the athletics coverage on the TV, had some dinner, relaxed and chatted. It was just what I needed.

Some ridiculous headlines and articles were printed in the papers after Edmonton, although I wasn't really that interested in what they had to say. By contrast, Kevin – who knew better than anyone my history of medical problems – was very angry about them; he wanted to issue a statement refuting the speculation that I hadn't any real physical problems and that I had given up lightly.

There does seem to be some misguided perception that I did spend too much time celebrating my Olympic gold medal. I can't really understand where that came from, and I find it infuriating. Maybe I give off the impression that I'm a party girl, I don't know. What I do know is that the few things I did do were high profile – my interviews with Parkinson and Frank Skinner, and my attendance at the BBC Sports Personality of the Year Awards, the BAFTAs and the Brits. But these were the highlights; they certainly weren't the norm, or part of a big celebrity circuit into which I threw myself. I did attend a charity ball and presented an award at the Pantene Beauty Industry Awards in November, but apart from that I spent a lot of time with my friends, either eating Chinese takeaways and watching videos in my flat, or going out to dinner. I really did very little else.

But even if I had gone out and partied all the time – why should it matter? How many people win an Olympic gold medal in their lifetime? Surely that *is* something to celebrate. In relation to this, there is also a misconception about what I earn from my athletics career. As a reigning Olympic gold medallist, a sprinter or a 400m runner, for example, will earn tens of thousands of pounds per appearance on the grand prix circuit for many seasons to come. As a multi-eventer, this just isn't the case. The majority of my earnings can only ever come from off-track commercial activity, and it saddens me when I am accused of doing too much in this area when it is my main source of income.

Another set of headlines and articles that struck me as crazy were the ones claiming that romantic problems had added to my decision to withdraw. This made me laugh, as it stemmed from a piece in the *Observer Sport Monthly*, published on the Sunday I got back to Britain, that picked up on a throwaway comment I had made about my love life being a mess and went on to make much more of it than they should have done. It would be true to say that my love life wasn't perfect at the time, but I have had turbulent times in the past and it has never affected my performances. I have always maintained that when I'm on the track I'm an athlete, and that the role of the media is to report on the facts concerning my performance – or lack of it – but that's where it should stop. Certain people in the media spotlight actively court attention to feed their celebrity status, but that is not, and never will be, me.

Sport is a lifestyle: it isn't nine to five, and it isn't Monday to Friday – it's a way of life, and as a result, relationships can be difficult. This is certainly the case with athletics. Athletes don't have clear weekends – so if your partner isn't in sport and has his or her time off when you're training or competing, it's not easy. I do not have a regular, designated rest day from training, so it is almost impossible for me to make proper plans from week to week. As a result, making arrangements that most people take for granted – such as a weekend away with a partner – can be almost impossible. The month away for warm weather training each year and the weeks away for the big championships abroad inevitably add to these problems. Some people do make it work, but invariably someone is left behind on their own. If you aren't spending quality time with the person you're in love with, then even the strongest and happiest of relationships will be tested. Unfortunately, my boyfriend, Jonathan, and I parted company during this year.

Any future relationship I may have will depend either on a change in my lifestyle, whereby I will be able to dedicate much more time to its success, or on the chance that I will find a partner who can cope with the demands of what I do. But whatever happens, I am sure that it will require me to make a bigger effort not to let athletics completely dominate my life.

I feel I have worked very hard over the last ten to fifteen years, but I've been driven solely by one goal – to be the Olympic champion – and in the process I have made a lot of sacrifices and neglected other things and people. I wouldn't have had it any other way – but now, as I get older, I do believe that there has to be room for other things in my life. There are two people in me: Denise the performer, and Denise the woman. Denise the woman does sometimes need attention, and if I ignore that side of me I will probably end up a lonely old spinster.

Life is all about living, and I've had some amazing experiences because of my career. But maybe, as Charles has suggested in the past, I should wake up a bit earlier in the morning, train earlier, and give myself an extra hour or two in the day to do something for Denise the woman. I need to be able to say, 'OK, I've worked really well in the past five to eight weeks of training, I'm going to try to keep a weekend free to do something special with my partner.' I don't know if that's feasible, but it's my ideal. Some people believe that the only way to get the best out of yourself is to dedicate yourself entirely to your sport. But if that *is* the right way, then I need to feel happy with it, and at the moment I'm not sure that I am.

I believe last year showed me the need to adapt and develop into the world in which I am now living, and the person I now am. This is not always an easy process, particularly as my profile becomes higher. It's about taking control, of being in control of all the areas in your life that matter and feeling whole and happy. Only then can you be in balance and harmony, and only then can you really excel.

* * *

So priority number one is to find my inner peace and happiness, to get more balance in my life and take time for myself. When I have achieved that, I know I will be in a very strong position to go on with my sport. It would have been great to have had the four titles under my belt at the same time: Olympic champion, European champion, Commonwealth champion and World champion, especially as the world title has always eluded me. However, all is not lost – the way I see it, I will definitely have another shot at it in Paris in 2003. I also want to be Olympic champion again. I am sure I have that in me, and there is something very special about being a double Olympic champion. I want to be satisfied, to know I have achieved everything I can before I hang up my spikes once and for all. As I look back on my career even now, I know I have done well: double Commonwealth champion, European champion, two-time silver medallist in the World Championships, Olympic bronze medallist and Olympic gold medallist – by anyone's reckoning, that isn't bad! But I know that there is more in me, I still feel that I haven't totally capped my potential.

2002 sees the European Championships and the Commonwealth Games, the latter of which will be held in Manchester. If I have to have surgery on my left ankle and foot, as I should really have done straight after Sydney, I'll be back into rehab again, so the preparation could be hard. However, I hold both those titles and will certainly be looking to defend them. They should both be very good competitions. The best heptathletes at the moment, such as Barber, Sazanovich and Prokhorova, are in Europe, so it will be a challenge, but I am looking forward to it.

I feel as if I am back to where I was after the Atlanta Olympics in 1996; I'm slowly rebuilding myself, reassessing my goals and my direction, and seeing how I can improve myself. Sometime ago I said, 'I have two Olympic gold medals in me and I'm going to get them, no matter what my other competitors do,' and I stand by that. The next year will see a lot of changes, but I'm very optimistic. You have to move forward, you have to evolve, and that's exactly what I intend to do.

If I look back on the journey through which this book has taken me, from Wolverhampton, a young girl with hope and ambition travelling on buses and trains in pursuit of a dream, it really does seem like a lifetime ago. If you had told me then about all I would go on to achieve, I simply would not have believed you. But I know there is still more to come, and who knows, it just might be the best yet.